IDENTITIES IN THE
LESBIAN WORLD

Recent Titles in **CONTRIBUTIONS IN SOCIOLOGY**
Series Editor: Don Martindale

BARBARA PONSE

IDENTITIES IN THE LESBIAN WORLD THE SOCIAL CONSTRUCTION OF SELF

CONTRIBUTIONS IN SOCIOLOGY, NUMBER 28

GREENWOOD PRESS
WESTPORT, CONNECTICUT • LONDON, ENGLAND

Library of Congress Cataloging in Publication Data

Ponse, Barbara.
    Identities in the lesbian world.

    (Contributions in sociology; no. 28)
    Bibliography: p.
    Includes index.
    1. Lesbianism—United States. 2. Lesbians
—United States. 3. Identity —Psychology)
I. Title.
HQ75.6.U5P66   301.41'57   77-84763
ISBN 0-8371-9889-5

Library of Congress Catalog Card Number: 77-84763
ISBN 0-8371-9889-5
ISSN: 0084-9278

First published in 1978

Greenwood Press, Inc.
51 Riverside Avenue, Westport, Connecticut 06880

Printed in the United States of America

10 9 8 7 6 5 4 3 2 1

This book is dedicated with much affection to Goldie Ivener, Al Sokanoff, Susan Schreiber, and my son, Dmitri—who were all there when I needed them.

CONTENTS

PREFACE

This book explores identities among women who love women, whom I call women-related women. It analyzes how identities are explained, constructed, maintained, and changed in the context of secrecy, stigma, and politics. The analysis is based on the experiences of women in both secretive and political-activist lesbian worlds whom I met and interviewed over the course of three years of field work in the lesbian community. The symbolic interactionist perspective informs this study, so particular attention is paid to the meanings these women give to themselves, their experiences, and their worlds.

The book is structured by three levels of analysis: the larger society, the group, and the individual. I first examine the imagery and meanings of lesbianism and of relationships between women from the standpoint of institutions and image makers within the larger society and analyze the underlying assumptions of these images. I then look at the lesbian world, veiled in secrecy, and the multiple effects of secrecy on relations between the larger society and the lesbian world, on relations within the lesbian world, and on the individual. The analysis moves to how identity is formulated in the lesbian world: *identity rules* and assumptions about lesbianism, bisexuality, and heterosexuality in lesbian groups are all considered.

The final emphasis of the analysis is on the individual and the various ways in which the individual affiliates with lesbianism and lesbians. In this section I compare the identity resolutions of the individual to the polar models of identity put forth in the larger society and the gay world, and suggest a more useful model for understanding identity.

ACKNOWLEDGMENTS

Many persons have contributed directly or indirectly to the writing of this book, but first were the many women who allowed me into their lives and shared their experiences with me. This book would not have been possible without their trust, confidence, and cooperation. I wish to acknowledge my gratitude to my colleagues and friends who offered their advice, criticism, and support to this project. Particularly, I want to thank Carol Warren for her guidance, encouragement, and criticisms of the original draft. Daniel Glaser and Judd Marmor were most helpful in criticizing earlier drafts of this work. I am very grateful to Joe Styles, who patiently read and critiqued earlier stages of the manuscript and offered me many valuable insights, I would like to thank Linda Mauldin for her assistance in handling the many details associated with the original manuscript.

I would like to acknowledge the help and criticisms I received from Murray and Rosalie Wax, as well as their helpful insights in formulating the book in its present stage. Sarah Wernick was invaluable to me in providing many helpful criticisms with respect to organization and clarification of the concepts presented herein. I would like especially to thank David Pittman for his support and suggestions. I am grateful to Barry Glassner, Jay Corzine, Peg Bortner, and Jan Boguslaw for reading early drafts of the manuscript and for their criticisms. I would like to acknowledge my gratitude to the Department of Sociology, Washington University, for the support they gave to this project. Earlier versions were supported in part by a Bio-medical Support Grant awarded by the University of Southern California and an N.I.M.H. Training Grant in Evaluation

Research, principal investigator, LaMar T. Empey. Last, but certainly not least, I would like to acknowledge my gratitude to Susan Schreiber, Susan Brown, Berda Morley, Helen Sloan, Sydney Jensen, and Julia Russell, who stuck with me through thick and thin, and especially to my son, Dmitri, who has displayed extraordinary patience and understanding for his working mother. I want to thank the women who typed far into the night, preparing many drafts of this book: Linda Tessier, Linda Mauldin, Kathy Valin, Irma Morose, and Jayne Hinds.

IDENTITIES IN THE LESBIAN WORLD

INTRODUCTION

Consider three women.

The first is a successful professional whose workmates think of her as a spinster. In fact, she is involved in a long-standing "marriage" with another woman, and within her small circle of close friends, she identifies herself as "gay."

The second woman was married for many years but is now divorced and lives alone. She has never conducted an erotic affair with another woman. She tells people she is a lesbian.

The third woman is a widow, who terms herself a heterosexual. She is in the midst of a long-term affair with another woman.

This study deals with these three women and many more. Such women inhabit a variety of worlds—some secretive lesbian worlds, others political-activist worlds. The focus of the study is to interpret and analyze the nature of identities, how they are maintained, and how they change.

I shall refer to the women in this study as women-related women. Women-related women include those who call themselves lesbian (or would probably be called lesbians by others) as well as women who call themselves bisexual, "sexual," "straight," or celibate but who have sexual or emotional relationships with other women. The subject of this study, thus, is identities of women who love women.

Conceptual Schemes

The text of this book is organized by concepts deriving from the social psychology of symbolic interaction and phenomenology. I have tried to present the materials so that a person unfamiliar with these areas of social psychology can nonetheless grasp much of my argument. But the reader who is familiar with the concepts that follow will be able to gain an increased appreciation of the situations and dilemmas of women-related women. Necessarily what is presented in the next few pages of this introduction is abbreviated: monographs have been written about identity and the self, and the professional literature contains considerable debate about such notions as *role taking.*

Identity and the Self

"What sort of person is she?" "Who am I" "Who are you?" are questions that trigger responses in terms of identity. Identities may signify who the individual "really is" or they may be ephemeral, having only temporary, or situated, significance. In particular situations, identities may not be relevant at all. But, as we shall note in this book, secret, stigmatized, and political identities may be important in contexts where identity is not usually an issue or is simply assumed to be unproblematic.

Identity is not inborn but is constructed and maintained in social interaction. This idea of identity emerges from the view of the self as process. The self arises in social interaction with others through learning to take the role of others. Role taking means acting toward oneself and toward the world as others do. It is a covert act that takes place in the mind and occurs before or instead of overt action. Thus a woman who engages in sexual acts with another woman may take the perspective of the larger society and define herself as lesbian.

However, role taking does not imply the learning of a *single* perspective. It may embrace many sets of others, some present and some remote. For example, the woman referred to above may learn to define herself as bisexual or simply sexual. Those with secret or hidden identities—for example spies, professional actors, and those vulnerable to stigma, such as the women in this study—may learn to take a dual or triple perspective toward themselves and the world: that of the larger society, that of others like them, and a quasi-independent view put together through the interpretive process of role taking. As Herbert Blumer stated in *Symbolic Interactionism,* "The human actor may perceive himself, have conceptions of himself, communicate with himself, and act toward himself. As these types of behavior imply, the human being may become an *object* to his

own action."[1] In the perspective used in this analysis the meanings of the
self are seen as given by human actors, rather than as inherently lodged
in selves. And the idea of change in inherent.

Social Identity and Personal Identity

A distinction must be made between who the individual conceives of
herself to be and how she is defined by others. Social identity refers to
who others think the actor is—that identity which she seems to possess.
Personal identity is who the individual holds herself to be—the individual's
ongoing subjective sense of self. Goffman refers to two types of social
identities, *virtual* and *actual*.[2] Virtual identity is that identity which the
actor seems to project. Actual identity refers to that identity which the
actor could be demonstrated to be, were all identity clues available for
assessment. This distinction is important in light of the secrecy that hides
the actual identities of many women-related women. But it is also important to remember that although the individual may attribute the same
identity to herself as others do, social identities are not necessarily the
same as personal identities.[3] The study of identities among women-related
women demonstrates that an individual's definition of self may or may
not correspond with what others think or believe and may withstand
persistent attempts at redefinition by others. McCall and Simmons note
that "our evaluations of self are in part derived from our *appraisal* of the
. . . evaluations of [others]. . . . But . . . we [can't] assume that the two
types of evaluations are identical, or usually identical, as some theorists
have seemed to imply."[4] When an individual regularly confronts audiences
that hold widely different sets of meanings about her identity, she lives
in a situation of strain. She typically handles this strain by giving weight
to one identity (and one audience) over others: one identity comes to be
conceived of as a "real" self, others as false and acted ones.

The Roots of Identities

Identities may have their beginnings in social roles and attributes—one's
place in the family, one's gender, one's age—or they may be based in certain qualities that the individual or others ascribe to the self. This study
reveals that among women-related women identities may be rooted in
feelings, whether these feelings are experienced or are assumed to be present. Finally, one's activities and affiliations with others may be the basis

for ascribing a particular identity to an individual. The many sources of
identity point up the importance of knowing the individual's interpretation
of the self.

Identity as Essence

Certain identities, such as lesbian, are commonly construed as pervasive
and unchangeable. These identities are based on what Katz calls *essences*,
inherent qualities "which may be manifested, reflected, indicated or represented by, but [do] not exist in, conduct."[5] Essential identities stemming from these essences are commonly perceived as going beyond an
embodiment of mere roles or attributes, referring to the state of *being*
of an individual rather than the mere *doing* of an individual.

A historian notes that gay people are frequently thought of as having
a gay essence by others:

Gay people were limited and reduced to their sexuality—even to its most
negative manifestations. *Homosexual* has been the term by which gay
people were simultaneously categorized, summarized and reduced to
less-than-human—denied their humanity on the basis of their sexuality.
. . . The term *homosexual,* with its emphasis on same-sex genital contact
directed toward orgasm, is particularly inadequate as a means of encom-
passing and understanding the . . . variety of same-sex relations.[6]

The reduction of women-related women to an essence characterizes
many theories of lesbianism and is a prevailing theme in religious pro-
nouncements on lesbianism. Interestingly, the notion of essence is imbed-
ded as well in the ways in which identity is conceived of in the lesbian
world. The themes of essence and essential identities are treated at length
in chapters 2 and 5, which analyze the construction of identity in the
larger society and in the lesbian world, respectively.

Identity Change and Transformation

Identities change, particularly those subjected to the special strains
and constraints of stigma and secrecy. The changes that identities undergo
may be of the everyday sort, reflecting the flux of social interaction and
the changing relevance of particular identities in changing courses of action.
Thus a person may think of herself variously as happy, tired, serious, lazy.

Other identity changes may be experienced as more thoroughgoing, more central and important—as *transformations* of identity.[7] Identities may designate *becoming* as well as being and having been.

Few, if any, women are intentionally socialized by the larger society to be lesbians. At the same time, as will be demonstrated at length in the chapters that follow, both the larger society and the lesbian world create pressures toward the adoption of lesbian identity for women who conform to their respective models of identity construction. In turn, such women may construct their own sense of identity that may or may not conform to the overarching models of straight and gay societies. The self-designations of women-related women usually involve a transformation of identity. Such changes in important ways of conceiving of the self are usually major events in a person's biography.

Labeling Theory and Self-Labeling

Labeling theory, which originated within the symbolic interactionist tradition, focuses on the labeling of individuals by others and the subsequent redefinitions of the self along the lines of the assigned label. This theory draws attention to the complex processes involved in defining and naming others and particularly emphasizes the significance of the differential degrees of power held by definers. In the following pages, the analysis concentrates on the definers of social reality, of selves, and of others that have import for the identities of women-related women.

All sociological approaches to the study of human social life must take into account and assign importance to the human actor on the one hand and the social group on the other. By employing the symbolic interactionist approach to the analysis of identities, this study stresses the centrality of the individual as choice maker and arbiter of her own fate, while recognizing the options and constraints placed on the individual by others. Symbolic interactionism is distinguished from more deterministic views of humans in its emphasis on the volitional character of the individual and in the important place it accords the individual in the interpretation and understanding of human behavior.

The social actor cannot be adequately understood or explained as a passive reactor to pressures from within or without—rather she must be understood in the context of the ways in which she orders and interprets herself and her world. Thus this inquiry places primary importance on understanding the meanings individuals give to their own experiences and to themselves. The development of concepts, categories, and theory in the analysis attempts to remain faithful to the character of the meanings given by the women whose lives and experiences I studied.

I propose a typology of identities that is based on the experiences of self and identity of the women-related women who were the subjects of this study. This typology is intended to debunk the polar conceptions of identity and sexuality that prevail in both gay and straight worlds.

EMERGENCE OF IDENTITY AS THE RESEARCH PROBLEM

Lesbian identity is conceived of by many women-related women as well as by many heterosexuals as a moral essence. It is frequently experienced by women-related women as "the true self." Others may also say that lesbian describes who a woman-related woman really is. This research focuses on the construction and maintenance of lesbian identity in contexts where it is and where it is not conceived of as the true self. In addition, it examines the social conditions that promote various understandings both of what lesbianism means and what lesbian identity is.

The issue of identity was not the original focus of my research; rather, it emerged as the focal point of investigation in the course of doing field work in the lesbian world. The study was originally conceived as one of several that were concerned with labeling theory, specifically the effects of labels on individuals and changes in the meaning of labels.[1] The original research plan was to inquire into the lesbian world as a setting in order to study the general process of destigmatization and the functioning of self-help groups in effecting the destigmatization of negative social labels. Thus, initially, lesbians were viewed as just one species within the genus "social category of stigmatized persons;" I viewed the lesbian world as simply one setting in which the general issue of destigmatization could effectively be studied.

To this end, I entered a gay organization reputedly concerned with changing the stigmatized meaning of the labels lesbian and gay. My approach to the study of the lesbian world was from the symbolic interactionist perspective. The emphasis that this viewpoint brings to the research enterprise is that the investigator should endeavor to understand the meanings that prevail among the actors in the world under investigation. A basic precept underlying this orientation is that to find out about people the investigator must go into their world and talk with them.

I chose to do field work in the lesbian world both for the reasons named above, which constitute my general orientation, and because little is known about the lesbian and her world. Scant research attention has been directed to lesbians and lesbianism by the three disciplines that have traditionally studied male homosexuality: psychiatry, psychology, and sociology. While some inferences about the female homosexual world can be drawn from the study of the male homosexual world, the former deserves specific investigation. I entered into the gay organization with the purpose of learning the meanings and analytic orderings of the members of the lesbian world—the ways, in short, in which lesbians order, categorize, shape, and render their world and themselves in relation to that world.

An Early Study in the Lesbian World

As a student, I had conducted an exploratory study into a secretive group of lesbians after being introduced to them by several friends who had identified themselves to me as lesbians. That very brief study had gone well in terms of gaining access to persons who seemed willing to talk with me and to include me in various social situations. During that investigation there were a few references to "when I would decide I was gay." This all took place with much good humor and in a general mood of jocularity. I paid it little mind.

At that time I had little insight into the critical nature of the circumstances through which I gained access to this group of women: I was presented as a *trustworthy,* discreet person, known to the gay women who introduced me into the group. In the social gatherings in which I participated, my status seemed unproblematic. Occasionally my researcher role would be brought to the fore, to which all attended with seemingly great interest. I perhaps gave too much credit to myself and my personability in accounting for the ease with which I moved around in the community, made observations, and asked questions. As I was to come to understand later, the only reasons I was so readily received were precisely because of my status as friend to several of the gay women and because of the assumptions that were made about my identity—all having little to do with my own social adeptness or lack thereof. But I am getting a little ahead of myself, in anticipating what happened in the course of the present investigation that led me to reflect back upon what was really going on in the previous research excursion into the community.

Choosing a Role in the Field

In instructing the student of social life in the research enterprise, most methodological guides emphasize the selection of a role for approaching the people in the chosen research setting. These guides describe various emphases on participation and observation on the field researcher's part, as well as the selection of overt or covert researcher status. In keeping with my own prejudices and notions about what would be the most efficacious stance for collecting data, I decided to be an overt researcher in the gay organization I had selected as the first point of penetration into the lesbian community. First of all, being more or less naive about the world I had chosen to study, I thought that I would be in a better position to ask questions and lend some legitimacy to my ignorance if it were clear that I was a researcher and not a member. My personal biases were also important in making this decision: though, no doubt, effective work can be and has been done by covert researchers, I feel more comfortable having my status known. At that time I had little idea of the way in which researchers are seen in the lesbian community. I shall return to this point—the situation of the researcher in the lesbian world—after I describe the settings and my entry into them.

Settings

The setting in which the initial phases of this study took place is a gay organization that is designed as a social service agency attempting to meet the needs of the gay community and is housed in an ancient two-story building near the downtown area of a large Southern city. A major purpose of the organization's activities is to decriminalize and destigmatize gayness. This purpose is rooted in the philosophy of the gay liberation movement, which emphasizes gayness as a viable and authentic life-style —not merely a reference to sexual behavior. To this end, the organization provides gay people with a wide variety of opportunities to interact and communicate.

In most instances, the programs of the organization are designed specifically for men or for women. The services include legal counseling and prison intervention programs (whereby persons who are arrested on gay-related charges are released to the organization), medical services (including a V.D. detection and prevention program as well as free physical examinations), housing and employment services. An important focus of organizational activities is the dissemination of information about gayness to the heterosexual community. This educational function is carried out in a variety of ways, such as public speaking at colleges and high schools and public service announcements on radio and television. The program most directly concerned with the destigmatization of the labels gay and lesbian is a many-faceted self-development program designed to facilitate self-acceptance and personal growth among gay people. This program includes peer counseling, gay awareness workshops, consciousness raising, rap groups, and crisis counseling.

These groups and encounters focus on handling gayness in a stigmatizing society and on other concerns such as gay experiences and relationships, the process of becoming aware of gayness, the meaning of gayness, and the acceptance of gay identity. In addition, these groups provide legitimating rationales and explanations of gayness and endeavor to give positive role models to the potentially gay person or to the individual who is having difficulty in acknowledging gayness.

A special type of group intended to deal with these concerns is called a growth group. Growth groups consist of eight to twelve women (there were growth groups for men also) and are conducted as ongoing group experiences for ten to twelve weeks. Growth groups resemble encounter groups in style and in much of their content. Their manifest purpose is to "help people get in touch with their feelings," specifically their gay feelings, with the aim of facilitating the acceptance of gayness and the acknowledgment (at least to the self) of gay identity.

Organizational Participants

Between sixty and one hundred women would attend the Thursday night women's groups each week. At least part of the constituency would change from week to week; therefore, categorizing it in terms of the usual sociological parameters is difficult, especially since other affiliations, jobs, education, family constellations, marital status, and age were not routinely discussed in the rap groups. According to organizational staff members and my own observations, however, the group was comprised of students, working-class women, and middle-class women. Most were white, but at any given meeting three to five black women and perhaps a few Chicano and Asian women would be in attendance. The women ranged in age from about eighteen to the mid-forties. There were notably few women older than fifty at these meetings. The organization expressed concern about the problems of reaching older gay women, believing that concerns about secrecy and differences in life-style kept them away.

The women who participate in the organization vary widely with respect to openness about their gayness. While it is true that many secretive women would not come to any organization that was avowedly gay, many who did come to the organization had formerly been extremely secretive about their lesbianism. In addition, women who were curious about lesbianism would attend the Thursday night meetings and other organizational functions.

In short, the gay organization that I chose as the initial site of entry into the lesbian community was involved with destigmatizing the category lesbian (and male homosexual) and providing an alternative set of meanings to the gay experience. It was concerned with helping people come to terms with being gay in a society that was perceived at best as being antipathetic to them and at worst as visiting condemnation upon them.

Entry into the Activist Setting

The first time I visited the organization was designated women's night. It was my intention to find the *controllers of entry* and to ask permission to conduct research there, but this did not happen that evening. Quite by accident, I found someone at the organization whom I knew from another setting. When she saw me, knowing I was a sociologist, she said, "If you are going to do research here, do it covertly, because there is already someone here doing research."

I then had occasion to observe the other researcher (though I was not observed in the very crowded room). She stood up at the back of the room and asked if anyone would be interested in being interviewed for her master's thesis. She added, "They think we're crazy, and I want to show through my research that *we* are not." I was somewhat surprised at the "we" reference and thought to myself that it might be more difficult than I had expected to gain entry into the setting, since a sociologist who was gay might be more acceptable than I. I met yet another sociologist—whom

I already knew—in the setting that evening (I began to wonder if everyone there was a sociologist), who said to me, "Don't be so naive—what difference does it make what you call yourself? The important thing is to get into the setting." While not being able to fault the utility of such an approach, I still remained clear in my determination to be an overt researcher without a "we" reference.

In the ensuing few days I received a couple of phone calls about my research but also more pointedly, about whether or not I was gay. I decided no time should be lost in getting to the appropriate gatekeepers to make my research plans known and to secure permission to be in the setting. I found the interest in my personal identity to be a bit untoward and discomfiting but essentially thought of it as idiosyncratic to the persons involved and plunged forward undaunted.

I called and asked for an interview with the research director, who, it turned out, was also a sociologist. I explained my interest in the problem of destigmatization to her and said that I wanted to do field work at the organization. I also said that I would be interested in interviewing some of the women after I had been there for a while and wanted to know how this might be handled. She expressed her fear that I might interview women "who came in off the streets" and who were not yet "aware of themselves," had not been inculcated with the organization's philosophy, or had not yet been helped, and that such women should not be presented as typical of the lesbian community. I said I would most assuredly not approach women as soon as they came in the door. I told her that all interviews would be confidential, and I further assured her that I did not assume that lesbians were sick or that lesbianism constituted pathology.

All in all, our discussion went very well. Yes, I could come to the organization and do research; yes, I could do interviewing, but she wanted to control who it was that I would interview. I argued that it would be interesting to interview women who had come into the organization comparatively recently as well as women who had been there for some time, to try and capture the changes that occurred over time.

The research director seemed pleased and interested in the research I had planned. She then said, almost as an afterthought, "I assume you are gay." I said no, I wasn't. She looked displeased and said that another non-gay woman who had come to do research at the center had become very uncomfortable with the women and made them feel self-conscious. I told her that I had no fears about this happening with me since I had done a brief exploratory study in the community a year or so before and I had not felt uncomfortable. I simply didn't see that as a problem.

I was again discomfited by the focus on my identity on whether I was gay or not. I couldn't see why that mattered. After all, I was a researcher —immersed in the ethics of social science, discreet, sympathetic, nonjudgmental. What difference did it make what went on in my personal life? Why was everyone so interested in whether I was gay or not? I was miffed, too. I had read about entry; I had followed the rules as diligently as possible; I had been honest; and now everyone was asking *me* questions. Entry into the secret community only a short time before had been relatively unproblematic. I harbored the secret conviction that I must be doing something wrong. Other researchers, I was sure, just presented themselves and were accorded access without so much focus on themselves.

In any event, I decided to pursue the research, albeit with some qualms. I immersed myself in the activities of the center, attended rap groups and consciousness-raising sessions, listened, observed, asked questions. I mentioned my researcher role on various occasions and received amused smiles, questions, and sometimes overt manifestations of disbelief.

The woman whom I had known from another setting became an invaluable aid in the research enterprise, as she had some power in the organization. She asked me to participate in several group functions at the organization. It seemed like a fair trade and would, I thought, be productive of data otherwise unavailable to me. It is important to realize that this was an organization staffed largely by volunteers. As a willing, even eager, person who wanted to become involved in all phases of the self-help program, I was most welcome. Within a short time it seemed as if I had established trust and was invited to participate in staff meetings, and it became clear that I could participate in as many organizational activities as I cared to. In fact, it became necessary for me to limit the number of my activities simply to allow time to record my observations and to attend to other aspects of the investigation.

In the meantime, throughout my involvement in various activities, persons I encountered made references, both subtle and direct, to my identity, implying, by turns, that I was straight, gay, bisexual. Most commonly, I was assumed to be in the process of "coming out" (realizing I was gay) and of coming to terms with being gay. Significantly, my own statements about who I was were interpreted in the light of this assumed struggle with myself.

Several months after I had become involved in the organization, I attended a gay consciousness-raising group, that included ten people involved in the staff. A senior member of the group, a man of about sixty, began talking about his experiences as a gay man, the insults and injuries he had sustained, and the route by which he had come to be an activist working exclusively for the concerns of gay people. He recounted that frequently he would be approached for help by gay people who were so ashamed or afraid of discovery that they would refuse to give their correct name or would ask that he not mention their affiliation with him since he was openly gay. Continuing around the room, the men and women spoke of their experiences as formerly secretive and now activist gays. To describe these experiences—which for most of the people there had included a great deal of personal loss and sadness in their lives—as "moving" hardly does justice to the ambience in the room. When my turn to speak came, I felt inadequate to the occasion and said that I did not share their experiences, though I was deeply and obviously moved by hearing them. I did not identify myself as a gay person, and I had begun to realize that that was extremely important to them. At that point I simply felt like an interloper, someone who really had no right to be there, for it did not seem like a research situation to me at all. I talked for a little while about myself, my own sexuality, my own life, half anticipating that I would be asked to leave. I felt extremely anxious and assumed that the research would probably have to be dropped since I was making it irrevocably clear that I was not one of them.

The response I received was truly amazing. Several women came over to me after the meeting and said that I really was a lesbian and would come to accept it; that what I had done was a beautiful thing; that I had really shared myself. I was dumbfounded. How was it that when I said I was not a lesbian, everyone kept saying I was? That night I received several phone calls from women who were concerned that I had become so emotional. They were appreciative of what I had done, they said—and again came the response that I really was a lesbian. My protest was to no avail. At that point I realized that I had been so caught up in trying to be honest that I had missed the critical nature of defining the world in terms of gay and straight from the perspective of gay people. I also began to understand some of the bases upon which attribution of gay identity were being made, one of the most important of which was seeking out the gay community.

It also became clear that this perspective was so pervasive that it made little difference how I presented myself, that I would be assumed to be any number of various things, and that what I said brought little to bear on these assumptions. The fact was that my own statements would be contradicted and interpreted within the framework of meanings in the gay world. I decided that these indeed were the data I should be attending to. What had seemed to be an idiosyncratic problem of doing research was in fact the research problem itself: the way in which lesbian identity and other related identities are constructed and explained in terms of the community's paradigm. The fact that I was a woman studying the woman's community, one who presented herself as not oriented in terms of pathology, carried with it the connotation that I was therefore really investigating my own sexual identity. In the eyes of the community, my research was simply a vehicle allowing me to do this.

The content and thrust of the various gay meetings I had been attending took on a new meaning for me. I began to notice the verbal and non-verbal responses to persons who said they were "just observing" or were "bisexual." I began to understand the complex and contradictory stance that the community has with respect to bisexuals and interested or curious heterosexuals and the pervasiveness of the assumption that persons who are *in* the community are most probably *of* it. In brief, I began to appreciate the overwhelming social significance of defining the other, the audiences to the self, in terms of the polar categories of straight and gay. I came retrospectively to understand that in my earlier research experience the real reason for my acceptance was that some perceived me as a trustworthy straight person, while others accepted me because they assumed I was in the process of discovering my "gay self."

Entry into the Secretive Lesbian World

After I had spent nearly a year in the gay self-help organization, it became clear that the people I was meeting there did not represent the gay community at large. Most of the people at the organization, I suspected, were more open about their gayness in front of more people than were gays in the general community. The many references that I heard about "coming out of the closet" (emerging from secrecy to openness

about gayness) led me to try to investigate the "closet," or the world of
the secretive lesbian.

There were few ties between the activist and the secretive worlds. By
and large, activists tended to associate with other activists, so the organization could not provide the contacts I needed. I reestablished contact
with the group of women whom I had met during the initial investigation
into the lesbian world. They proved to be extremely helpful in introducing
me to their friends, who then introduced me to others. In general, the
pattern of contacts into the covert gay community was that of snowbal-
ling, as initial introductions produced referrals to others who subsequently
introduced me to still more women. Contacts with members of some
friendship networks thus branched into contacts with others.

The intensity and duration of my relationships within the covert community varied from the renewal or continuation of friendships to the limited, interview situation—though I typically had many contacts over time
with most of the women referred to in the text, both those from the organizational setting and those from the secretive community. Field work
in the community and theoretic sampling,[2]—that is, purposive efforts to
contact persons representative of particular sectors of the community,
such as older women, ex-lesbians, bisexuals, and male-identified women
—produced a cross-sampling of women with a variety of identity stances.

The Sample

The women I observed, talked with, and interviewed, located through
either the organization or friendship networks, I differentiate as activist
and secretive lesbians, respectively. However, finer distinctions among
these women and others I shall refer to later should be noted. The lesbian
world is composed of many different kinds of groups, some bonded together for reasons of sociability and others grouped together by a shared
interest in various political philosophies, such as gay activism, feminism,
radicalism, and separatism.

Gay activism is concerned with destigmatization of the category lesbian
or gay and with law reform and the civil rights of gay people. The influence of feminism in the community is wide and varied. Some secretive
women, as well as activists, for example, identify themselves as feminists,
while others do not. In turn, the interpretation of feminism by some
activist lesbian feminists has led them to take a separatist stance. These

women wish to disaffiliate themselves from men, including gay men, insofar as possible. Within the secretive world, similarly, some lesbians avoid contact with the straight world when possible, but because of the trust I established within the community, I was able to gain access to some of them.

The seventy-five women I interviewed ranged in age from sixteen to seventy-six. The greatest number were in their thirties (36 percent), followed closely by those in their forties (25 percent) and those in their twenties (21 percent). Eight percent were in their fifties, 6 percent in their sixties, with one in the teen age category and one seventy-six years of age.

The majority of women were white and middle-class. Only 4 percent of the sample were black and, therefore, no generalization to the experience of black lesbians is possible. Approximately one-third of the sample had been married, including two who had gotten married as a cover for their lesbianism.

Most of the women in the sample are conventionally employed and 77 percent are in various professions. An additional 18 percent are in responsible administrative capacities in the business world or are freelance artists and writers. Seventy-four percent of the women interviewed have had at least some college education: of this group, 80 percent (forty-four) had completed a bachelor's degree and 37 percent (sixteen) at least a master's. Among these sixteen women, six have Ph.D.'s or are in the process of completing their dissertations.

Eighteen percent of the sample live a life-style that is strongly influenced by their political stance. That is, they are living in feminist collectives or communes, or their work life—choice of jobs and recipients of their services—is strongly influenced by their political-sexual philosophy. For example, one therapist in the sample chooses to work exclusively with gay clients, another with women, and two others are employed by an organization dedicated to the lesbian alcoholic. Within the framework of my methodology, I endeavored to obtain a theoretic sampling of women who had particular kinds of experiences: those who had labeled themselves lesbian, those with similar experiences who had not done so, and women who formerly had relationships with women but no longer did so. I was most fortunate in having women in all these categories make themselves available to be interviewed. This does not mean that I have definitively sampled the lesbian world, nor does what I present here represent all

women-related women. As indicated earlier, these findings cannot be
generalized to persons of other socioeconomic classes or races without
much caution. I am confident however, that this sample of women is
fairly representative of white, middle-class, women-related women who
have struggled with and to some degree answered the question, "Who
am I?"

Interviews

   Field work in both activist and secretive communities was supplemented
by in-depth interviews. I did not begin interviews until I had been in the
secretive community for about seven months, and the interviews were divided fairly evenly between activist and secretive lesbians. All interviews
were open-ended and focused mainly on specific concerns with identity.
They were designed to probe how women identified themselves, to determine the chronology of identities, to learn the meanings of lesbianism, to
comprehend the ways in which an individual affiliated with the social
category lesbian and with the community to understand the conditions,
circumstances, and experiences that led to adoption of a lesbian identity,
and to note changes in the experience and meaning of the self over time.
In addition, I investigated the history of the respondent's sexual-emotional relationships and her subjective experience of herself in relation to her
identity and her life history. These interest areas guided all interviews,
both at the organization and in the covert community, yet if someone
spontaneously stressed a particular area that represented a unique slant
on an issue or presented a new issue entirely, I explored this novel concern
in the interview.

   The analysis that follows draws considerably from interview material
as well as from the three years of field work in various parts of the community. However, the analysis is not limited to interviews, but draws
upon experiences and information gained from interacting with women
whom I did not interview but with whom I spent much time in various
formal and informal situations.

   In the text I use quoted material that is representative of a particular
point of view with respect to identity-related concepts in the community.
Negative cases are employed to indicate the diversity and changeability
of sexuality and identity in the lesbian world. Overall usage of identity
terms is detailed in chapter 4.

The Role of the Researcher in the Lesbian Community

Methodological treatments of the researcher role imply that the researcher chooses a role, enacts that role throughout the course of the research, and is rather unproblematically accepted to be who she presents herself to be.[3] It is assumed that the role chosen by the researcher and the role perceived by the researched are one and the same. But the foregoing account of my entry into the gay organization indicates that the role the researcher chooses may vary independently of the community's perception of her.

Within various sectors of the lesbian community there are assumptions made about researchers that serve in some instances to facilitate and in others to impede research. The researcher may be welcomed because she is thought of as a spokesperson for the lesbian community, or she may be unwelcome if she is seen as seeking to support theories about lesbians and homosexuals that presume pathology. Again, the researcher, particularly the sympathetic researcher, may be seen as really gay or as using the research as a "cover" for a personal exploration of gayness. A researcher of the same sex as respondents in the lesbian or male homosexual worlds is, of course, most likely to have assumptions made about her or his identity. Warren noted, however, that women researchers investigating the male world may also have their motives and identities questioned.[4]

Sociologists may be perceived as "do-gooders" who will "tell the truth" about the gay world.[5] However, this perception of the researcher is not an unmixed one, particularly in the radical or politicized segments of the gay community. Women and men in the gay liberation movement tend to be quite conversant with the literature on homosexuality. They know well the names of analysts who are perceived as antipathetic or hostile to lesbianism or homosexuality and who maintain the view of homosexuality as pathology, such as Socarides, Bergler, and Beiber. In addition, more politicized sectors of the community are wary of social scientists who—though rejecting the supposition of pathology—do not acknowledge their own supposed gayness or are unwilling to state in public forums that homosexuality is fully on a par with heterosexuality. One researcher, whose work in the male homosexual community led her to conclude that homosexuals manifested not more, and in some instances less, pathology than a control group of matched heterosexuals,[6] was criticized by some activists because she reputedly said, when asked

if she would want her own son to be homosexual or heterosexual, that
she would prefer the latter.

In my researcher role I was perceived as a "wise" spokesperson for the
gay community or as an outgroup member who knows the secret of the
ingroup, as a full member, or a new, potential member. It became clear that
the way in which I was perceived was an inextricable part of the data and
the data-gathering process. I was required, therefore, to take a theoretic
stance with respect to myself as well as to the world I was investigating.
Douglas defines a *theoretic stance* as standing back from, reflecting upon,
and reviewing the phenomenon taken for granted in the common-sense
experience of the natural stance: "To take the theoretic stance is to treat
the everyday world as phenomenon."[7]

Through disciplining myself to see the ascriptions of others as phenom-
ema that were meaningful and understandable in terms of the world under
study and that illuminated some of the salient features of that world, I
became part of my own data. My experiences as a researcher, and my re-
flections on these experiences, enabled me to explicate critical features
of the construction of identity in the lesbian world. In the pages that
follow, I will attempt to take the reader through the process of compre-
hending the meanings of lesbian, moving from a common-sense point
of view external to the lesbian world to an appreciation of the complexity of identity formation among women who love women—a complexity
further complicated by stigma, secrecy, and politics. In the process of
discovering how identity is constructed by women in the lesbian world,
it became clear to me how I was inadvertently fulfilling the conditions
for lesbian identity—all having little to do with same-sex sexual activity.
Before moving to examine the ways in which these women experience
and define themselves, let us look at the pervasive image of lesbians that
informs our society and the assumptions and beliefs that underlie this
image.

SOCIETY AS A SOURCE OF MEANINGS OF LESBIAN IDENTITY

Public Opinion

Stigma surrounds lesbianism in our society.

In the late sixties, a Gallup poll showed that 93 percent of respondents regarded homosexuality as a sickness; a CBS television poll showed that 76 percent of respondents felt that homosexuality was a sickness; and a Louis Harris survey showed that 63 percent of respondents believed that homosexuals were harmful to American life. In addition, a 1969-1973 study conducted by [the Institute for Sex Research (Indiana)] showed that the attitudes toward homosexuality of the three thousand people interviewed were on the whole strongly negative . . . 86 percent . . . objected to homosexual relations without love, 79 percent objected to homosexual relations *with* love.

According to the institute's survey, 60 percent of those sampled disapproved of the fact that nine states do not forbid sex acts between persons of the same sex that are done in privacy between consenting adults.[1]

The public opinion polls cited above are an indicator of the meanings that lesbianism has in our society, meanings that reflect the ideas about lesbianism put forth by important sources of imagery in our culture. In this chapter, I will examine the sources of these meanings and the assumptions that underlie them.

An important underpinning of the negative imagery of lesbianism is the way in which *sex-related identities* in general are commonly construed. Our first focus, then, will be to look at prevalent understandings of these identities. I propose that there is a commonsensical, unexamined assumption about the ways in which these identities are interrelated and a presumption about the direction they should take: I call this assumption the *principle of consistency*. This principle influences how people think about sexual identities on the level of folk theory and is ensconced in Judeo-Christian religious and legal views of sexuality. It is the underlying construct in so-called scientific theories of sex-related identities.

The second part of this chapter examines the views of lesbianism that are held by powerful institutions and reality definers in our society— religion, law, social science, and popular literature—and their relationship to the principle of consistency. Understanding common-sense and scientific views of lesbianism is important because the ways in which we *define* people, and the theories we develop about what causes them to be the way they are, influence how we treat them and what we think ought to be done about them.

This study suggests the necessity of a much more complex view of women who love other women than that found in public opinion, religious and legal views, or scientific theory. The negative imagery of lesbianism in the larger society is a mirror against which alternative meanings— those of subcultures, affiliative groups, and individuals—are reflected, reversed, studied, rejected, or otherwise taken into account.

Sex-Related Identities

The negative meaning of lesbianism within the larger society derives from ideas people have about the relations among sex-related identities. These relations are commonly construed as a set of expectations which I call the *principle of consistency*. This principle assumes that the elements of sex assignment, gender identity, sex roles (or gender roles), sexual object choice, and sexual identity vary together. Before detailing the principle of consistency I shall define each of these elements in turn.

Sex Assignment

Sex assignment is one of the primary ways an individual is socially categorized. Sex assignment as a male or female is made on the basis of physical appearance, which is commonly understood to indicate gender. In a particular instance there may be a difference between the sex that an individual is believed by others to be (the sex the individual apparently is) and the true genetic or chromosomal sex. Similarly, there may be a difference between the gender an individual deems himself or herself to be and the gender others think he or she is. Generally speaking, however, an individual's chromosomal or genetic sex, the gender claimed by the self, and the gender assigned to the individual by others agree. If others believe that the individual is a boy or a girl and proceed to interact with the individual as a member of that sex, the individual is most likely to hold the same view. Sex assignment and gender identity are congruent for most human actors.

Gender Identity

Gender identity, the experienced sense of maleness or femaleness, is based on sex assignment at birth. It is the inner sense of being male or female—corresponding with the body's form and structure. Money and Erhards define gender identity as the "sameness, unity, and persistence of one's individuality as male, female, or ambivalent, in greater or lesser degree, especially as it is experienced in self-awareness and behavior; gender identity is the private experience of the gender role, and the gender role is the public expression of gender identity."[2] Gender identities are an important dimension of the private experience of self.

Gender identity is thought to have its roots in biology, in the constitutional differentiation between male and female that is manifested in chromosomal, gonadal, hormonal, and morphologic sex. Money emphasizes, however, that in understanding the emergence of gender identity, stress should be place not on the comparative weights of genetics and environment but on their interaction.[3] The biological or phyletically written factors have their greatest influence prenatally, while after birth, it is difficult to separate social influences from biological influence.

Postnatally, the programming of psychosexual differentiation is by phyletic decree, a function of biographical history, especially social biography. . . . the social biography program is not written independently of the phyletic program, but in conjunction with it, though on occasion there is disjunction between the two. Once written, the social biography program leaves its imprimatur as surely as does the phyletic. The long-term effects of the two are equally fixed and enduring, and their different origins are not easily recognizable. Aspects of human psychosexual differentiation

attributable to the social biography program are often mistakenly attributed to the phyletic program.[4]

Gender identity implies a whole series of expectations and meanings
with respect to gender role and sexual identities.

Gender Role

Gender identity is the foundation upon which gender role, or sex role,
is based. Money and Erhardt define gender role as "everything that a person says and does, to indicate to others or to the self the degree that one
is either male or female, or ambivalent; it includes but is not restricted to
sexual arousal and response."[5] Gender role involves seeing oneself as a
masculine or feminine being, learning those behaviors and acquiring those
qualitites that are considered masculine and feminine in a particular culture.

The public aspect of gender identities, are an important aspect of most
social identities and gender roles are central to an individual's sense of
personal identity. Gender roles are directly relevant in many kinds of
social interaction and are often taken into account in the course of conduct that is not *apparently* related to issues of sex or sexuality.

For example, one's legitimacy as a social actor in particular settings
may be called into question by virtue of the fact that one is "giving off"
signs of the "wrong" gender role.[6] The successful enactment of gender
roles has implications for the ways in which individuals will be approached
and for the kinds of interactions judged to be appropriate with them.

Duberman notes that gender roles are learned behavior, usually related
to one's biological sex but not necessarily determined by it.[7] She states,
however, that gender identity and gender role are frequently confused:

In our society men are thought of as biologically (inherently and un-
changeably) aggressive and women as biologically nurturant. Gender roles
are seen as naturally identical with [gender identity]. . . . To be born male
does not guarantee masculinity . . . to be born female does not guarantee
femininity. . . . Masculinity and femininity must be learned within a social
context.[8]

Sexual Object Choice

Sexual object choice refers to the gender of the persons toward whom
a human being directs his or her sexual feelings and sexual activities. It is

assumed in folk and scientific thinking that the socially and biologically "natural" sexual object choice is cross-gender, that is, the opposite sex. Sexual socialization—the processes of teaching, training, and learning the sexual meanings of the self—includes learning the behaviors and attributes deemed appropriate for a given gender. Part of sexual socialization is learning appropriate sexual object choices—those persons toward whom it ıs socially permissible to direct sexual and romantic feelings and with whom it is proper to engage in sexual acts.

In our culture, it is presumed that sexual object choices are naturally heterosexual and stable. Sexual object choices and the implied sexual activity connected with these objects lead to the construction of sexual identities.

Sexual Identity

Sexual identity refers to one's social and/or personal identity in terms of preference for sexual activity with a particular gender. As a social identity it is intimately related to sexual activity and sexual object choice: choices of recipients of love and sexual attention have effects on an individual's public sexual identity, there may well be differences on the level of the individual between sexual object choice and sexual identity. As socially construed, however, sexual identity has a clear reference to sexual activity or lack thereof, and an equation is commonsensically made between sexual activity and sexual identity. The only sexual identity that receives wide support in our culture is that of a heterosexual, and the heterosexuality of social actors in the larger society is usually taken for granted. Sexual identities may be highly individual and idiosyncratic, however, they include heterosexual, homosexual or lesbian, and bisexual. These identities are generally presumed to be stable over the life span.

The Principle of Consistency

I propose that the above-named elements of sex-related identities—sex assignment, gender identity, gender role, sexual object choice, and sexual identity— are presumed in our society to relate in a congruent and coherent manner, which I identify as the principle of consistency. This principle consists of assumptions about the development and relations among sex-related identities with respect to both gender sex and sexual identity. Once one of the above elements is given, the rest are presumed to follow or to co-occur. For example: a biological female should experience her gender identity as essentially female and should have a feminine gender role identity. Her sexual socialization should direct her toward men as sexual object choices, who would be similarly consistent in their sex-related identities, and her sexual identity should be heterosexual. Disruptions of the principle of consistency in the area of sexual object choice— that is, when the sexual object choice is deemed incorrect or deviant— typically lead to conjectures about gender role and gender identity. Efforts to explain these variations or "mistakes" in sexual object choice eventuate in theories that focus on "problems" or "errors" in sexual socialization or on anomalies in gender sex. Because of the close linkages between these identities, incongruent or variant sexual behavior is believed to have implications for gender identity, sex role identity, and sexual identity.

The principle of consistency has the status of an unexamined belief underlying both common-sense and scientific ideas about sexuality. It is a reasonable belief about the development of and relations among sex-related identities for *some* people and is a useful predictive model for this group. Yet, it does not admit of variations in the relations among sex-related identities. By accepting the principle as a given, theories attempting to explain variations obscure, rather than illuminate, the understanding of those who do not conform to its expectations. Assuming the universality of the principle of consistency means that efforts to explain variations in sexual behavior and sexual identity must resort to the idea of mistakes, either on the level of biological gender or on the level of socialization or psychosexual development. Further, because the principle of consistency is an unquestioned assumption about the inexorable direction of sexuality, variations or differences from this direction are usually taken as evidence of an essential difference. Thus the identities of those who do not conform are cast as *essential* identities— stemming from an immutable, pervasive moral essence.

The principle of consistency and the idea of essential identity are important in understanding the thrust of prevalent images and theories about lesbians. The principle of consistency presumes connections between sexual identity and sexual object choice on the one hand and gender identity and gender role on the other, so theories using this principle explain same-sex object choices among women by assuming masculinization of gender identity and gender role. Empirically, however, it can be shown that the relations among sex-related identities, roles, and sexual activities are problematic. An "incongruent" sexual object choice and lesbian sexual acts may or may not mean a lesbian sexual identity. Similarly, such a choice or such activities in the experience of an individual may, though they usually do not, have implications for gender identity and gender role.

Noting that the attitudes associated with sex-linked identities are complex, Gagnon and Simon observe that there is a normative constraint to ignore the sexual aspect of most conventional social roles, even those for which an assumption of sexual activity can safely be made. "However, where sexual activity is identified with a role, our sense of the dimensions of this sexual component is often widely exaggerated."[9] The larger heterosexual society usually views the social role of lesbian in sexual terms, and the sexual aspect of that role takes on such a high degree of significance that lesbians are seen primarily as sexual beings. Other characteristics of lesbians are typically subsumed under their sexuality or are ignored. According to the logic of the principle of consistency the focus on lesbian sexuality is connected with assumptions about problems in gender identity and in gender role of the lesbian. The concept of *inversion* is thus often equated with lesbianism.

The Inversion Assumption

Commonplace social notions about what constitutes appropriate sexual expression and behavior for each sex have come to be thought of as an expression of an underlying natural order. Men, by biological mandate, choose women as sexual objects; women, correspondingly, are responsive to men. Variations in sexual conduct such as homosexuality are explained in terms of the assumption that same-sex sexual object choices entail a reversal of gender sex and of sex role. Thus, if a woman chooses another woman as a sex object, she is presumed to be a masculine woman and relationships between women are presumed to mirror heterosexual dyadic roles. Homosexuality frequently connotes inversion both in commonsense thinking and in scientific theories.

Inversion, according to Tripp "implies nothing about the sex of the partner; it refers to a reversal of the commonly expected gender role (or sex role) of the individual, whether animal or human."[10] However, in Tripp's terms inversion does *not* mean a wholesale role reversal for the individuals involved. Rather, it refers to the passive or active role in sexual activities for men and women, respectively, regardless of the sex of the partner in these activities, as opposed to a normative framework that prescribes passivity for women and aggressiveness for men.

Tripp notes that in the past homosexuality and inversion were mistakenly thought of as identical. Properly understood, inversion is a natural part of mammalian sexuality, in both its heterosexual and its homosexual expressions. This point becomes clearer when contrasted with what inversion is not—that is, male/female, procreatively oriented, "missionary position" sexual activity. Tripp states that the inversional alternative is powerfully established in mammalian biology and is not properly characterized merely as a *convenience reaction* but is positively stimulating in itself. In Tripp's analysis, homosexuality can be called inversion only in the sense that some nineteenth-century writers had in mind: a reversal of what one expects a person's sexual object choice to be. Inversion does not imply the masculinization of lesbians (nor the feminization of male homosexuals).[11]

Tripp observes that the logic of ascribing inversion to homosexuality stems from the impulse to "heterosexualize" homosexuality.[12] This term means simply that the logic of heterosexuality is applied to homosexual relations: for example, if a woman has sexual relations with another woman, the prescribed sexual object choice for men, she must really be manlike or masculine. Tripp notes that the ascription of cross-sex motivations and attributes that some lesbians and male homosexuals make about themselves is understandable in this context. He adds that the heterosexual model is a pervasive cultural framework for *all* sexuality, particularly in a culture that is repressive to homosexuality.

Inversion, then, is more accurately thought of as an aspect of both heterosexuality and homosexuality and not as the exclusive character of and explanation for homosexuality. Nonetheless, ideas about lesbianism and male homosexuality are linked commonsensically with the concept of inversion.

Religious Images of Lesbians

Fundamental to the social meaning of identities, especially those having sexual content and/or moral significance in this society are the related views that emanate from the Judeo-Christian tradition. The religious outlook on sexuality and morality serves as the basis for both legal and secular customs and laws. Ancient Jewish religious institutions included *kadesh* (male homosexual temple prostitutes) so early Jewish writing reflects horror of homosexuality only in special circumstances. However it came to be identified with idolatrous pagan behavior after the return from exile in Egypt, thus becoming an anathema to Jews.[13] Both Judaism and Christianity have condemned sexual acts that fall outside the context of marriage and the family. In invoking the concept of natural law, religious thinking tacitly assumes the principle of consistency by deeming *unnatural* any acts and persons that do not conform to its logic. Natural law, which originates in Aristotelian thought, is a notion about the nature and essence of the natural moral order. It is a teleological concept meaning that the goals or ends of processes are posited as active agents in their realization.[14] Embodying the idea that purpose and goals inhere in acts and objects, it implies that the natural and intended goal of sexual activity is procreation. Thus natural law, incorporated into the language of the church and, later, of the legal statutes, is used to condemn sexual activity that is not procreative.

Rule remarked that historically lesbians have lived not so much outside the law, both religious and secular, as beneath it.[15] The absence of proscriptive laws for women implies the low value placed on their activities in a situation of male dominance and authority. Yet, despite the lack of stated scriptural or dogmatic basis, the religious institution yields an image of lesbianism as unnatural and sinful. Although it is difficult to trace the historical development of evaluative prejudice, it seems that the pejorative attitude toward lesbians stems in part from extending biblical injunctions about male homosexuality to include lesbianism and in part from the interpretations and elaborations of dogma by early Christian churchmen.

Love between women received little specific attention in Judaic law, though male homosexuality was unconditionally condemmed: "If a man lies with a man as with a woman, both of them have committed an abomination; they shall be put to death, their blood is upon them."[16] Women were not mentioned in the law. In later rabbinical law, while men were still condemned to death for homosexual relations, lesbians were simply disqualified from marriage with a priest.[17]

The destruction of Sodom and Gomorrah has usually been understood as evidence of divine displeasure with homosexuality, though the traditional understanding of this parable has recently been subject to question.[18] However, the interpretation of God's wrath that has come through non-rabbinical writings into the Christian tradition is the narrow construction of a condemnation of homosexuality.

Though love between women was not specifically forbidden in the Old

Testament—indeed, it was not explicitly mentioned— the inferred religious disapprobation of lesbianism was expressed in secular matters. Klaich observes, for example, that with the official recognition of Christianity in the Roman Empire the works of Sappho (the poet of love between women) were censured. Lesbianism was acceptable in Sappho's lifetime under certain conditions, such as citizenship status of the partners, and at ages considered appropriate.[19]

There is one place in the New Testament that makes specific reference to lesbians:

For this reason God gave them up to dishonorable passions. Their women exchanged natural relations for unnatural and the men likewise gave up natural relations with women and were consumed with passion for one another, men committing shameless acts with men and receiving in their own persons the due penalty for their error.[20]

Rule notes that it could be argued that the above passage refers to men and women having "unnatural" relations with one another, especially given Saint Paul's antisexual stance.[21] This stance, she observes, is evident in the proscriptions of early churchmen with regard to sexuality: "John Chrysostom thought lesbian practice even more disgraceful than homosexuality among men because women should have more shame than men." Rule conjectures that this might be because women came to be interpreted as sexually responsible for the Fall.[22] Concern over the possibility of sexual relations between women in convents spread to proscriptions directed at lay women as well. In *Summa Theologica,* Aquinas directly addressed homosexuality and invoked natural law in condemning such practices. The natural law argument provides the underpinning of anti-homosexual legislation and of sentiment regarding homosexuality in the church today.[25] By A.D. 1260 severe punishments for lesbianism emanated from the legal school at Orleans—women were to be mutilated for first and second offenses. For a third offense she was to be burned. The church itself did not always carry out the punishments but provided the rationale for secular law. Fears of lesbianism became entangled with concern over heresies and later with fears about witchcraft and the suppression of non-Christian cults. In brief, the Judeo-Christian tradition presents an imagery of lesbians as sinners and for a significant part of its history has provided the rationale for punishments in consequence of it its judgments.

In recent decades, there has been concern in some quarters of the church with the oppression visited upon homosexuals, both male and female, and for the part the church has played in this oppression. A consequent effort to reformulate religious views of homosexuality toward at least a less condemnatory attitude, if not acceptance, is emerging among some clergy. The words of Treese perhaps exemplify the most thorough going acknowledgment of the church's traditional position vis-a-vis sexuality and the need for change:

In the realm of human sexuality, I, as a churchman, feel moved to confess that a great deal of the blame for preserving, if not indeed creating, the fears and guilt of sex which permeate our culture, lies at our feet. The failure to see sexual relationship in any other light but the functional one of reproduction has resulted in the limitation of sex to the purely physical with no concept at all of the depth of significant interpersonal trust, empathy and love of which sexual intercourse, at best, is the expression. . . . the pall of centuries of sin-obsessed taboos and misanthropic caricatures of human nature still blankets our culture and informs our mores.[24]

These statements by a churchman should not be read as a wholesale change of the traditional position of the church. As Martin and Lyon note, the "good news" is yet to come for lesbians.[25] The official position of the church remains unchanged.

The church's influence extends far beyond the church itself. Its dicta with respect to homosexuality—and sexuality in general—are reflected in contemporary secular laws that can be invoked against the lesbian. In many instances the language and logic ensconced in contemporary secular laws reflect those of the medieval Christian church and bypass modifications in attitudes that may have gone on in the church itself.

Wainwright Churchill characterizes contemporary Western culture as sex-negative, deeply phobic about sex that does not have the "alibi" of procreation:

In its overesteem of sexual chastity, expressed in both the obsession with monogamy and the obsession with celibacy . . . in its attempt to apply rigid controls to sex and even to suppress it as a dangerous force by the use of almost every conceivable technique (including legal statute), Judeo-Christian culture expresses, even more emphatically than ancient Roman culture, the sadomasochistic conception of sex as an innately violent, foul and criminal drive.[26]

The impact of the Judeo-Christian culture is evidenced in both the language and the intent of the laws that exist in the large majority of states today. Before looking at contemporary laws that potentially can be brought to bear against lesbians, male homosexuals and for that matter, many heterosexuals, I will summarize briefly the close ties between Judeo-Christian sexual and moral proscriptions and secular law.

Lesbians and the Law

When Christianity became the state religion in Rome, the laws of religion were fused with those of the state. The tradition formalized in religious law and custom pertaining to homosexuality was codified into the law of the land. The language and intent of secular law reflected the opprobrium of homosecuality in religious thought and revealed its bias toward procreative sex within marriage. (The term *sodomy* itself stems from the biblical parable of Sodom and Gomorrah.) Homosexual acts apparently were considered too embarrassing to discuss and were referred to as "that abominable sin not fit to be named among Christians."[27]

After the advent of Christianity, Roman rule, which had been fairly tolerant of heterodoxy of custom and belief, came to require spiritual conformity.[28] Homosexuality became equated in people's minds with fears of natural disasters, famines, and treason. Emperor Justinian—of whom it was said, "No Roman Emperor so nearly assumed the position of temporal Pope"—passed the statute in Roman law that became the model for subsequent laws against homosexual intercourse.[29] After Justinian's codification of the law, sodomy never again received intelligent or even rational treatment in the legal sanctions of Judeo-Christian nations until certain reforms in the penal code of France were carried out some thirteen hundred years later.[30]

The Christian church adopted the ancient Jewish sex codes and formalized them into the eccesiastical laws that governed medieval Europe and provided the basis for the English common law. (English common law in turn, was the foundation of colonial law in the United States and of many current laws.) Medieval Europe was the site for overwhelming clerical concern with sins of the flesh.

During the Middle Ages heretics were accused of unnatural vice as a matter of course. Indeed, so closely was sodomy associated with heresy that the same name was applied to both. In "La Coutume de Touraine Angou" the word herite, which is the ancient form of heretique, seems to be used in the sense of sodomite. . . . In medieval law, sodomy was also repeatedly mentioned together with heresy, and the punishment was the same for both.[31]

Churchill suggests that the reasoning behind the connection of heterodox sexual practices with threats to established secular authority could be summarized like this: "Anyone who would practice 'pagan love' is a heretic, all heretics are witches possessed by the Devil, and all heretics and witches attempt to subvert the authority of both Church and State and are therefore traitors."[32] Even in modern times fears about homosexuality are mixed up with ideas of treason.

The French Revolution and the influence of rationalist philosophers saw the reform of laws concerned with sexuality in many parts of Europe. The penal code was limited to manifestly harmful acts, while acts such as fornication and homosexuality were left up to the individual.[33] The Code of Napoleon, which embraced these liberal ideas, influenced the laws concerning sexuality in France, Belgium, Denmark, Sweden, Greece, and many other European countries. Some countries specified the age of consent, but even so, the view of the behavior was considerably mitigated and both parties were likely to be exonerated if both parties were underage. In more recent times France has slightly changed its law to discriminate against homosexual activity of those under twenty-one years of age.[35] Anglo-Saxon countries, however, retained their "fierce morality" and did not undergo the mitigating effects of the Napoleonic codes.[36] Churchill observes: "It is curious that in the United States, where the force of French philosophy made itself felt in the political views of the Founding Fathers, no such reform was incorporated into the penal codes." These remain much more under the sway of a Calvinist philosophy particularly in areas that can be considered as "moral." "American law about sexual morality remains medieval in precept and practice, and all other Anglo-Saxon countries as well as Germany, Austria, and Russia retain modified versions of medieval law."[37]

In 1958 the Wolfenden Committee in England studied the question of homosexuality and the law and made a series of recommendations for reform in this area. After much debate the new Sexual Offences Act of 1967 removed the legal penalties for homosexual acts in private between men over twenty-one. This act, however, deals with the suggestions of

the reformers only gingerly and still contains the potential basis for pro-
secuting homosexual acts between consenting adults.[38] Considering the
United States, one researcher commented: "The present emphasis on
sexual conformity in America may be felt at the level of the federal government; a person even suspected of homosexuality is barred from any
government work. It is the policy of both the Armed Forces and the
Civil Service Commission to exclude any individual suspected of homosexuality from military or civilian service.[39] Private communications from
several respondents as well as from persons familiar with military practices
indicate that even today there is considerable apprehension about being
labeled as lesbian in the service. Churchill notes that "in the United States
homoerotophobia has reached proportions unmatched elsewhere in the
world today."[40] Until relatively recently, all but one of the fifty states'
laws prohibited homosexual activities between males even when carried
out in private between consenting adults.[41]

Sodomy laws form only part of the legal sanctions that are of potential threat to homosexuals. Archaic statutes (about dress codes, failure to
register as a sex offender, prohibition of solicitation) and many laws regarding public behavior (such as loitering, disturbing the peace, idleness)
as well as sexual misconduct laws and licensing requirements can be (and
have been) invoked against gays in many states. In fact, arrests specifically invoking sodomy laws are very rare.

Churchill remarks that

to all these . . . criminal statutes must be added the enormous burden of
the special, so-called sexual psychopath legislation now in force in at least
twenty states. The Barr-Walker Act in Pennsylvania is one example of this
type of legislation. . . . Simple, unaggravated homosexual acts between
consenting adults sometimes come within the scope of this extraordinary
legislation. Even more frightful is the application in some states of these
laws to persons who are merely *accused* or *suspected* of some sexual ir-
regularity.[42]

The patterns of meeting others and establishing relationships among
lesbians differ significantly from those of many gay males (a topic that
will be discussed at length later). Lesbians therefore are extremely infrequently—even potentially—subject to laws regarding public violations.
In the original wording of statutes lesbianism was not specifically mentioned and in fact has come under considerably less legal scrutiny than has

male homosexuality. In some instances this was due to the fact that less attention was given to behavior among women; in others, due to the wording of the law. However, many laws are now being expanded to refer to women and lesbian activities explicitly. Georgia recently enacted legislation specifically leveled at the lesbian.

A set of laws that have been invoked with respect to lesbians are those concerning custody of children. Lesbian or homosexual parents may lose custody or visitation rights in spite of ideal relationships with their children. Having a relationship with another woman can be considered to constitute a material change in circumstances such that an initial custody decision may be reversed as in *Risher* v. *Risher,* a recent Texas court case. In this case, the mother not only lost custody of her children but was ordered to pay child support. In an unusual move, the judge specified that legal costs be paid by the mother at every possible stage of appellate review.[43]

Several writers have noted that where laws specifying homosexual acts have been removed from the books, no real change in the circumstance of the homosexual has obtained: "In the one state, Illinois, in which this type of law was abolished, some citizens complain that the police continue to impose restrictions on homosexual activities by recourse to other laws that have been reinterpreted to cover the prohibition of such activities."[44] This has always been true. As noted above, many of the laws under which homosexuals can be prosecuted are so vague in their wording that almost any sexual act apart from procreative sex in marriage can be interpreted as coming under their purview. Current Arizona law, for example reads:

A person who willfully commits in any unnatural manner, any lewd or lascivious act upon or with the body or any part or member thereof with a male or female person, with the intent of arousing, appealing to or gratifying the lust, passion, or sexual passion of either such persons is guilty of a felony punishable by imprisonment for not less than one year nor more than five years.

Also:

A person who commits the infamous crime against nature with mankind or animal shall be punished by imprisonment for not less than five nor more than twenty years.[45]

Much heterosexual activity is also proscribed under the vague and archaic wording of laws. A current attempt with respect to these Arizona
laws is to remove proscriptions from consensual heterosexual sexual behaviors while retaining sanctions against consenting homosexual behavior. Laws such as those cited above are under challenge in some states
simply because they are unenforceable.

The continuing existence of archaic laws—even if they are unenforceable—has psychological ramifications for the self-concepts and life options
of gay people. Also, the fact that legal sanctions can potentially be brought
to bear against gay people cements negative attitudes that others have
about such behaviors and about gay persons. Further, the possibility of
legal sanctions for homosexual behavior has the net effect of leaving gay
people susceptible to blackmail attempts.

Eighteen states, under general criminal code revisions, have removed
laws against sexual activity in private by consenting adults, Illinois having
been the first. California is the only state that specifically decriminalized
homosexual acts between consenting adults, while two states that rescind-
ed laws affecting homosexuals, Indiana and Arkansas, are currently engaged in efforts to reinstate anti-homosexual legislation. Even if the re-
moval of statutes has not materially affected the arrest rates of homosexuals, the emotional benefit from their repeal was well put by one respondent:

The very idea that one *could* be arrested for one's sexual-emotional relationships is traumatic for most sensitive persons. People who conform
to the canons of reasonable conduct find it an abomination as well as
frightening that they *could* come to the attention of the law because of
some caprice or maliciousness on the part of others. (Tape-recorded interview)

The relationships among public opinion, popular imagery, and powerful institutions are complex and interweaving. Religion and law draw
upon and interact with political and economic spheres. They inform and
are informed by the context of social relations in which they develop. In
turn, the concerns that they formalize are introjected into the beliefs and
images of public opinion. The public then becomes the supportive matrix
for the maintenance of institutions. This reciprocal relationship becomes
evident in the images of lesbians that emerge from these institutions and
that characterize public opinion and in the invocation of natural law as

a rationale for this imagery, which parallels the logic of the principle of consistency. Lesbianism is seen as a moral essence—a quality that pervades and defines the whole person. Religion presents the lesbian in terms of sin, the law in terms of crime, and psychiatry in terms of sickness.

Many researchers in the area of homosexuality have remarked on the affinity and interdependence among religious, legal, and psychiatric thought about homosexuality. For example, Churchill says:

It is not too much to suppose that the extraordinary prestige that psychiatry enjoys in this age of conformity may be explained to a very large extent by the complete dedication that this branch of the healing arts has to precisely the same values and, one must add, precisely the same illusions that receive support from the other moral institutions of our culture.[46]

The picture of lesbians and homosexuals that arose from psychiatry brought about a transformation in social definitions and understanding and a change in vocabularies from a language of sin to one of sickness.

Medical and Psychiatric Images of Lesbians

We will now examine the imagery of lesbians that derives from psychiatry, psychology, and sociology. The literature from these disciplines is viewed as an object of study rather than as a received body of knowledge and is examined with respect to the similarities in the images of lesbians they present. The underlying assumptions of theories of lesbianism will be shown to conform to the principle of consistency and to imply the essentiality of lesbianism.

The disciplines first concerned with studying lesbianism and male homosexuality were medicine and psychiatry. Most of the theoretical treatments of lesbianism from these perspectives employ assumptions of the principle of consistency in sex-related identities and ascribe essentiality to lesbianism. The principle of consistency as the underlying assumption about the relationship among sex-related identities finds its clearest expression in psychiatric theories about the etiology of lesbianism.

Simon and Gagnon note that the study of homosexuality with few exceptions suffers from two major defects: "It is ruled by a simplistic and homogenous view of the psychological and social contents of the category 'homosexual' and at the same time it is nearly exclusively inter-

ested in the most difficult and least rewarding of all questions, that of
etiology." They note that the homosexual, like most significantly labeled
persons, has all his or her acts interpreted through the framework of his
or her homosexuality.[47] These flaws are evidenced in the theories of
lesbianism put forth by Krafft-Ebing.

Krafft-Ebing

Krafft-Ebing was among the first medical doctors to deal with lesbianism. His view of lesbians—pejorative in the extreme—embraced elements of both the consistency principle and the attribution of essential
identity. Krafft-Ebing believed that lesbianism was rooted in constitutional features and heredity; thus he focused on the study of differences in
physical form and structure among lesbians. Failing to find any physiol-
ogical difference between lesbians and heterosexual women, he concluded
that lesbianism was a "natural predisposition that was the consequence or
sign of degeneration and was to be found only in individuals who were
tainted hereditarily, usually by insanity.[48] He thus proposed a genetic
explanation for lesbianism. Klaich comments on Krafft-Ebing's theory:
"In other words, lesbians were born queer: it was in their genes, which
were degenerate. No outside influences worked on such women: their
tendency developed spontaneously from an inbuilt predisposition."[49]
To account for lesbianism in women who had had previous heterosexual
experience, Krafft-Ebing hypothesized that lesbianism could be an acquired phenomenon but that it had an underlying congenital base. This,
he postulated, had been stimulated by some injurious influence such as
fear of pregnancy, exposure to all-female boarding schools or, more pernicious of all, excessive masturbation.

Krafft-Ebing defined homosexuality as the "total absence of sexual
feelings toward the opposite sex." His search for gender sex anomalies,
specifically physical indications of masculinization, illustrates his belief
in the linkage between sexual behavior and gender identity and sex-role
identity as well as his belief in the ontological status, or the status of
being, of lesbianism. His assumption that lesbians are masculinized women
is evidenced in the following: "Uranism [lesbianism] may nearly always
be suspected in females wearing their hair short, or who dress in the fashion of men, or pursue the sports and pastimes of their male acquaintances;
also in opera singers and actresses who appear in male attire on the stage
by preference."[50] Krafft-Ebing regarded suspiciously any women who
showed a disinclination for traditionally defined female sex roles, such

as a preference for intellectual activity to dancing, an interest in the sciences rather than art, and disappointment at not being permitted to go to college.

Although Krafft-Ebing later came to think of lesbianism in terms of a biological failure that could be lived with, for some time he rather contradictorily held the view that it was a pathological condition that should be exorcised. Failing this, women so afflicted should strive to become "neutral" and not engage in any sexual activity whatsoever. Nevertheless, Klaich notes that many lesbians, "long suffering under the criminal/sinner stigma, welcomed the congenital theory."[51]

In contrast to Krafft-Ebing, other theorists focusing on the biology of lesbianism and invoking the consistency principle have been sympathetic to the subjects of their study. Havelock Ellis, for example, was "urgent in arguing a case for biology" which he hoped would provide the basis for legal and social reform.[52] He stated that "homosexuality is a highly abnormal aberration and yet it seems to supply a greater satisfaction than any other aberration can furnish."[53] Ellis felt that, ideally, homosexuals should be celibate, but he was tolerant of their sexuality. In support of law reform, he stated:

But there can be little doubt that we shall gradually break down the false notions and rigid attempts at legal and social prohibitions which have caused so much trouble and confusion. . . . In so doing we shall purify our spiritual atmosphere and strengthen our moral code by removing from it prescriptions which were merely a source of weakness.[54]

Freud

With the turn of the century, Freud's tentative, heuristic exploration of lesbianism signaled a shift from Krafft-Ebing's absolutist and condemnatory statements. But Freud's etiological theory of lesbianism represented a clear instance of the consistency principle, directing attention toward the search for disruptions in the psychosexual developmental process. And it incorporated the image of the masculine lesbian.

Freud considered lesbianism a practice that deviated from the usual. It was, in his view, not necessarily neurotic, nor did he think it necessarily could be cured. He sought to explain homosexuality within the general context of his theory about female sexuality but also assigned importance to constitutional factors. The preoedipal child, Freud said, is naturally bisexual and focused on the mother. A girl's activity is centered on her clitoris. When the young girl discovers she has no penis, she experiences a feeling of castration. She achieves heterosexuality by transferring her libidinal attachment from her mother to her father and entering the feminine phase of passive sexuality. At a later stage of development the young girl "may replace her father with another male figure who will give her, in a non-incestuous situation, a symbolic penis—a baby."[55]

Through appropriate sublimations of her purported wish for a penis a girl may obtain a successful heterosexual resolution to the oedipal castration complex. However, if the young girl's attachment to her father is too strong, she may reject all men because her incest fears become transferred to them, and she may become lesbian: "In this instance, the girl is said to be fixated in an 'immature' level of sexuality, stuck with a feminine oedipus complex." Another way, according to Freud, in which lesbianism may arise is when a young girl fails to enter the oedipal phase at all and clings to active sexuality. She fails to reject her mother as a love object. In this case, the woman is stuck with a masculinity complex. Finally, a woman may become a lesbian even though she has successfully gone through all the stages of sexual development because she suffers a trauma and regresses to a "lower" stage of development.[56]

Freud saw the proper stance of psychoanalysis with respect to lesbianism as discovering the "psychical mechanisms" that lead to a woman choosing another woman as her love object. He felt that the "cure" of lesbianism was difficult, if not impossible.

One must remember that normal sexuality also depends upon a restriction in the choice of object; in general, to undertake to convert a fully developed homosexual into a heterosexual is not much more promising than to do the reverse, only that for good practical reasons the latter is never attempted.[57]

Although Freud was clearly not as pejorative with respect to lesbians as were some of his followers or his predecessor, Krafft-Ebing, he nonetheless presented an image of the lesbian as "immature," "regressive," and "masculine"—an image that not only is echoed by his adherents in the field but informs the lay public image of the lesbian as well.[58]

Pathology Theories

Many psychiatric researchers assume that lesbianism is pathological, or sick, and reduce the study of individuals to the study of a "condition."

In so doing, such theorists embrace the notion of essential identity and assume the consistency principle in their search for disruption in the "normal" psychosexual developmental process.

Caprio's theory of lesbianism deserves attention because when it was published, it was the only full-length psychiatric work dealing specifically with the topic. Other works on homosexuality at that time were largely devoted to the male homosexual and only peripherally concerned with lesbians. Caprio, a psychiatrist, wrote *Female Homosexuality,* which demonstrates the essentialization of lesbian identity by imputing negative qualities to lesbians.[59] His analysis of lesbians was based on data from his patients, interviews with prostitutes, and (amazingly) fictional case histories from *Life Romances* magazine. Caprio's views are considered somewhat of an anachronism today in the psychiatric community;[60] nonetheless, his irresponsible use of sources is unfortunately the basis for stereotype assigned to psychiatric theories by many women within the lesbian community.

Caprio sees lesbianism as a potential threat, "capable of influencing the stability of our social structure." Labeling the lesbian as "emotionally unstable and neurotic," he states that "we" should attempt to "understand" her as a sick person who possesses a form of sexual immaturity leading to "a type of existence that carries with it complications and ultimately results in frustration and loneliness.[61]

One of the most vigorous proponents of the sickness theory is Edmund Bergler, who in his book *Homosexuality: Disease or Way of Life?* theorizes that lesbianism results from oral regression. He states that lesbians are masochists whose sexual behavior is a futile attempt to substitute a clitoris for a nipple as a result of their unresolved weaning problems.[62]

In equating lesbianism with abnormal sexual development and neuroses, different theorists emphasize different kinds of neurotic patterning: Ernest Jones traced homosexuality in women to extreme oral eroticism and "very strong sadism."[63] de Saussure emphasized penis-envy and an identification with the father.[64] Deutsch characterized lesbianism as a perversion—the result of a fixation on the mother—attended by "murderous rage" that was subsequently transformed into love for women.[66] Rado saw all women as basically masochistic with a wish to be violated in sex but then stated rather paradoxically that some women "escape" into homosexuality because they fear "mutilation" by pregnancy and childbirth.[67] Others thought a critical factor in the etiology of lesbians was regression to the mother-child relationship.[68]

Additional explanations that have been proposed for lesbianism are various "fear theories." Rosen catalogues some of the fears that have been posited as causal, most of which are linked with the consistency principle: fear of growing up and assuming adult responsibilities, fear of rejection or castration, and fear of the opposite sex.[69] Other proposed etiological factors are desire to conquer and possess the mother, neurotic dependency, heterosexual traumata, tomboy behavior in early childhood, prolonged absence of the mother, and masturbation with a resultant clitoral fixation. Too, certain social factors such as heterosexual taboos and all-girl groups have been imputed as causal by some analysts. In line with the consistency principle, other theorists have suggested genetic, constitutional, and endocrine abnormalities as causing lesbianism. A review of these theories by Perloff concluded that there have been no definitive findings.[70] Marmor concurred that no definite constitutional or genetic factors have been found to be of etiological significance.[71]

Many of the theories put forth to explain lesbianism have been very simplistic and quite uniformly negative. Romm and Kaye, though certainly far from unique, exemplify this trend. Romm says that

homosexuals of both sexes are human beings who have given up hope of ever being accepted by their parents and by the society in which they live. They are basically unhappy because normal family life with the fulfillment of having children can never be within their reach. The label "gay" behind which they hide is a defense mechanism against the emptiness, the coldness, and the futility of their lives.

Romm goes on to characterize lesbianism as a psychosexual aberration stemming from the inability to handle "the stress of heterosexual relationships."[72] Kaye et al. add more fuel to the negative fire. In a study of twenty-four psychiatric patients, they conclude that lesbianism "is a massive adaptational response to a *crippling* inhibition of normal heterosexual development" (emphasis added).[73] Like Krafft-Ebing, they provide a list of cautions or signs that indicate potential lesbianism: "seeking physical fights in childhood, dislike of dolls, trend toward excessive play with guns, preference for boys' games and a tendency not to play house, a tendency to see themselves as tomboys, and the development of strong crushes on women during puberty."[74] Kaye and Romm invoke the consistency principle in their search for disruptions in the normal psychosexual developmental process. Their theories also support the view of the lesbian as a masculine woman, deviating from traditionally conceived femininity.

Charlotte Wolff, a British psychiatrist, presents a sympathetic, yet ultimately damning, view of lesbians that employs the notion of "the masculine lesbian." She affirms that sex that has procreation as its aim is the only real and authentic sexuality. Though lesbianism is natural to all women, Wolff states, it is "tragic, because of the impossibility to complete sexual fulfillment and particularly childlessness." She asserts that her respondents described lives of resignation and unhappiness, those who described themselves as happy, we are assured, were dissimulating.[75]

Lesbians, according to Wolff, have a labile gender identity that might be interpreted as a sign of immaturity or arrested development but in her view is the retention of the capacity to change from feminine to masculine feelings and attitudes. "I have no doubt that lesbianism makes a woman virile and open to any sexual stimulation and that she is more often than not a more adequate and lively partner in bed than a *normal* woman" (emphasis added). However, she quickly moves to assure the reader that there is only one authentic and fulfilling kind of sexual expression—heterosexuality. "However happy physical relations between homosexual women may be, they are deprived of the last step [presumably procreation] and have to come to terms with a void."[76]

The above psychiatric theories of lesbianism assume pathology and then proceed to illustrate this assumption in their theoretical explanations. Referring to such studies, Naomi Weisstein sees problems with much of the research done by clinicians in that "[they] have never considered it necessary to offer evidence in support of their theories . . . The problem with insight, sensitivity, and intuition (in 'years of intensive clinical experience') is that they can confirm for all time the biases that one started out with."[77] Szasz also cautions against the self-confirming logic of the clinicians: "Nearly all psychiatric concepts have their roots in intuitive inspired truths, that is, faith in the unexamined prejudices of our culture."[78] Ernest Van den Haag avers that using the term *sickness* with respect to homosexuality is an indication "of disguised moral disapproval, whether the user is a layman or a trained therapist.[79]

In addition, it is important to remember that most studies of lesbianism in psychiatry are based on patient samples. In this vein Marmor points out the fallacy of making generalizations about homosexuals on the basis of clinical impressions. He conjectures that were psychiatrists to characterize heterosexuals on the basis of experience with heterosexual patients, a similar picture of psychopathological heterosexuals might arise. He argues that "the psychiatric characterization of the homosexual . . . as psychopathological is fundamentally a reflection of society's disapproval . . . and psychiatrists are unwittingly acting as agents of social control in so labeling it." Further, he cautions that the psychiatric classification of homosexuals is not just a harmless theoretical [issue]: The social and legal consequences of sterotypically labeling an entire group of human beings as mentally ill—or suffering from psychopathology, a euphemistic alternative, are quite serious. . . . Psychiatric labeling of homosexuality as ipso facto a form of mental disorder lends authoritative weight to the basis on which homosexuals are often subjected to discrimination in employment, discharged from military service without honor, deprived of various legal rights, and sometimes confined involuntarily in mental institutions."[80]

Marmor contends that the idea that homosexuality is pathological rests on three premises: "(1) that homosexuals are the product of disordered sexual development, (2) that they represent a deviation from the biological norm, and (3) that they are uniformly deeply disturbed, unhappy people." According to Marmor, these three assumptions are simply restatements of this society's moral disapproval of homosexual relations. Other cultures have widely varied attitudes toward homosexuality, some viewing it positively or neutrally, others negatively. Moreover, he cautions, "it would be a serious error to assume that this society's current reaction to homosexuality is sacrosanct or eternal."[81]

Marmor states that his position with respect to lesbians and homosexuality expresses the majority view among psychiatrists today, which stands in sharp contrast to the earlier and traditional views put forth by the discipline. These opposing interpretations of homosexuality define a heated debate within psychiatry between those who conceive of homosexuality in terms of disease and those who do not. In December 1973 the American Psychiatric Association dropped homosexuality from its nosology of psychiatric disorders. Marmor reports that a recent referendum upheld this decision, revealing that the majority of American psychiatrists no longer regard homosexuality as a clinical entity.[82]

The changing views among psychiatrists concerning lesbianism and homosexuality are supported by another trend in the study of lesbians. Though presaged by the work of Havelock Ellis, this tradition had its more contemporary start with the research of Kinsey, a zoologist.[83] An image of lesbians quite different from the traditional psychiatric picture emerges from the research of Kinsey and others who focus on non-patient populations of lesbians.

Non-Patient Studies of Lesbians

Researchers such as Kinsey, rather than assuming the logic of the consistency principle and ascribing essential identities to the subjects under study, attempt to treat the issue of lesbianism as one behavior in the constellation of human activities and attributes. These observers point out the prevalence of homosexual behaviors in the population at large and emphasize degrees of homosexuality—not all of which eventuate in the assumption of a homosexual identity. Most of these non-patient studies are from the discipline of psychology (with the exception of Kinsey). They attempt to characterize the whole personality of lesbians rather than focusing only on sexual behavior and in some instances provide comparisons with matched groups of heterosexuals.

The studies of sexual behavior among non-patient populations of men and women put the issue of homosexuality in a new context.[84] According to these findings, homosexuality—or more particularly, homosexual behavior—was not limited to a small group of psychiatric patients but was part of the sexual experience of many persons. Kinsey's sexual behavioral rating scale, with values of 0 to 6, represented various degrees of heterosexual and homosexual behavior. The 0 end of the scale signified a completely homosexual behavioral history.

Kinsey concluded that sexuality is best understood not in polar terms but rather in terms of a continuum. In a sense then, Kinsey presented homosexuality as a normal variation in sexual experience. He stressed the importance of social learning in influencing the direction of sexuality. His findings, briefly summarized, were:

The data indicate that the factors leading to homosexual behavior are (1) the basic physiologic capacity of every mammal to respond to any sufficient stimulus, (2) the accident which leads an individual into his or her first sexual experience with a person of the same sex, (3) the conditioning effects of such experience, and (4) the indirect but powerful conditioning which the opinions of other persons and the social codes may have on the individual's decision to accept or reject this type of sexual contact.[85]

The 1960s saw a proliferation of studies of non-patient lesbians. In the main, the results of these various studies contradict both the earlier psychiatric images of lesbians as neurotic, immature, and unstable and the idea that lesbians have hostile or fearful conceptions of the feminine role.

Armon, for example, tested all the major psychoanalytic theories about lesbians with the use of projective tests and found no significant difference between homosexual and heterosexual women on the following dimensions: dependency, hostile-fearful conception of the feminine role, disparagement of men, hostile-fearful conception of the masculine role, confusion and conflict in sexual identification, and limited interpersonal relations. She concluded that "the failure to find many clear-cut differences which are consistent for the majority of the group would suggest that homosexuality is not a clinical entity."[86]

Other studies supporting the view that lesbians are not necessarily neurotic include that conducted by Hopkins. Comparing lesbians with heterosexual women, she found that lesbians were more independent, resilient, reserved, dominant, bohemian, self-sufficient, and composed.[87] Freedman, Saghir and Robins, and Thompson, McCandless, and Strickland all concurred that there were no significant differences between lesbian and heterosexual control groups on neuroticism. They used a variety of psychological tests, the Adjective Check List, and the Semantic Differential Tests in comparing the two groups. Thompson, McCandless, and Strickland found that lesbians scored somewhat higher on self-confidence.[88]

In contrast to studies that claim that lesbian relationships are unstable and unhappy, Loney's study of non-patient lesbians led her to the conclusion that most lesbians were involved in stable ongoing relationships.[89] Seigelman's study corroborates the findings of Hopkins, Freedman, Saghir and Robins, and Thompson, McCandless, and Strickland. Seigelman found in a comparison between heterosexuals and lesbians that "the lesbians are better adjusted than are the matched control group of heterosexual women."[90]

Sociological Analyses of Lesbians

The scant sociological studies of lesbianism are of two types: those which deal with lesbians in prison settings and those which deal with non-institutionalized lesbians and focus on descriptions of selected aspects of lesbianism. None of these studies addresses the issue of identity per se. Some of the prison literature, however, does make a distinction between "real" and "situational" lesbians, that is, the "jail-house turn-out," a woman who has sexual relations with women as a matter of convenience while in prison, where no men are available. A real lesbian is a woman whose sexual and emotional relationships are with other women irrespective of whether she is in a "man-deprived" situation or not.[91]

In the prison studies, lesbians are presented as the epitome of masculinized women, in contrast to the feminine (that is, the "not real lesbian jail-house turn-out"). Giallombardo characterizes the relationships between girls in prison as mirroring the patterns of an extended family, with lesbians taking the male roles.[92]

The studies of non-institutionalized lesbians include an alternative model of psychosexual development and descriptions of various aspects of lesbian careers and life-styles. As discussed above, the Freudian concept of psychosexual development derives from the notion that sex drive is instinctive and that childhood experiences significantly pattern the subsequent course of adult sexuality in terms of sexual object choice: "Both adolescent and adult sexuality were viewed as being in some measure re-enactments of sexual commitments developed, learned or acquired during infancy and childhood."[93] Two sociologists, Simon and Gagnon, challenge this notion and in contrast to Freud posit a discontinuity between childhood and adult sexuality.[94] They see adult sexuality as mutable, amenable to social influences. They acknowledge that children's sex assignment will almost without exception determine their gender role training, which will then influence their later sexual commitments and capabilities. However, they argue for the precedence of social and cultural factors in psychosexual development. They particularly note the effects of sex socialization on the disparate sexual development of boys and girls, a practice that might be seen as militating toward same-sex object choices. In brief, males and females are socialized to regard sex and love in opposing ways. Females are trained to be nonsexual and romantic; males to be sexually active and nonromantic.

Males—committed to sexuality and relatively untrained in the rhetoric of romantic love—interact with females who are committed to romantic love and relatively untrained in sexuality. Dating and courtship may well be considered processes in which persons train members of the opposite sex in the meaning and content of their respective commitments.[95]

Simon and Gagnon's formulation of psychosexual development takes into account the possibility of changes in the orientation of sexual activity, sexual object choice, and implicitly, sexual identity without harking back to childhood experiences for an explanation. They suggest that sexual socialization practices tend toward men and women having quite different (and in some instances opposing) sets of needs and responses. This, in turn, implies that the development of same-sex relationships can be partially understood in the context of these contrasting patterns of sexual socialization for men and women. Simon and Gagnon also focus on continuities in conventional feminine styles of interaction in the initiation and maintenance of intimate lesbian relationships. They observe that romantic, emotional attachments usually precede sexuality for women in lesbian relationships as they do in heterosexual relationships.[96]

Other sociological studies concerning lesbians include Warren's summary of the perceptions of lesbians and "fag-hags" (heterosexual women who seek the company of gay males) among upper-middle-class male homosexuals.[97] McIntosh, Simon and Gagnon, and Bell criticize the emphasis on etiology in the study of lesbianism and homosexuality and note the common characterization in the literature of lesbianism and homosexuality as a condition.[98]

The sociological literature on non-institutionalized lesbianism avoids the characterization of lesbians as unidimensionally masculine and emphasizes the diversity of lesbians in terms of social class, race, and background. And yet this literature possesses another kind of unidimensionality that must be questioned: the definition of lesbian in most sociological studies assumes an equation between activity and identity.

Warren remarks that our cultural message about homosexuals and lesbians is that "people who do those kinds of things *are* that kind of person," (emphasis added) and that this common-sense view prevails in social science literature as well as popular stereotype.[99] This review of the literature supports Warren's contention. Both theorists and the lay public make a common-sense connection between activity and identity, resulting in a mystification of both sexual activity and sexual identity; both see lesbianism as a moral essence that permeates the entire person. With few exceptions the prevailing image of the lesbian in sociology is rooted in popular stereotype and everyday common-sense meanings within the heterosexual society, not in the meanings that women-related women construct for themselves.

From the foregoing summary of the principal theories of lesbianism, it should be clear that the predominating characterization in most social science literature is negative and entails a moral rhetoric. These theories and images imply an ideology of consistency between gender identity, gender role (or sex role), and sexuality that leads to sexual identity. Further, there is the implication that particular sexual behaviors will eventuate in a particular sexual identity. There is growing diversity among those concerned with defining and understanding lesbianism. Before looking at the impact of this diversity on popular opinion, let us examine another source of images of lesbians and lesbianism—that found in popular literature.

Popular Literary Treatments of Lesbianism

Literary treatments of lesbians vary widely, from novels where lesbians are the central characters to pornography written for male consumption. Only a brief exposition is attempted here, but it can accurately be stated that until the 1970s most of the literary works about lesbians stressed the themes of masculinized women and pathology.

The imagery and notions about lesbianism in popular novels in most instances reflect and mirror the conceptions presented in the psychiatric literature. The lesbian is shown as sick and unhappy, immersed in tragic relationships, and doomed to misery. In reviewing lesbian fiction, Martin and Lyon note that prior to the 1960s unhappy endings characterized most literary treatments of lesbianism. Indeed works that were not outright condemnatory were liable to be judged obscene—as was the fate of *The Well of Loneliness.* After the 1960s, Martin and Lyon assert, "Happy endings were 'allowed' in some instances, implying that lesbian couples might be able to establish fulfilling alliances but the quality of the literature still left much to be desired."[100] In a similar vein Rule found that: "self-sacrifice, moral guilt, a twisted psychology, and heterosexual salvation are still the preoccupations of many novels published today."[101]

One book in particular, *The Well of Loneliness,* deserves specific mention because for so long it was the only widely available full-length treatment of lesbianism that had a lesbian as its central character. Rule remarks that *"The Well of Loneliness,* a 1928 novel by Radclyffe Hall, remains *the* lesbian novel . . . either a bible or a horror story for any lesbian who reads at all."[102] She asserts that this novel has influenced millions of readers in their attitudes toward lesbians.[103]

Radclyffe Hall's book was designed as a sympathetic portrait of the lesbian experience, a plea for understanding for "those who through no fault of their own have been set aside from the day of their birth." Endorsing the theory of lesbianism as a congenital condition, Hall was conversant with the works of both Krafft-Ebing and Ulrichs but tended to favor the view of the latter, a lesser-known psychologist. Ulrichs contended that inversion was an inborn natural orientation, that legal and social recognition be given to inverts, and that they be allowed to marry.[104]

Basically, *The Well of Loneliness* is the story of a young woman distinguished by her masculine style and manners—her discovery of her "lesbian nature," her acceptance of herself, and the way in which she resolves to live. Stephen Gordon was so christened by her wise and understanding father, who perceived and understood "her true nature." He resolved to raise her as a son, not only training her in physical fitness but also providing her with a "proper" education. Her mother rejected her and then condemned her outright when she discovered her in an affair with a married woman. "And this thing that you are is a sin against nature."[105]

Stephen goes through a series of experiences, an affair with a maidservant, a romance with a married woman. She is excoriated, rejected, and shamed, but throughout it all, she displays a fine sense of martyrdom and masculine restraint. Stephen longs for the companionship and understanding of men; the virtues with which the author invests her heroine are deemed masculine virtues. Hall's presentation of women, however, manifests no identification with them—they are either vacuous, stupid, and shallow or virtuous, loving, and shallow. Stephen's tutor, who is herself a "hidden invert" is presented as a sad state of affairs, indeed: "She was what came from higher education—a lonely, unfulfilled, middle-age spinster." Mary, the woman that Stephen loves, is presented as the epitome of wifely virtue.[106]

The denouement of the story is that Stephen gives up the love of her life to Martin, who also loves Mary. Realizing that she is not a true man like Martin, she can never make Mary happy and cannot protect her, Stephen has no choice but to be a martyr to her love.

The Well of Loneliness has survived not because it was a good novel, but rather because it was the only full-length novel with a lesbian as the central character. Rule asserts that its survival depended on its misconceptions: "It supports the view that men are naturally superior, that, given a choice, any woman would prefer a real man unless she herself is a congenital freak."[107] Martin and Lyon comment, "Unfortunately, to the uninitiated the book perpetuated the myth of the lesbian as a pseudo-male, and many young women . . . emulated the heroine, Stephen Gordon."[108]

Perhaps the best known of lesbian novels, *The Well of Loneliness* is not atypical of the way lesbians are presented in popular literature: at best victims, martyrs, suicides, and tragic figures; at worst depraved and predatory women. Some of the literature dealing with lesbianism has been veiled in a context of mysticism and exotica, other examples can be described only as trash.[109] *The Children's Hour,* a play by Lillian Hellman, was the early exception to the negative trend in literature concerning lesbianism.

Starting in the 1950s, however, a new kind of lesbian literature began to appear, one that is markedly different from its forebears in being unapologetic and putting forth the positive aspects of relationships between women. These later novels, like *The Price of Salt, A Place for Us,* and *Winterlove,* are not concerned with the masculine/feminine dichotomy and do not restrict themselves to tragic endings for their protagonists.[110] In addition to fiction, there is emerging a new genre of literature under the combined aegis of humanism, women's liberation, and gay liberation, challenging accepted definitions of both homosexuality and heterosexuality. The first book of this type was Martin and Lyon's *Lesbian/Woman,* which related their own experiences as lesbians and included anecdotal material from the lives of hundreds of lesbians they have known.[111]

Diversity among the Image Makers

As has been indicated at some length above, widely diversified opinions about lesbians exist among society's image makers. Different theorists and researchers attribute to lesbians all manner of characteristics—from congenital degeneracy to an abundance of independence, self-reliance, and glowing mental health.

Other views of lesbians have emerged from non-patient studies. Some of the diversity of opinion stems from recent challenges to Freudian theory, which undergirded many psychiatric and psychological studies in the past.[112]

In Leif's review of the tenor of psychiatric opinions about homosexuality, he states that psychiatry is much less sure today about what constitutes healthy sexuality than it was ten years ago and points to a current attitude of exploration in the discipline, in contrast to past certitudes about sexuality. Brecher traces some of the recent changes in attitudes among psychiatrists to their experiences with patients, who now frequently present an exploratory point of view regarding sexuality. He states that psychiatry has come a long way since Krafft-Ebing's "deeply damaging" notions about lesbianism and male homosexuality, but he notes that "Krafft-Ebing's writings and views still remain amazingly popular. Newspaper accounts about sexual offenses continue to cast a Krafft-Ebing-like aura around sexual deviation."[113] Thus, even though the images that psychiatrists and psychologists hold of lesbians are undergoing a change in the direction of a more positive, less pejorative view, the impact of the traditional psychiatric theories continues to reflect and support popular notions about lesbianism. In the public domain, the traditional psychiatric views of lesbianism that entail the consistency principle, essentiality, and sickness continue to hold sway, though the profession as a whole may have changed its views.

Struck with the recent diversity in theories of lesbianism from the psychotherapeutic community, Klaich poses a question: "Since the psychotherapeutic community disagrees so violently as to whether homosexuality is or is not a sickness, why does the American public insist in overwhelming numbers that it is?" She suggests that the majority of popular books and articles on homosexuality (the public's source of information) are written by therapists who endorse the sickness theory. She cites as examples a review of one such book, run as a front-page news story by the *New York Times* and entitled "More Homosexuals Aided to Become Heterosexual," and a *Time* magazine story based heavily on Bergler's book, *Homosexuality: Disease or Way of Life? Time* essay warned readers "that whatever pity they might have in their hearts for homosexuals," they were nevertheless not to let this emotion becloud the realization that they were "face-to-face with a 'pernicious disease.'" She also cites as evidence the widespread presumption of pathology in media presentations about lesbians; in one made by David Susskind, he invited a group of lesbians to one of his shows and then proceeded to pronounce them all "sick."[114]

The popularization of a negative perspective on lesbianism is put forth by books purported to be "all about sex," such as *Everything You Always Wanted to Know about Sex.* In his two-page treatment of the issue of lesbianism—found in the section on prostitution— he dismisses lesbian sexuality as futile with the comment, "one vagina plus one vagina equals zero."[115]

Summary

Thus, the literature on lesbians, both scientific and popular, exemplifies the meanings of lesbian identity on a societal level. Their most elaborate expressions are found in traditional psychiatric etiological theory but are present in religious imagery and the law as well. These socially shared meanings of lesbianism employ the consistency principle and ascribe essential identities to lesbians. To review, the consistency principle is a common-sense assumption or rule about the relations among sex assignment, gender identity, and gender role, which in turn entail expectations about sexual behavior and sexual identity. Violations of these expectations in sexual behavior have implications for how gender identity and gender role will be viewed; that is, the lesbian will be interpreted as masculine. Theories that invoke the consistency principle direct their explanatory efforts to identifying biological anomalies on the one hand or evidences of faulty socialization on the other. Thus, lesbianism as presented in classical psychiatric theories implies both an essential identity that affects the whole person and a masculinization of women.

The attribution of essential identities in theoretical explanations of lesbians is evinced in the reduction of human actors to the status of a condition. Attributing essential identities then leads the theorist to view all other qualities of the individual as emanations of the attributed essence.

The most important criticism of such theories is that they cannot be disproved and thus do not meet criteria for scientific theories. In short, the large majority of the theories presented above simply illustrate their implicit underlying assumptions. Theoretical presentations about lesbianism and the popular images of lesbians and lesbianism reflect and reinforce one another.

The picture that emerges from this review of the images and meanings of lesbianism that obtain in many significant institutions in our society, particularly those that perform socializing functions from which people learn to name and order their worlds and themselves, is almost unrelievedly negative. Nevertheless, the lesbian, in developing definitions of her own self and meanings of her own lesbianism takes these images into account, if only to reject them. These images from the larger society form the template against which other images and meanings are measured and compared.

Within the lesbian community alternative meanings of lesbianism come to supplant these socially shared understandings. These new meanings develop under the protective aegis of secrecy—the overriding condition of the relations between the lesbian world and the larger heterosexual society. Secrecy, in a significant sense, implies social separation between the two worlds, a separation that in turn promotes the articulation of a subculture where alternative meanings of lesbian identity can emerge. The chapter that follows details the ways in which secrecy distinguishes and forms the lesbian world, its influence on relations between the gay and straight worlds, its effects on the quality of life in the lesbian world, and its implications for creating altered meanings of lesbian identity.

SECRECY: THE CONTEXT OF COMMUNITY AND IDENTITY AMONG LESBIANS

The stigma and negative imagery surrounding lesbianism in the larger society produce separation between straight and lesbian worlds. The lesbian world exists under the protective cloak of secrecy, becoming a subculture of the larger society. Secrecy dominates relations between the lesbian world and the straight world and affects the character of life within the lesbian world as well.

The strains and lures of secrecy for those in the lesbian world promote and sustain commitment to the lesbian subculture and identity, in turn, the commitment attenuates relations with the larger society. I will focus first on the accomplishment of secrecy and its effects on interactions between straight and lesbian worlds and then on its effects upon life within the lesbian world itself. Finally I will look at disclosure and its relationship to secrecy, community, and identity.

Secrecy, Stigma, and Audiences to the Self

Simmel defines two types of secret society. The first is a society whose very existence is not known; the second, pertinent to the lesbian world, refers to groups whose existence is known but whose members are not.[1] In his analysis of secrecy, Simmel notes characteristic conditions for the emergence of secret societies, conditions relevant for understanding the development of lesbian subculture. First, a secret society tends to arise under conditions of public "unfreedom" when legal or normative proscriptions regarding persons or behavior necessitate the protectiveness of secrecy. Homosexual activity is proscribed by law and negatively sanctioned by social custom; homosexual persons are potentially or actually stigmatized in most non-homosexual settings. Second, a secret society develops only within a society already complete in itself. Lesbian groups exist as a subculture within the context of the larger heterosexual society, in some ways mirroring its cultural patterns and in some ways opposing them.[2] Third, secrecy tends to extend in importance beyond the secret itself and to permeate every feature of the secret world.[3] Secrecy affects the relations between participants of gay groups and members of the larger heterosexual society. Secrecy affects, as well, the internal relations of the lesbian subculture.

The perceived need for secrecy stems both from the ever present possibility of stigma and from the perception, prevalent in the lesbian community, of heterosexual hostility toward homosexuality. The lesbian who wishes to conceal her gay identity must know whether her audience is straight or gay. In fact, the relevance of categorizing others as straight or gay is a concomitant of becoming gay and of handling gay identity with others. Intrinsic to the sense of gay or lesbian identity is the definition of oneself as different from heterosexual others and the realization that one will be defined as different by straight audiences. This sense of difference is accompanied by the realization that disclosure of the gay self before certain groups may be problematic. The secret has profound effects on the social relations of secret keepers. The definition of an audience as straight or gay, therefore, has implications for the decision by a secretive lesbian to initiate a relationship with a particular audience and for the course such a relationship will subsequently take.

The Heterosexual Assumption

A feature of social interaction among heterosexuals that facilitates the maintenance of secrecy for lesbians is the *heterosexual assumption*—the assumption that parties to any interaction in straight settings are usually presumed to be heterosexual unless demonstrated to be otherwise. The pervasiveness of this assumption and other prevailing norms of social interaction, such as a tacit agreement to accept interactants at face value, make it highly improbable that sexual orientation will be raised as an issue.[4] The heterosexual assumption is obviously functional for covert lesbians, though some feminists and activist gay women see it as a de facto denial by heterosexuals that alternatives in sexual identity and life-style exist. Thus a routine assumption of social interaction in the straight world facilitates secrecy for gays in straight settings and illustrates a feature of gay knowledge about interaction with straight audiences that is part of the "passing" vocabulary of many secretive lesbians.

In and Out of the Closet

In the argot of the lesbian community, *in the closet* generally means being secretive about the gay self with non-gays, though sometimes a lesbian may be in the closet with certain gays as well. A lesbian is *all the way in the closet* when only she knows about the gay self or when only the two parties to a gay relationship are aware of the gay self. She is *almost out of the closet* when most significant others know that the person is gay. One is in the closet, in short, with people from whom the gay self is concealed. A fifty-six-year-old respondent characterized the closet and how it affected her life:

There are all kinds of degrees of being in the closet. There are some people who are so in the closet that only they and their lovers know. All the rest of the world is dealing with a masquerade. And then, there are the kind of people I have known, the kind of life I have lived, where you have a circle of gay people that you move around with. And so, you have some social life with them and then there is the rest of the world that you deal with during the week, during the daylight hours. (Tape-recorded interview)

When a woman begins to identify herself as a lesbian, she is usually already enmeshed in a network of social relations with heterosexual persons. With respect to these established relationships as well as with new relationships, the issue is whether to conceal or to reveal her newly emergent gay identity.

Fear of stigma limits disclosure to those inside the lesbian world. Lesbians usually seek to keep their gayness secret from outsiders by employing strategies such as passing, restriction, separation, and counterfeit secrecy. Different strategies are used with different audiences, such as persons known in the world of work, the family of origin, friends and associates, and fellow gays.

Handling Stigma

Passing refers to acceptance as being "just like everybody else" when in fact some aspect of the person's character or biography, if known, would serve to set the individual apart from others. In this analysis virtual identity refers to the straight mask presented to some audiences by the gay actor, while actual identity refers to the gay self.[5] For the secretive lesbian, passing refers to the accomplishment of a virtual straight identity among straight persons. Passing entails a variety of strategies by the lesbian, including attentiveness to the details of speech, affect, dress, and demeanor and, sometimes, the construction of a "straight front" in concert with male accomplices. On the other hand, elaborate strategies may be unnecessary since lesbians' secrecy is in part protected by the heterosexual assumption.

Strategies of Passing

In addition to relying on the effectiveness of the heterosexual assumption in straight settings, many lesbians employ one or several passive or active strategies of passing. These strategies involve impression management, the camouflaging use of dress and demeanor, and, sometimes, a conspiracy of others. Often, passing requires the conscious management of oneself, others, and situations. Thus, Lyman and Scott note that passers must develop a heightened awareness of ordinary events and everyday encounters.[6] A covert lesbian who wishes to pass becomes concerned not only with obscuring the gay self but also with presenting a convincing straight front to straight audiences. A woman who wishes to pass must be alive to the subtleties and nuances of communication and relationships, to the details of speech and other cues to identity in social interaction. The following comment is by a fifty-eight-year-old woman who has defined herself as a lesbian since adolescence and who presents a straight image in most straight situations. She suggests the extensiveness of impression management involved in passing as well as the tension it can occasion:

When a person is in the closet, you know, they're . . . operating on all levels, and, uh, with, ah . . . considerable tension. I mean you always know thirty seconds ahead of what you say, you know what you are going to say. And you get—I got so used to that, I became almost inarticulate when I had a chance to say whatever I wanted to say. I lost a lot of spontaneity of speech because—because I'd formed the habit of always knowing what I was going to say. Changing genders where necessary—it spread into anything then. I think that is the most oppressive—when you figure how important speech is to you. And then having to monitor [yourself]. (Tape-recorded interview)

Conversations that are relatively matter-of-fact for straight people may occasion elaborate impression management for the secretive gay woman. One strategy used by gays who wish to pass as straight within straight settings is to remain netural in the face of detrimental remarks about gay people. Some respondents stated that they felt they had to silently withstand casual slanders about gay people or risk drawing attention to their gay selves. They reported that they often experienced derogatory remarks about gays as being directed, albeit unwittingly, against themselves. The following account illustrates the inner conflict that passing, by acting nonchalant, might bring about:

I: How do you react when you hear people saying things about gay people or about lesbians and stuff? Does it make you mad?
R: Yeah, well, it does. It depends on who's saying it and what they say. It does irritate me, yeah. But usually I'm so hung up on trying not to act like it means anything to me that I don't feel anything too much. I'm too concerned with the way I'm reacting. It's real hang-up of mine. I wish I didn't feel that way. I care less now than I used to, however. It's just a thing where with some people it could be a stigma, that's why. And I hate to think that I'm influenced by the opinion of people who would maybe have that narrow a mind but I can't help it. There are people who I think would, if they really knew for a fact, might just change the relationship just enough, you know, that I wouldn't like it. I don't know, maybe I'm wrong, maybe it shouldn't, but you see I don't know these things. So I prefer to keep it on—let them think what they want but I don't want to get into confessing it or discussing it or being blatant about it. (Tape-recorded interview)

Simon and Gagnon note that it is easier for gay women to pass than it is for gay men.[7] It occasions little suspicion in the straight community for women to live together, and further, a category of asexual single women is both believable and acceptable in the larger society. Some gay women, however, choose to reinforce their straight image by referring to boyfriends or by having a male friend accompany them on appropriate occasions. The men who serve as a legitimating cover for gay women are frequently gay themselves. A fifty-two-year-old lesbian recounted the way in which a male friend was used to provide a covering rationale for her distress when her twenty-five-year relationship with her female lover ended:

I always took one of the gay fellows to office parties. One in particular, a good friend of mine, is the vice president of a big company; so we played this game for years and making like he and I had been living together. And during the time the break-up with B was going on, my boss threw a big going-away party for one of the guy's fiftieth birthday and I took along this other gay fellow. And this just threw everyone into a tizzy, you know, and I said, "Well, Tom and I have been having problems," so they would think that all this emotional crisis that I had was over him. It turned out well; they think I had been living with him and all that and they think that's the problem. But it was a terrible thing to have to sit there and you couldn't talk—there was nobody to tell it to. (Tape-recorded interview)

The use of a male companion as a cover may be functional for maintaining secrecy but, ironically, success in passing may exacerbate a subjective sense of isolation. As indicated above, techniques for maintaining secrecy are a double-edged sword. Secrecy maintenance avoids the problems of stigma and discreditability. Simultaneously, however, it prevents truly intimate interaction with those unaware of the passer's secret.

Nonverbal Cues to the Self

Modes of dressing and management of appearance are nonverbal ways of giving information about the self. An important aspect of passing, therefore, is to conform scrupulously in dress and appearance to the feminine styles prevalent in the straight community. Lesbians are aware of the masculine stereotype of lesbians held by the straight world, so it is not unusual to hear very feminine-appearing lesbians express concern about features of dress that they fear might be clues to the gay self. Dress style and appearance can be used as protective coloration to conceal or reveal information about the self.

One respondent spoke about the way in which she used such cues when she felt that her gayness was in danger of being exposed:

Sometimes I would feel that things were getting a little too close for comfort. I would feel uneasy, and, uh, so I would do the super-feminine bit. It's not too difficult for me to do, if I really work myself up to it. I used to be able to do it and enjoy it, but I've had times when I've gotten kind of nervous so I sent up smoke screens as much as possible. You recostume a little bit, you change your mannerisms, you psych yourself out and you bring up topics that are terribly okay, just do the whole thing. It's like guys who are straight but worry about what people think of them and get super-jock. You just select the parts of the role that are the best signals and you send them off. [Laughter] (Tape-recorded interview)

Implied in her remarks is the keen awareness of role as a social construction that one finds in the lesbian world. In connection with this idea Warren notes that actors in the gay world are by virtue of their secret situation immersed in the sociological perspective.[8] Interaction with the straight world is rendered both problematic and ironic by a process of self-consciously approximating approved roles and manipulating both self and others to present a particular image. The secret lesbian becomes a detached observer of the process of role construction by the fact of her reflective distance in role accomplishment.

Passing requires concealing gay identity and suppressing clues to gayness. It implicitly entails relativizing the self in accomplishing an acceptable public identity and may involve the conscious construction of the self for an audience. The context of everyday face-to-face interaction presents the secretive lesbian with the challenge of achieving a straight social identity. In the very process of constructing a straight image, the gay self is reiterated in inner awareness. The constraint reported by lesbians in having to hide their true identity works to increase commitment to that very identity. Within the walls of the self the individual lives in a gay time, but with the world outside she interacts with a straight mask.[9]

Restriction

Among the women with whom I spoke, a few prefer to avoid straight people altogether as potential friends. For these women, the world of work provides the single avenue of contact with straight people. Relationships with work associates are maintained at an instrumental level only. In a very special sense, the "real lives" of these secretive lesbians are spent with gay people in gay spaces that demarcate the gay subculture: the time, places, and people that are significant to these women are all gay. In line with Simmel's observations about the intensity of relations among secret-sharers, the gay audiences before whom the straight mask is dropped assume great importance for the hidden lesbian.[10] Correspondingly, gay time and gay space are given a greater accent of reality than is the straight world. The gay subculture becomes the real world, where the authentic self is revealed. Lesbians whose world of sociability is exclusively gay describe themselves as living a "totally gay life."

Not surprisingly, women who restrict contacts with the straight world perceive the greatest differences between the categories gay and straight and express the greatest social distance from the straight world. Simmel and Warren both note that secrecy may promote the sense of superiority in the way of life of the secret subculture.[11] This notion is exemplified in the comment of one gay woman who maintained she had "nothing in common with straight people":

When I'm around straight people, I can be very shy and uncomfortable, because I can't be myself. So it's probably all tied together. I like gay people more, to me they're much more interesting, maybe I'm able to talk about myself and my marriage[12] so that makes them more interesting. (Tape-recorded interview)

As these remarks imply, concealing the gay self before straight audiences serves to strengthen commitment to audiences where the maskless gay self can be unproblematically presented.

Separation

Within the lesbian subculture, separation of gay and straight friendship worlds is described as "living a double life."

Oh boy, I've lived a double life like you wouldn't believe all my life and sometimes the pressure was so enormous I thought I was going to explode. We'd sit around and have coffee, the girls in the office, and they'd say, ". . . This woman looks like a man. . . . Oh my god, that's a queer," and I'd sit there and listen to this kind of stuff and . . . until I'd just get violent sometimes. And there's been a few times when it's been all I could do just to keep from jumping up and saying, "Look, you guys have lunch with me, we've socialized together for fifteen years. I'm queer!" I've wanted to do it so bad that you know, I, uh, almost explode! Because you know . . . Why? I mean, what would I have accomplished anyway—I would have lost more than I had gained. (Tape-recorded interview)

This woman expressed with a great deal of feeling the twin themes that typify the experience of very secretive women: the frustration imposed by secrecy and the certitude of rejection by straight friends should the gay self be revealed.

Among activist women, leading a double life did occur, though not to the extent characteristic of secretive women. Being secretive among one's friends, with one's family, or in the work world and at the same time being an activist in the gay community was experienced as dissonant by these women. One activist lesbian, unwilling to reveal her gay self to straight friends, spoke about the incongruity between her political and personal lives when acting as a group leader at an activist meeting:

This is hard for me. I am the leader [of the discussion group] and I wish I were in a better place as an example. I feel very gay, I live an entirely gay life-style, that is, my involvement sexually as well as socially is with women, with a woman. And yet I am not entirely comfortable with my gayness. For example, my neighbor is like a sister to me. I've known her for ten years and yet I have never told her I am gay. I am very closed about being gay with many people. It has gotten better over the years. I go back twenty years being gay. I don't feel entirely comfortable within myself about it . . . in terms of sharing it, and yet more and more of my life is devoted to making it possible for gays to live without oppression. (Condensed from field notes)

The separation of gay and straight worlds is the modal pattern among secretive lesbians and is characteristic of some activist women, in at least some areas of association. Although activist lesbians report that this tactic engenders a subjective dissonance and raises the conflict of disloyalty to activist gay audiences (if not to straight audiences as well), it allows the maintenance of relationships with the heterosexual world and with the lesbian world with minimal risk of rejection from either.

Living a double life can be accompanied by a sense of alienation—and can escalate the fear of discovery. Not only may the secretive lesbian be a silent audience to the deprecation of gay people, she must also be able to negotiate relationships skillfully so that straight friends remain unaware of gay friends. Handling a double life requires the most stringent management not only of the self but also of situations and others who might give clues to the gay self. Relationships with the straight world, though uninterrupted, are nonetheless less meaningful when the true self must be concealed. At the same time, though gay friends are privy to the gay self, their friendship claims may be limited by the extent to which the gay actor is committed to maintaining friendships in the straight world; for, under the conditions of living a double life, social time must be divided between gay and straight friends. Straight friends must be handled in such a way that they are unaware of the existence of the individual's commitment to the gay world. This boundary between gay and straight friendship worlds comes to be zealously guarded, not always to the advantage of gay friends, as the following account illustrates:

At a party one evening a group of women discussed the disadvantages of people dropping in without notice. "Sometimes, if I'm not expecting anyone, I won't answer the door. I think it's terrible; what if you are entertaining some straight friends or something and some big dyke comes in. You know, people tell me I shouldn't feel that way, that I'm ashamed of my friends, and well, maybe I am, I don't know, I just feel that way." Another woman concurred: "No, no! I can understand it, I mean. You have to choose who you're going to tell, you have to keep things separate. I mean I agree with you. (Condensed from field notes)

Most of the women that I spoke with in both secretive and activist communities did not want to isolate themselves from friendships with straight people. Yet initiating or maintaining relationships with heterosexuals confronts the lesbian with decisions about disclosure or concealment of her gay identity. Both lines of action entail tension. Disclosure risks the possibility of rejection, while concealment carries the tension of secrecy and conscious management of the self. Many women elect to handle these tensions by keeping their gay lives and straight friends separate, revealing the gay self only to gay audiences and donning a heterosexual mask for straight friends. However, many gay women experience the fearfulness of disclosing the gay self to straight friends as contributing to alienation. Obviously, secrecy precludes the possibility of social supports from the straight world. A secretive lesbian spoke about the lack of acknowledgment and social supports in terms of oppression:

Well, like most oppressed people I didn't realize it. Now I realize that my private life wasn't okay. To have to sit around and go to endless wedding and baby showers and buy gifts and things and no one celebrated my emotional highs with me—and, uh, then when you are in an emotional hole, there is no one to hold your hand as any woman can expect when she breaks up with her boyfriend. (Tape-recorded interview)

Such lack of reciprocal sharing in straight/gay relationships tends to promote a sense of isolation; and the gay woman may see herself successively cut off from meaningful interaction with heterosexual others while correspondingly strengthening her bonds with the lesbian subculture.

The World of Work

Typically the work world is a straight environment in which the lesbian must keep her gay self hidden. Although the necessity for passing may be perceived as more or less urgent with respect to particular audiences of friends and acquaintances, the consequences of breaches of secrecy in the world of work are usually seen as grave, potentially reaching far beyond mere disapproprobation to include the curtailment of a whole career.

Some professions are regarded as more "sensitive" with respect to gayness than others. Women in the teaching profession and women who work with children, for example, feel it incumbent upon them to be very secretive about their lesbianism in the work world. Several women whose work is involved with schools in some capacity stated that they feel inhibited about becoming involved actively or noticeably in the gay community: they feared that if they became identified as gay, they might be fired. The following respondent indicated that although she was with the activists "in spirit," she herself could not be an activist for these reasons:

[I am] aligned with the gay movement in the terms that the feminist movement is. But as far as being active—no. At the present my reasons would be self-protectiveness, in terms of, I don't know if it's a cop-out or not, but in terms of my employment, and . . . I work for [a large public organization] and I work in the school system in the area, and I think there would be negative repercussions if I were active and found to be active, by my agency, and, yeah, I'm not willing to take the risk. I could not be an open activist in the gay movement, I cannot be on the barricades there at the present time, um, and in some respects I doubt that I would be at any time in the near future. (Tape-recorded interview)

The necessity of maintaining secrecy about the gay self places considerable strain on what might appear to be extremely ordinary situations involving co-workers. For example, conversations about relationships or leisure-time activities can be problematic for the secretive lesbian, and casual exchanges about social life can constrain her to being noncommital about her friendships and associations. The perceived need for secrecy about a gay identity in work settings can have profound effects on establishing extra-work relationships with colleagues and may eventuate in tactics of restriction or separation. The problem of having to hide the gay self becomes exacerbated when the successful negotiation of one's business career involves business-connected sociability, a feature of many

professional and business circles as an individual's career advances. I asked
one woman, prominent in the business world, how she handled business-
connected entertaining:

I haven't handled it very well up until now. I haven't done any business
entertaining at home and that's a subject that's about to come up, because
we've just moved and taken an apartment where I now can entertain quite
easily . . . and I'm not quite sure, how I can handle it—it's quite a problem
on my mind right now. Most of the people with whom I'm associated in
business are *very* conservative in every respect—I know specifically that my
boss in particular has a big thing against gay women, because he's been very
overt about it, never dreaming that he's stepping on my toes. I've been
very uncomfortable. I never give in to the urge to say anything and I don't
like that: there is a great deal of discomfort for me in any kind of dishonesty—it is so tied up with the quality of life, so that anything less than
honesty makes me acutely uncomfortable and I get paranoid.
  When I went into this relationship—I never really resolved the relationship of this relationship to the rest of me and my life. I just cut off anything that made me feel uncomfortable about being in this relationship.
Of course, I cut off part of myself. (Tape-recorded interview)

The need for wearing a straight mask in the world of work is part of gay
folklore—a folklore that is documented by the experiences of some gay
women. Among the lesbians I interviewed, two had been expelled from
college and one had lost a teaching position for reasons related to lesbianism. But even among women who have not had such personal experiences,
the experiences of others, the stories that circulate about such incidents,
and a pervasive belief in the likelihood of negative consequences accompa-
nying disclosure in the work world are strong deterrents against revealing
the gay self to these audiences. The reluctance to reveal the gay self in
work situations serves to prevent the work world from being a source of
sociable relationships and enhances commitment to accepting audiences
of gay others.

Counterfeit Secrecy

  Lesbians who conceal gayness from straight audiences usually express
the conviction that the attempt at secrecy is effective and that the straight
masks they present are unquestionably accepted. However, in the experience of some of these women, relationships with friends and family are

more accurately characterized as patterned by the tacit negotiation of mutual pretense through which the gay self is not acknowledged. I call this pretense *counterfeit secrecy.*

Glaser and Strauss, in their discussion of awareness contexts, refer to the state of silent "collusion" between actor and audience as a "mutual pretense awareness context," whereby both parties to an interaction know a secret but maintain the fiction that they do not.[13] Both audience and gay actor cooperate to maintain a particular definition of the situation and both parties tacitly agree not to make that which is implicit explicit by direct reference to it.

Such tacit negotiations function to smooth over a potentially disruptive breach of social expectations. Social actors frequently prefer to ignore a violation of social expectations and to act as if "nothing unusual is happening" in order to maintain the flow of interaction.[14] This purposive ignorance is an important feature of social interaction that gives rise to counterfeit secrecy. Straight people often act as if nothing unusual is happening when presented with gays or with gay situations, providing that no one makes the implicit explicit. Making the violation obvious by naming it or pointing it out would, of course, force acknowledgment of the pretense or give rise to covering tactics.

A respondent in her late fifties commented on the quality of those relationships with straight friends and neighbors characterized by counterfeit secrecy:

I: Were you open about being gay?
R: Well, you know, certainly not verbally, no. But it was that life that so many of us had led. Technically in the closet but where the neighbors, the people you work with, have to know! How can they avoid—but they don't want to put it into words: "Don't tell me, don't tell me." But they would ask my friend[15] what she was going to cook for dinner, and I would interchange with neighborhood men about how to fix the lawn mower, how to build this and that [laughter], and we're talking. It was role playing that we had not constructed but they simply sensed that these were the appropriate people to talk about these things. We used to be just aghast at the assumptions that these people acted on, and yet, uh—nothing was ever said. And this didn't happen just once in my life but in several different relationships where we lived a suburban life or were together in the street and, uh, it seems that people are willing to take you as you are if you just don't burden them with any names. You know, that is my experience with the closet. (Tape-recorded interview)

In relations where counterfeit secrecy prevails, interaction flows smoothly, suggesting a kind of acceptance. However, this seeming knowledge and seeming acceptance cannot be tested for fear of rejection. The whole structure of this ambiguous acceptance is founded upon *not* acknowledging the gay self and thereby functions to confound the possibility of disclosure. In this way, the etiquette of counterfeit secrecy entails discretion that becomes more and more difficult to disrupt as time passes.

An important concomitant of counterfeit secrecy is denial. Denial may be manifested by continued questioning of the gay woman about boyfriends, by references to future marriage, or by other tactics that presume heterosexuality.

The Family of Origin

Few audiences rival the place of the family in terms of intimacy and importance to the individual. After a woman has acknowledged herself as a lesbian, she may be confronted with the decision of whether or not she should reveal her gay identity to her family. The typical intimacy of family relations creates its own pressures toward disclosure: Simmel notes that intimacy makes secret keeping particularly difficult.[16] Disclosure of the gay self to the family of origin, however, raises the specter of rejection from an audience that a lesbian may consider important, for the lesbian typically (and often not incorrectly) has an image of her family as disapproving heterosexuals.

The family, in terms of both proximity and intimacy, is so situated that the management of secrecy is difficult, and the gay self may be inadvertently revealed. During the time a young woman is living at home there are many more opportunities for the family to observe her and to draw conclusions about her personal life and relationships than would be available if she lived away from home. Occasionally, the family's discovery of the gay identity of one of its members occurs dramatically. In the case of this young woman, a spurned lover broke the bond of secrecy:

I had been seeing this woman for about a year, and the relationship ended on a rather sour note. She called my parents and informed them that I was a lesbian They [my parents] thought maybe I should go to California and that it would help me to get over this relationship, this woman. They always thought it was other people that were exerting a bad influence on me. They thought that going away would keep me away from those influences. (Tape-recorded interview)

The parents of another woman surmised their daughter's lesbianism from the fact that she spent all of her free time with another young woman:

I: Do your parents know you are gay?
R: They found out about it. They found out about my affair in college. I don't think I elected to tell them, and of course they shrieked to the roof. . . . They refused to talk about it, or think about it, from that day to this. It was traumatizing for them.
I: Did you talk about it with them when they found out?
R: No, no. They didn't want to. . . . My mother . . . never said another word about it. And that was in 1959 and this is 1974. (Tape-recorded interview)

The consequences of ruptured secrecy, or inadvertent disclosure of the gay self may be that future references to gay identity and acknowledgment of the lesbian's personal life are proscribed within the family. The gay self is considered inappropriate as a legitimate topic of conversation; the lesbian is unacknowledged as lesbian by her family. Thus, counterfeit secrecy commonly characterizes relationships between the lesbian and her family.

The following respondent traces the development of counterfeit secrecy in her relationship with her parents:

R: Well, I was going through a rather dramatic jilting and, uh, I was going to the school psychologist and she told the dean. The dean put a private detective on my tail and as a result everybody I associated with was called in and interrogated and a whole bunch of us were expelled—and so that made me a little more closety.
I: Did your parents know why you were expelled?
R: My family knew that I was in trouble, they knew that I had trouble, but I refused to discuss it with them other than I was having some problem and I could handle it myself, and I didn't want to discuss it with them because I didn't want them to bear what it was at that time. Since then it's different.
I: Your parents now know that you are gay?
R: Yeah. They know. We've never discussed it in absolute specifics but we've discussed it in generalities. My sister knows and we've discussed it. My sister and I talk quite freely, but my father has been very much aware of my gayness for a long time, probably before I was myself. My mother, of course, knew but it was a very difficult thing for her to accept, and so I finally sat her down one day and said, "Look mother, you know like,

um, I'm a good person, I've been moderately successful, I've done well
and, uh, I got married.[17] It saved your face from having an old maid in
the family. But I have to go my own route and want you to respect me
and love me." Well, I knew she did or I couldn't have said that. . . . *I didn't
lay it on them.* You know I didn't blatantly hit 'em with it, but *I just discussed it terms that we didn't have to be that specific but it was certainly
understood what it was that we were discussing.* (Tape-recorded interview)

Denial is shown in the following account by a lesbian whose mother had
been apprised of her daughter's lesbianism:

My mother will ask me occasionally, "How is your love life, dear? Have
you met any nice boys?" And I can just see her clapping her hands over
her ears and saying inside, "Oh, please! Don't tell me!" And I don't. I just
say, "Oh it's fine," or "Yeah, groovy!" It's an unspoken thing in our
house. We don't talk about things like that. *My brother used to know, but
we never talk about it. There are boundaries on the things we talk about.
It's funny how people know, and refuse to know, and won't talk about it.*
(Tape-recorded conversation)

Some families persist in treating the lesbian as if she were in a transitory
stage that will be replaced by heterosexual relationships and marriage;
which in specific instances, this may be the case. Others fail to accept the
evidence of their senses and interpret their daughter's relationships with
women with a kind of deliberate naiveté:

When my parents came to visit us, I showed them through the house.
They saw our bedroom with one double bed in it. But it's like if we don't
name it, don't talk about it, it's not real, it doesn't really exist. (Tape-
recorded interview)

In the experience of some lesbians, parents and family think of the lesbian as sick and hope for a cure. The following account indicates the
stress generated in family relationships by treating the lesbian as sick.

My parents sent me to a psychiatrist to be cured. He said, "I don't know
what your parents want me to cure you from." To this day, that's the way
they think about it, as something to be cured from. "You can't be happy.
There is no way you can be a lesbian and be happy," they think. That's
all they pray for, a big miracle. I mean that's the way they perceive it.

But I tell her, "Mother," I said, "what is happiness for you is not happiness for me." We don't talk about it. It used to really bother me but it's gotten to the point where she's more unhappy than I could ever be. There is nothing I can do about it. I have done my best to try and get her to accept it, you know. I've said to her, "You've got a good kid. She's doing good things and she's bright and she's got a nice home and I've got nice friends and I'm telling you I'm happy." But it's not enough. I can't change her. I finally came to terms with the fact that it was her trip, not mine. (Tape-recorded interview)

Depending on the individual's desire for candidness in relations with family members, relations may be strained because of the family's perceived lack of acknowledgment or of acceptance of lesbianism. Secrecy, counterfeit secrecy, and the tensions generated by the acknowledgment of an unacceptable gay identity may all result in the lesbian's feeling separated or cut off from her relatives. One woman who has defined herself as gay for the past forty years describes the sense of isolation from family and friends that resulted from not acknowledging her relationship with her roommate of fifteen years:

I've hated the idea of all my life having to hide my feelings in front of family and friends and business acquaintances, business associates, and, uh, certain other friends other than my, uh, homosexual friends. This is because honesty is the one thing I believe in more than, uh, anything. I cannot stand not being honest about my feelings and this has been hard on me, but I've had to do it and I've carried it off. (Tape-recorded interview)

The usual pattern of relationships between the lesbian and her family of origin, illustrated in the accounts above, was counterfeit secrecy, combined with an implicit denial of the woman's homosexuality.[18]

Consequences of Counterfeit Secrecy

Secrecy has many ramifications for relations between those who have the secret and those who do not.[19] In general, these consequences are isolation and exclusion from the each others' worlds. The same consequences can be seen with counterfeit secrecy. Further, in relationships where the secret is no secret at all, both actor and audience structure their relations in ways that deny the authenticity of the gay self.

Counterfeit secrecy undoubtedly facilitates the appearance of amicable relations. Knowing that one is excluded from confidence, however, has an impact upon the behavior of those who interact with gay people. The person who has not been granted the right to know is also constrained not to admit knowing that which has never been acknowledged. Relationships between the concealers and the persons from whom something is concealed are weakened by the facsimile of secrecy as a barrier, paralleling the barrier of real secrecy, is raised against true intimacy. In order that relations not be disrupted, the gay self must remain masked, so counterfeit secrecy, like actual secrecy, colors relationships with a sense of inauthenticity. Some women experience the lack of acknowledgment of the gay self as tantamount to rejection. If one must obscure or deny the true self in order to maintain a relationship, then the implication is clear that the true self is unacceptable. Such relationships, no matter how intimate they are supposed to be in terms of conventional social roles, become limited in their intimacy. Lesbians who maintain counterfeit secrecy with others affirm that they feel cut off from being themselves, just as do gay women who maintain real secrecy. Counterfeit secrecy and the fear of disapproval its rupture would bring render others unavailable to provide emotional support of the lesbian. Thus, in ways quite similar to real secrecy, counterfeit secrecy serves to attenuate relationships and to promote commitment to the gay subculture where the gay self is validated.

The inadmissibility of the gay self creates an impetus for further commitment to that very self and to gay audiences that honor and respect the gay self.[20] Secret keepers tend to seek out the company of the secret society in order to compensate for the problems of isolation and to create a place where the maskless self can be revealed.[21] Finally, the gay self, just because it is a secret, achieves overarching importance for the lesbian. Simmel notes that that which must be hidden assumes a greater importance and seems more real than that which can be freely revealed: "What recedes before the consciousness of others and is hidden from them . . . is . . . emphasized."[22] Thus, the consequence of counterfeit secrecy, like real secrecy, is the reiteration of gay or lesbian identity in inner awareness.

Secrecy: Recognizing One's Own

The veils of anonymity are often as effective with one's own as with those from whom one wishes to hide. An unintended consequence of secrecy is that it isolates members of the subculture from one another. The secrecy characteristic of lesbian life has implications for the ability to recognize and meet other lesbians, which in turn has ramifications for identity. An individual may be blocked in identifying herself as a gay because secrecy prevents her from meeting others like herself.

The difficulty of meeting other gay women is frequently a topic of casual conversation among women-related women. This problem is of particular relevance for novice lesbians. The following account illustrates the difficulties encountered by one woman who wanted to meet other women similar to herself in both sexual orientation and social class:

I was more aware of . . . the male community. . . . Who knew there was a female community? [Laughter] The bars were absolutely the only way to meet a female community unless you were at one of the girl's schools back there, you know, Skidmore, Elmira, Vassar, those places there'd be some. I didn't know one lesbian in college for four years. Who ever talked about it? No one ever talked about it. I wanted to know other women and I didn't know anything about it. I had seen people at Fire Island but I couldn't relate to that. Most of the people I met in the bars were from a different background. A lot of people who had really good jobs didn't want to go into the bars. They had too much to lose. So I met a very small part of the gay community—people who didn't have that much to lose—in the bars. I think that's still true to some degree. That there's a whole big social community going, male and female, of people who are making a lot of money and have really good jobs and still can't take the risk. (Tape-recorded interview)

This account exemplifies the barriers to meeting others like the self that are the inadvertent consequences of secrecy. The coming out process is complicated for many women by the relative inaccessibility of supportive others, and the sense of difference that the novice lesbian experiences can be exacerbated by not being able to locate the world of her own.

It has been emphasized that gay women who are passing must be particularly alert to the character of their audiences. Thus it can be inferred that a gay woman would be more likely than others to spot someone who, like herself, is passing for straight, as she would be aware of the nuances of passing.

Goffman makes the distinction between "giving" and "giving off" cues. By giving cues, he refers to consciously and voluntarily transmitting a signal to another about the self; but in the second instance, giving off cues means the involuntary transmission of messages about the self, messages that one might not wish to transmit.[23] Remaining secretive about the gay self and yet wishing to contact others like the self who, more likely than not, will also be trying to pass in straight settings means that one must be sensitive to cues given off by others. At the same time one must be wary about giving off cues to gayness oneself.

People who pass are alive to another's passing techniques and strategies. The failure to say certain things (for example, to specify the gender of an individual referred to in a conversation), secretiveness about one's personal life, expressed lack of interest in males, the fact of never having been married, the presence of a roommate, and the consistent failure to present a male companion at appropriate times— all can start speculation on the part of a gay woman that another woman may indeed be gay.

When I meet new people, I generally assume that they are straight. Then if I find out that they are single, have never been married, or have a room-mate, I start to wonder. (Conversation from field notes)

A standard feature of gay lore is that "it takes one to know one." It seems to me that this is not due to any mystical sixth sense but rather to a sensi-tivity—honed by the experience of passing—to the nuances of various cues. The following account illustrates the belief that one can always tell one's own and at the same time indicates some of the pragmatic ways in which gay people go about discerning secretive gays around them.

I was very closeted and wearing dresses to work and all that and this girl came to work and she really came after me! And I thought it was obvious to everyone in the place. "I'll take you to lunch. Come to my house, we'll have a drink after work," and "Tell me about yourself," and it was much more than just your friendship type of thing and when finally I acquiesced and figured "what the hell" and went over and we had a talk and I asked her, just that, I said, "Well, how did you know I possibly would be inter-ested in you?" And she said, "It takes one to know one," and I find that that's true. I usually always . . . in our crowd we used to call it getting a hum, you know, I can always tell if a girl is gay or if she's looking to be turned out.[24] It's just an intuitive humming kind of feeling. If a woman is attracted to another woman, if she's of that tendency, and she is sitting across the room looking at me, there will be a look in her eyes similar to that of a man, when he finds you attractive. Perhaps I pick up on this be-cause I'm not bad looking, and if a woman is attracted to women, she will look at me in a way that is different or in a way that is different from your heterosexual woman, I guarantee you! It's a look of interest, there is a warm spark in the eyes, and it's different. I can tell. (Tape-recorded interview)

Although this account indicates the way in which small cues, such as eye signals, are put together to identify another gay person, it is highly atypical in suggesting immediate pursuit on the basis of such a hunch. There is, after all, considerable risk that one could be wrong, and gay lore is replete with stories of such mistaken identity.

It is usually the case that such a hunch or intuition about an individual would be followed up by a subtle process of testing the gay hypothesis without taking risks to the self or risking disclosure for the other. Lyman and Scott call these identity negotiations *giving signs of a double identity.* Some lesbians refer to this inferential process as "dropping pins," by which is meant the casual mention of gay places, gay people, or gay events. If the person responds by acknowledging that she knows the persons, places, or events ("picking up the pin"), it is tentatively assumed that she is gay. This inferential process usually takes place with seeming nonchalance and in an indirect manner so that at any point up to the actual verbal disclosure of the gay self, parties to an interaction can signal that they are really not gay after all and withdraw with impunity. As may be imagined, these negotiations frequently take place with straight audiences being none the wiser. Many secretive gay women, however, feel that it is too dangerous to engage in such identification games in straight settings. In such instances secrecy may be effective in concealing the gay self not only from the straight world but from other gays as well.

Effects of Secrecy on Life Within the Gay Subculture

Simmel comments on the tendency of secret societies to claim its members in a total sense. The secret excludes all persons and groups external to the secret, serving to bind the members of the secret society together more closely than ever.[25] The inclusive secrecy of the lesbian subculture has some specific implications for lesbian identity: it creates an atmosphere for exploring lesbianism, provides a source of positive meanings for lesbianism, and helps sustain lesbian identity once it is established.

From the secret subculture alternative meanings of identity emerge. In chapter 5, the context of these alternative meanings is described, but for the present it can be stated that the secrecy of lesbian subculture tends to aristocratize lesbian identity. That is, lesbian identity is defined in a positive way, as special and superior to heterosexual identity. Simmel notes the aristocratizing function of secrecy on the identities of members of secret societies, while Warren makes similar observations with respect to the positive effect of the male gay community on the identities of its members.[26]

The secrecy around gay life provides a protective milieu for trying on a lesbian identity in a favorable ambience. Once lesbian identity has been acknowledged and accepted, the lesbian subculture created by the binding and separating powers of secrecy supports and strengthens commitment to that identity, through association with validating others.

Within the subculture, the bonding nature of secrecy is evidenced in the rapidity with which friendships, at least on a superficial level, are formed. While it is true that the more enduring bonds of friendship are developed over time in the lesbian subculture (as is true in the larger society as well), the mutuality of gayness makes the more casual forms of friendly interaction readily accessible within the protective framework of the subculture. The mutual identification of the other as gay serves to facilitate the initiation of casual friendship and sociability.

Simmel comments on the necessity of staying on good terms with other members of the secret society.[27] In this regard, most lesbians I met perceive the lesbian world as small, one in which it is difficult to extend the boundaries of friendship networks. This perception leads to maintaining the form of friendship, if not the content. Friendship groups in the lesbian subculture are thus strengthened by the lack of alternative ways for meeting other gay women. To a greater degree than is true of the male community, lesbian friendship groups are an important source of romantic and sexual relationships, while gay bars serve a much less important function in this regard than is the case for homosexual males.[28]

Friendship groups among lesbians are frequently comprised of couples in long-term relationships. The breakup of a long-term relationship can be at least temporarily disruptive to the social life of one or both parties to the relationship in a manner analogous to what may happen in a heterosexual friendship group when a marriage breaks up. There is, however, an important distinction between the two: the gay woman does not have alternative sources of gay social life readily available to her. There is thus considerably more pressure in the lesbian world for friendship groups to keep their members than in the larger heterosexual society.

Secrecy tends to intensify differences between the gay subculture and the straight world and to promote cohesion in the secret society. Similarly, secrecy promotes escalation between perceived differences in gay and straight identities. A final consequence that has import for both gay and straight worlds was noted by Simmel: secrecy tends to exclude all those not explicitly included by the secret.[29] Secrecy tends to amplify the sense of difference and to increase the barriers between people, as is shown in the mythologies held by each group about the other. The effect is a mystification of both worlds. Among gays the straight world is frequently caricatured in monolithic terms of intolerance and hostility; the straight world, for its part, not only tends to see the lesbian in stereotypic terms but also has the power to enforce the consequences of its stereotypes. By its very nature secrecy renders correctives to these stereotypes problematic, if not impossible.

Disclosure

The disclosure of lesbian identity is intimately linked with secrecy. Disclosure is intrinsic to secrecy, and revelation has a special allure for secret keepers.[30] According to Simmel, power adheres to secrecy through the knowledge of what revelation can do: "The secret . . . is full of the consciousness that it can be betrayed, that one holds the power of surprise, turns of fate, joy, destruction, if only perhaps of self-destruction." Secrecy thus puts up a barrier and simultaneously tempts one to cross this barrier by disclosure.[31]

Passing, restriction, and separation all involve the keeping of the secret. Disclosure, on the other hand, involves revealing the secret to given audiences. The most salient distinction that gay women make with respect to other persons is to categorize them as either straight (heterosexual, that is, potentially hostile) or gay (homosexual, that is, potentially friendly). This distinction is particularly important with respect to making friends and building friendship networks because the intimacy of friendship escalates the tension toward disclosing a gay identity. Goffman distinguishes between the *own* and the *wise* as two categories of ingroup and outgroup persons (Goffman's general term for nondeviant outgroup individuals is *normals*). The own are the ingroup, whose members share both the stigma and the secrecy of stigma. The wise are those outgroup persons who know ingroup secrets, either because they have been effective in piercing secrecy or because they have gained the trust of ingroup members.[32] Within the lesbian subculture, yet subtler discriminations are made: not all of one's own are considered trusted audiences to the gay self and so, like straight (that is, *normal*) audiences, are presented with a straight mask. Different commitments to disclosure can bring about conflict within the subculture as well as with those external to it. The ethos of openness that increasingly characterizes politicized sectors of the gay community has served to disrupt its boundaries. For some secretive gays, the new openness is perceived as liberating and legitimating. For others, it has created a new class of dangerous own who, by opening the closet door, may take others, less willing than themselves, with them.

The social meanings of disclosing the gay self to straight audiences can be adequately appreciated only with reference to the secrecy of which it is an opposite. Disclosure of the gay self occurs with an awareness that the secret, once revealed, cannot be hidden again. Disclosure also means that with every person to whom the secret is revealed, a trust is given in which the risk of further disclosure is inherent. Nonetheless, some lesbians do select particular straight audiences to whom they reveal the gay self.

Some heterosexuals are differentiated by some members of the lesbian community as being safer than others for the presentation of a gay self. These include straight people with whom the relationship predates coming out; straight friends who have successfully demonstrated the qualities of empathy and discretion; and feminists who are ideologically encouraged or constrained not to stigmatize lesbians and to be supportive of the lesbian life-style. Special audiences of straight persons such as therapists or lawyers would usually be considered safe audiences to the gay self and had been found to be supportive of the gay self in the experience of most of the women with whom I talked.

One activist lesbian remarked that the pressure within certain feminist groups toward acceptance of lesbianism as an alternative life-style helped mitigate, for her, the risks of disclosure:

You know, if I've gotten bad reactions [from disclosure], I don't know about it. But you have to remember that I'm doing this mostly with feminists and there would be a certain kind of social pressure on them from other people if they indicated that it did bother them. They're in a funny position right now because they supposedly can't think that there's anything the matter with [lesbianism]. (Tape-recorded interview)

Four of the women with whom I spoke have never revealed their gayness to straight friends, even in relationships of considerable duration. Considerably more of my respondents, however, expressed great apprehension about having their gayness revealed to further audiences of straight people although they had straight friends who were aware of their gayness. Subsequent disclosures do not necessarily become easier despite having previously experienced acceptance from heterosexual friends.

The timing of disclosure is considered problematic by many. To disclose the gay self at the beginning of a relationship with non-gays runs the risk of immediate rejection by a relatively untested audience and opens up the possibility of accusations of being "blatant." To wait until a relationship has been established, on the other hand, means that the secretly gay woman may be accused of dishonesty in her relationships with her friends. Thus lesbians who wish to maintain or initiate relationships with straights perceive themselves in a "damned if I do, damned if I don't" situation.

Disclosure to straight friends is usually a gradual process. Some lesbians report a preliminary period of feeling others out prior to disclosure. Persons to whom a gay identity is to be revealed might be sounded about their attitudes toward gay people or toward minorities in general. A stage-setting tactic reported by several respondents was to engage a prospective audience in conversation about prejudices against minority groups. Agreement about the unfairness of prejudice would create the background for the revelation of the gay self.

The following nonactivist lesbian is unique in being very open about her gayness; nevertheless, the groundwork for disclosure she describes is mirrored in the accounts of other gay women:

I: What kind of reactions have you gotten being so open?
R: What kind of reaction? There's two ways of approaching it. If you know a person is going to be open to what you have to say, you just go ahead and say and your instincts are pretty true.
I: How can you tell?
R: I don't know; it's a feeling I get. If you know that they're going to be uptight, you lay the trip. You reverse the role and you start talking in such a way that "it's horrendous how people will pick certain things about people's life-styles to be prejudiced against." And you start to say things like "I can never understand how somebody can look at somebody else and say, 'You're not a good human because you're black,' or 'You're not a good human being because you're Jewish,' or 'You're not because you're Catholic' "; I say, "I never can understand that kind of thing. I've never hurt anyone, and I'm Jewish, I'm a lesbian, I don't go around raping little children," and that sort of thing [Laughter] and right away there's no possible way! Even if that's what their feelings would be, it would put too much of a burden on them: they'd have to admit that they're assholes. You just switch the tables. (Tape-recorded interview)

Modes of Disclosure

Modes of disclosure include both direct and indirect verbal and non-verbal forms. For example, the family's awareness of a woman's gay identity usually occurs through observation of cues rather than by direct disclosure on the part of the lesbian. As already indicated, as a close audience to the individual, the family is ideally situated to notice cues to the gay self.

A respondent described the method of disclosure by implication that she had initiated with straight friends after years of secrecy:

If it is quite clear up front that this is part of my life, um, then I don't have to go through all that crap with these people, little stupid games of easing into it, getting to know someone really well and then trying to figure out, you know, like how do I break it to them, because I may lose this friendship because it'll be too much for them. Or I can ignore it and never state it and always have a huge chunk of things I'm stifling. . . . I don't come out and say, "I'm lesbian," but when I'd come in with some-one it would be pretty clear. I'd say, "She and I have done this," or "She and I have done that"; I'd try and be as natural as I would be with a guy, if I was going with a guy, but not having to make this—blowing trumpets, making an announcement when I walk into the room. (Tape-recorded interview)

Thus, implications and inferences may be the vehicle by which the gay self is disclosed. Such a technique entails simply not hiding the gay self. The straight audience is presented with the everyday concerns accompa-nying gayness or with cues to the woman's gay identity.

Nonverbal Disclosure

An identifiably gay style, an appearance that approximates popular stereotypes of lesbians, has repercussions for relations with the lesbian world as well as with the straight world. It can serve to circumscribe rela-tions with more secretive lesbians. As gayness can be ascribed on the basis of association alone, some very secretive lesbians avoid being seen with any obviously gay friends. Such women state that they are fearful that associations with identifiably gay persons may evoke suspicions as to their own gayness. One woman talked about the limits she places on relationships with friends who might draw suspicion to her:

Now they don't go—they don't have anything to do with straight people, and truly sometimes I was embarrassed to be with them. They were so

butchy looking—I felt like I didn't want to go out with them to the store—
what if we would meet some straight friends or something? I'm ashamed
to admit it—it's shitty to feel that way about friends, but I can't help it.
(Tape-recorded interview)

Though the tactic of concealing one's friendships with other gay people
was widely accepted within the lesbian subculture as expedient and understandable, even necessary for the preservation of secrecy, it nonetheless
caused conflict for many gay women.

It is clear that the perceived necessity for secrecy influences the selection of friends in the gay world as well as in the straight world. Highly
secretive lesbians cannot afford to have extensive relationships with men
and women who are obviously gay. In addition to meeting other criteria
for friendship, gay friends are chosen with an eye to the plausibility of
their straight masks and their lack of detectability in the straight world.

Verbal Disclosure

A critical feature in most accounts of disclosure is the emphasis placed
on the verbal assertion of gayness. It is "putting it into words" that marks
the irrevocable breaking of secrecy. According to this logic, behaviors and
situations are capable of multiple interpretations and imputations, but
words are not. Frequently, it is only through such a verbal assertion that
a straight audience will be acknowledged by a gay actor as really knowing,
and it is through words that counterfeit secrecy may be forfeited or bro-
ken. Knowledge of gay identity through direct disclosure by a gay person
is distinguished by many gay women from all forms of proximate knowledge, like strong suspicions, guessing, or hunches. Thus disclosure to
straight friends—precisely because of the importance and irrevocability
it entails—may serve to intensify the bonds of friendship. The friend becomes the wise and shares the special knowledge of a secret world. The
intensity that marks the relations of secret keepers is thereby extended
to special audiences not intrinsically part of the secret world.

Disclosure as an Ideology

Disclosure has a special emphasis in the lesbian community at the
present time, and both secretive and activist lesbians have developed lines
of action in response to this special emphasis. The tension between secrecy and disclosure among lesbians exemplifies Simmel's observation that
disclosure is always just under the surface of secrecy, creating a constant

tension toward breaking the secret.[33] Simmel asserts that pressures develop in secret societies that predispose its members toward disclosure; as these societies sustain themselves, enduring over time, the strength of assertion comes to replace the protection of secrecy.[34]

Over the past several years, with both the advent of gay liberation and the rise of the feminist movement, there has been an increasing resentment of the strictures of secrecy. An ethos of openness has been developing in certain parts of the gay subculture, a phenomenon that has evoked a wide range of responses from the community. The reactions of secretive lesbian groups toward activists and activism span the range of possibilities (with the exception of disinterest). One woman in her sixties, who remains quite secretive about her own gayness with straight friends and family, nevertheless expressed enthusiasm for what she perceived as a movement toward legitimation of homosexuality through the new openness about gayness by activists:

You asked me how I felt about the gay liberation thing and I'll tell you I think you have to go overboard on anything, way overboard, before you —to the extreme before you back up, then you're a step ahead of where you were before, and this is why I have such faith in the kids—nothing is going to change till we go to these extremes. . . . You have to demonstrate, you have to make a scene before you make the slightest impression on anybody. (Tape-recorded interview)

Women such as this one categorically state that secrecy is the worst feature of gay life. Paradoxically, some who find secrecy oppressive also find the openness in the gay activist community to be very threatening. They feel that activism will draw attention to gay women, who heretofore were largely unnoticed.

Most of the time they associated homosexuality with men and now, you know, they've started looking at women and—before we were kind of back over here and it never occurred that two women—two women who aren't even gay at all probably have people looking at them and I'd just as soon not have that kind of attention. What's the benefit of it? Because nobody is really going to accept this. Not in my lifetime. (Tape-recorded interview)

Other lesbians state that they cannot identify with the activists on the basis of either activist techniques or personal style. Some emphasize what they perceive as class differences between themselves and the activists and characterize activist lesbians as "having nothing to lose":

> And you see the public is still not seeing that there are good and bad in this life, too. And, unfortunately, the ones they've seen aren't ones I'd run around with, either, at least some of the ones I've seen on television. Why, they're not my caliber that I would associate with. . . . You get a lot of mouthy women up there, who go hollering around and they're obnoxious—some of—a lot of them are—I guess they are out there fighting the battle for us but I'd rather see some women up there who look like women, presidents of companies that had responsible jobs saying their piece, on a little higher plane. (Tape-recorded interview)

Many secretive lesbians have an ambivalent attitude toward secrecy, perceiving its necessity and at the same time desiring disclosure from the "right" kind of people in order to educate the public about the diverse individuals under the umbrella of homosexuality.

Lesbians whose secret status depends upon the ignorance about lesbianism in the heterosexual world fear the liberationists who emphasize the truth about gayness. For their part activist lesbians develop rationales to account for their openness, which they express in political terms. In a political sense, they maintain, disclosure is a consciousness-raising technique, making people aware of gayness as a life-style, a refusal to hide the gay self. According to some gay activists, concealing gay identity is tantamount to being ashamed of it.

Most overt activists say that they feel a sense of personal freedom in no longer having to mask their gay identity, but they do acknowledge that "doors may be closed to them" in the future for having done so. On the other hand, most activists observe that identifying people by sexual orientation is in itself oppressive and thus consider this emphasis on disclosure a temporary, situated phenomenon that at some future point will no longer be necessary.

> I feel that it was necessary to state that I was a lesbian because it's almost like flaunting it and why would I flaunt that sort of thing? And, um I'm hoping that I'll reach a point in, say, three years where I won't ever have to designate myself by any stupid arbitrary word. . . . But politically, it's absolutely essential, because every time I say that [I'm a lesbian], it's so much easier for someone, um, I hate to use the word *closet*, but for some who don't feel free . . . to be whoever they are, someone who spends all

their time hiding. It makes it so much easier for them to be comfortable with it, comfortable with themselves, you know, and the more of us who are willing to say, "Hey! I'm a lesbian, and we are different from each other, and there is no such thing as a stereotypical lesbian," the freer everyone else will become. But I'm hoping in another couple of years it will be absolutely unnecessary. (Tape-recorded interview)

Effects of Disclosure on Identity

In general, it can be stated that disclosure of lesbian identity functions to support that identity and to promote commitment to it. To assess the supportive effects of disclosure on lesbian identity, two features of disclosure should be taken into account: the context of disclosures and their meaning, as related to the anticipated audience response.

Disclosure takes place either in the gay world or in the heterosexual world. The meaning of disclosure is tied closely with the anticipated response to disclosure an anticipation which, of course, differs considerably according to whether the audience is perceived as gay or straight.

Within the context of the lesbian subculture, a supportive milieu for gay identity, disclosing facilitates entry into gay groups. Such disclosure not only provides entry and promotes the informal forms of friendship and sociability available in the lesbian world; it also allows the discussion and elaboration of this identity with a validating and positive audience of others like the self. Thus, the acknowledgment of lesbian identity promotes the destigmatization of lesbian identity. As might be expected, disclosure of the lesbian self to other lesbians in the context of the lesbian world is usually done for the purpose of making entry into particular groups or of initiating sociable relations with others. The mutual disclosure of lesbian identity is usually the necessary, if not sufficient, condition for the initiation of sociable relations within the lesbian community, unless an individual is assumed to be a trusted wise.

Disclosure within the context of the heterosexual world may be seen as related to three kinds of anticipated response: acceptance, neutrality, or rejection. All three ultimately function to provide direct or indirect support for lesbian identity and to promote commitment to that identity. As is the case with disclosure in the lesbian world, the fact of disclosure itself serves to facilitate the elaboration of gay identity. This is clear when an anticipated positive response to disclosure is realized, for lesbian identity is then given direct support by the audience, and the heterosexual audience in turn becomes the trusted wise. When a neutral response or a rejection is realized, paradoxically, gay identity receives indirect support by virtue of the fact that the individual seeks the company of supportive lesbians and thus becomes closely bound to audiences composed of her own.

Within the more politicized and activist sectors of the lesbian community, disclosure is undertaken as a conscious tactic designed to educate heterosexuals with respect to the existence and diversity of lesbianism. In addition to the educative possibilities incidental to such disclosures to heterosexual audiences, the effect on the disclosing individual is to promote solidarity with lesbians. Again, such political disclosures serve to strengthen commitment both to lesbian identity and to the lesbian world.

Some radical groups within the lesbian community engage in what Humphreys has termed *stigma confrontation*.[35] Stigma confrontation entails the unequivocal statement of lesbian identity (or gay male identity), not so much to educate as to confront. Some of these radical women endorse a separatist philosophy and, therefore, acceptance by heterosexuals is not one of their concerns. Rather, they emphasize the education and liberation of other lesbians. While such groups take an explicitly unapologetic stance of openness toward the straight world, their open stance is ultimately directed at other lesbians in efforts to promote solidarity and to provide support for other women in the coming out process. The net effect of such politically motivated, purposive disclosure is an intensified commitment to lesbian identity and lesbianism as an alternate life-style. In addition, it promotes destigmatization of lesbian identity and increases solidarity among lesbians.

One demurrer should be added. A few of the women I spoke to referred to women who disclosed their lesbian identity to heterosexual others in a "confessional" way because they were reputedly distressed about being lesbians. Such women were not included in this sample. The effects of such self-labeling with the intent of change to a non-lesbian identity fall outside the purview of this analysis. It remains the task of future investigators to explore the ramifications for identity among women who use disclosure as a technique of disidentifying with the social category lesbian.

Summary and Conclusions

The secretive lesbian creates her social identity in the matrix of the lesbian subculture. She may choose to conceal her gay self by passing or by restriction and separation of the audiences to the self. The emergence of lesbian identity renders problematic the presentation of the self to heterosexual audiences as it entails the risk of stigmatization and may occasion material loss. In making decisions about relationships and weighing the merits of secrecy and disclosure, the lesbian takes into account the stigma that inheres in lesbian identity in the larger society and the risks attendant to the revelation of gay identity outside the lesbian subculture.

It has been emphasized throughout this chapter that one of the most significant aspects of being or becoming gay is that it fundamentally alters the relationships of the self to others, based upon the perception of hostility toward gayness on the part of heterosexual society. The relationship of the gay self to the straight world is mediated through secrecy. Secrecy isolates the gay subculture from the straight world and offers refuge to those with lesbian identity through protection and validation.

The requisites of secrecy necessitate the categorization of others as gay or straight. These become the primary typifications through which interaction is filtered. The interactive process of indicating to the self that the self is gay, and that the other is gay or straight, serves to reiterate the primacy of these categories and to emphasize the differences between them. At the same time, the process of repeatedly bringing lesbian identity into private awareness through the exigencies of secrecy serves continuously to elaborate and emphasize its importance.

The meaning of certain regularities observable in the gay subculture is illuminated in the context of secrecy within the gay world. It was noted, for example, that gay referencing functions to reinforce the basis of commonality in the group and to demarcate the gay world from the straight world.

Warren observed that the stigmatization of the gay world ensures that all gay space and time will tend toward secrecy.[36] In multiple ways secrecy contributes to the formation of the gay subculture, intensifies commitment to gay identity, and binds the gay self to its own. By the same token, the importance of disclosure and assertion, newly emphasized in sectors of the gay community, is grounded in the context of the secrecy of that world. But in addition, factors that develop within the secret society militate toward disclosure. The posture of the secret society toward the larger society is ultimately one of vulnerability: the possibility of discovery threatens to rend the safety it offers.

SUPPORTS FOR LESBIAN IDENTITY IN THE LESBIAN SUBCULTURE

A fundamental social law is that social separation leads to cultural differentiation.[1] In the last chapter I emphasized that secrecy forms the social structural situation of the lesbian and is the condition of relations between the larger heterosexual society and the lesbian community. The secrecy of the lesbian world effects a separation between heterosexual and homosexual worlds of meaning that promotes the development of a complex and distinctive lesbian subculture. This subculture, in turn, gives rise to alternate meanings attached to lesbianism and lesbian identity.

However, it is not directly through the separation of isolated individuals that alternative definitions of lesbianism develop. Rather these estranged individuals are integrated into groups within the subculture. Group integration forms the basic condition for the emergence of new cultural meanings of lesbianism and for group support of lesbian identity.

Groups in the Lesbian World

This study concerns two kinds of gay groups—secretive and activist—which provide different, but related, kinds of identity support. These two general kinds of groups are differentiated into subtypes that overlap in various ways with one another. Secretive groups bound together for sociability vary in socioeconomic composition, degree of secretiveness, separation from others, and accessibility even to other gay women. One subset consists of groups that adopt various approximations of male-female role styles. These styles may *appear* similar to those adopted in some activist groups. However, in the latter the adoption of masculine clothing connotes disparagement and confrontation of feminine role stereotypes as well as a preference for nonrestrictive clothing. Activist groups are comprised of feminist, gay liberationist, and separatist elements. They include self-help groups, which, in turn, have various ties with feminism, Marxism, gay liberation, and separatist philosophies. There are also groups characterized by egalitarian relationships, which may be either secretive or activist, as may be bisexual groups, and various combinations of these different group types.

These different groups emphasize two kinds of concerns with the issue of identity: concerns with security and concerns with the content or meaning of gay identity. Groups most concerned with security and the preservation of secrecy about the lesbian identities of their members focus on the protection of their members from untrustworthy or unknown others who might reveal the gay identities of group members. Groups that focus on the content of lesbian or gay identity, such as feminists, activists, radicals, self-help groups, and some role-playing groups, are engaged in the formulation or reformulation of the meaning of the categories gay and lesbian. Of course, both of these identity concerns may overlap in a given instance, for they both entail an emphasis on identity that supports lesbian identity and create pressures for its adoption.

Concerns with Security

Many of the secretive groups in the lesbian community develop for purposes of sociability and leisure-time activity. They function as forums for personal friendships and potential sources of sexual-emotional relationships with other women. Although these secretive groups may not deal explicitly with the content or meaning of lesbian identity, they are concerned that members or potential members so identify themselves in order to secure or protect their secret status. Entry into one of these secret friendship networks usually requires the prior acknowledgment of gay identity by potential members. Persons who are not sure whether they are gay or not are sometimes viewed as potentially threatening to the secrecy of the group, so failure to have a lesbian identity may severely limit acceptance into such community groups on security grounds. Of course, there are exceptions. As elaborated earlier, an outgroup nonstigmatized person who is allowed to share the ingroup secrets is known as *wise*.[2] Trusted heterosexuals or bisexuals, by virtue of their discretion, sympathetic stance, and personal qualities of likeability, may be accepted as group members. Other wise persons may possess some special attribute or service that allows them membership in secret groups. Thus, in order to gain entry into these secret groups, one must either be a lesbian (or a gay male) or must be trusted by at least one of the group members who will testify as to the potential member's discretion.[3]

Concern with the Content of Lesbian Identity

Other groups within the lesbian community, particularly those that hold ideologies of feminism and gay liberation, are concerned with the content or meaning of lesbian identity. The central issue in these groups is the reformulation of lesbian identity as a positive identity choice. Lesbianism in such group implies an alternative life-style. In addition to whatever sociability functions these groups fill, they also have an educative purpose addressed to the novice member who is in the process of coming to grips with gay identity. They are concerned as well with changing the negative imagery gay women may have about their lesbian identities. Some of these groups, such as self-help groups, have institutionalized their concern with reformulating identities and formally provide activities specifically dealing with the issue of lesbian identity. I call such attempts at change and reformulation *identity work*.[4] Within these groups there may be more latitude extended temporarily to bisexual and heterosexually identified women who engage in lesbian activity. Identity statements of heterosexuality or bisexuality are tolerated, being interpreted as a phase in the process of realizing one's gayness or in terms of an individual's having trouble facing her gayness. In these groups lesbian identity receives attention and support, and the ambivalent or the uncommitted receive pressure toward conforming to the identity norms of the subculture. It should be noted that these pressures toward adoption of lesbian identity do not lead in unilateral fashion toward its acceptance. In fact, they may be the basis for disidentification with lesbian identity, and for the maintenance of *idiosyncratic identities*—a point that will be treated further in the chapters that follow.

The Mutuality of Stigma

The gay subculture provides protection for its members by maintaining secrecy about members' identities vis-à-vis the larger heterosexual society. Even most gay activist groups, some of whose members are very open about their own lesbian identities, tend to be secretive and protective about members who do not want to be publicly identified as lesbian. The protective cloak of secrecy extends beyond persons with a lesbian or gay identity to persons within the subculture who define themselves as bisexuals or hetero-sexuals. Thus a rather paradoxical effect of secrecy is not only that it sepa-rates persons and groups from the larger society but also that it provides shelter for neophytes, the undecided, and the curious.

Lesbians recognize that whether or not a particular individual acknow-ledges a gay identity, the heterosexual world may ascribe a gay identity to her on the basis of lesbian associates and that such an ascription would be discrediting and problematic in the heterosexual world. The individual who is in the lesbian subculture though not of it, therefore, receives the pro-tection of the group and is not betrayed to the straight world. With few exceptions, an operative rule in the lesbian community is the protection of all participants from the stigmatizing straight society: whatever ingroup sanctions the community might exercise against persons who deny (or refuse) a lesbian identity, they generally exclude exposure of gay activity or gay associations to the straight world. Even in the politicized sectors of the subculture, there is a prohibition against "pulling the cover" of a gay person or a potentially gay person in front of straight audiences.[5] Thus, the mutuality of stigma, possibly motivated by fears of "return uncovering," affords protection for persons who maintain bisexual or heterosexual identities but have lesbian relationships.

Functions of Gay Groups in Providing Identity Support

Stigma confronts women-related women in the larger society, and identifying as a lesbian is difficult in a negative and stigmatizing context. The identity supports provided by groups in the lesbian world are import-ant in neutralizing and overcoming the stigmatizing effects of the judg-ments of the heterosexual world. All gay groups within the gay subcul-ture serve certain general functions that support the identities of their members, including changing the meanings of the category lesbian through *normalization* of the lesbian world, *nihilation* of the straight world, pro-vision of *ideological justifications* for lesbianism, and *aristocratization* of lesbianism in the face of stigma.

Normalization

On a very general level, the lesbian subculture serves to change the negative meanings of lesbianism through normalization, the process of making gayness routine. The normalization of lesbians and lesbianism is a function of intensive association over time, causing the unusual to become routinized through affiliation.[6] According to respondents, the experience of relating to lesbian women breaks down stereotypes. An individual who sees many gay women finds them indistinguishable from heterosexual women (except for their sexual object choice) and comes to view the lesbian community as extremely heterogeneous in composition. Association over time serves to neutralize stereotypes and render lesbians quite ordinary.

For a long time, even when I was going with B, I called myself straight. *She* was queer, and I was straight. [Laughter] I don't know how that jibed, but 'cause I was still fighting it. But once we went to the [gay] bar it changed my whole life because I thought, gee, there are other gay people, people who looked like me and who I could relate to. I have a choice. I didn't realize that I had a choice. It was just B and I, just the two of us in the world . . . and then to see all these gay women! I really had not expected it or known they existed. I expected to see a lot of gay guys. So I started getting away from her and relating to other women and I guess that's how I finally came out (Tape-recorded interview)

The process of normalization is facilitated by two features of the lesbian subculture, the *homosexual assumption* and *gay referencing*.

The Homosexual Assumption

The homosexual assumption operates in a way similar to the heterosexual assumption in the heterosexual world. In gay settings or among gay people, individuals are generally assumed to be gay unless proven otherwise. Here, as with the heterosexual assumption, identity is unproblematic unless it becomes an issue.

The assumption provides a framework for the discussion and acknowledgment of gay identity and other issues related to gayness, such as gay relationships, gay events, gay places, and other gay people. The homosexual assumption also tends to limit identity questions for individuals who have gained initial entry into lesbian groups. Groups whose main purposes are sociability and leisure activities show relatively little concern with the issue of identity once an interactant has gained entry. They make the homosexual assumption. However, some groups, such as those engaged in identity work, routinely raise identity as an issue. In radical circles the initial declaration of lesbian identity may be quid pro quo for acceptance into the group. Identity is more likely to be a focus of conversation in these groups than in those gathered together for reasons of sociability.

Gay Referencing

Gay referencing means the practice of specifying people, places, and events as gay or straight in conversations among gay people. If a gay interactant fails to make the necessary specification when referring to persons or places, it is asked for: "Is he/she gay?" "Were there gay people there?" "Are your neighbors gay?" Gay referencing has three functions: first, it linguistically separates the subculture from straight society; second, it reinforces the basis of solidarity for the group; and third, it provides tacit permission for the discussion of things of interest to gay people. Although it may be impossible in the straight world, within the subculture gay identity, interests, gay issues can be acknowledged and validated as important; gay relationships can be celebrated. Gay referencing facilitates the acknowledgment of lesbianism and emphasizes gay-related issues in group interaction. Not only is the basis of commonality enhanced in conversation, but the relevance of categorizing the world in terms of straight or gay—including attributing gayness to oneself—is reiterated. Simon and Gagnon have observed in their study of the lesbian community that the socialization process in the gay world emphasizes sexualization of that world.[7] The basis for solidarity in a common sexual orientation is further extended and elaborated in social interaction by gay referencing.

Gay referencing serves as a device for introducing terminology and perspectives of the subculture to the newcomer as well as for emphasizing the common bond of the group members. Gayness becomes a lens through which the rest of experience is focused. Through reiteration, gay referencing effects a normalization of gayness and simultaneously increases the relevance of gayness as a standard against which experience is measured.

Nihilation

Nihilation refers to techniques developed by members of stigmatized groups for shielding themselves from stigmatizers through symbolic denial of the legitimacy and the efficacy of the more powerful group. Nihilation, like gay referencing, serves to set off the gay from the straight world; it emphasizes the legitimacy and validity of gay experience by attempting to "conceptually liquidate" the straight world and thereby to render it harmless.[8]

Nihilation is accomplished at several levels within lesbian groups and with varying degrees of seriousness and playfulness. At its most theoretical level, nihilation suggests that the stigmatizing heterosexual society is fundamentally no different from the stigmatized gay group.[9] For example, a subcultural explanation for the stigmatizing behavior of heterosexuals is that heterosexuals who are anti-gay are really reacting fearfully to their own gayness. Illustrating this nihilating rhetoric is the angry statement to the straight world made by one radical lesbian:

I tell you, the function of a homosexual is to make you uneasy. And I will tell you what we want, we radical homosexuals; not for you to tolerate us, to accept us, but to understand us. And this you can do only by becoming one of us. *We want to reach the homosexuals entombed in you, to liberate our brothers and sisters, locked in the prisons of your skulls.* . . . We will never go straight until you go gay. As long as you divide yourselves, we will be divided from you—separated by a mirror trick of your mind. We will no longer allow you to drop us—or the homosexuals in yourselves— into the reject bin; labelled sick or childish or perverted. And because we will not wait, your awakening may be a rude and bloody one. It's your choice. You will never be rid of us, because we reproduce ourselves out of your bodies—and out of your minds. *We are one with you* (emphasis added).[10]

This statement, directed at the society at large, invokes the notion that all people are gay. This idea, echoed in the rationales and explanations for the perceived hostility of particular straight people toward gay people, is illustrated in the following account:

I was sitting in this conference room when this woman came in. I could swear she was a gay woman. She was really flirting with me, and I have to tell you that I would be the last one in the world to pick it up, but it was really obvious. . . . All of a sudden—and I mean it was like out of the blue—she started this whole diatribe about lesbians and how they were sick and had made bad choices with their lives—it was craziness! The whole subject was hardly related to what it was we were talking about. It was really awful, she was obviously getting a lot of support from the straight people there. I was so furious I couldn't speak—and I'm sure that she was

gay, just sure of it. Why else would she have to go on such a crazy trip
about lesbians? (Tape-recorded interview)

Apart from attributing the stigmatized attributes to the stigmatizers and
asserting the fundamental gayness or bisexuality of everybody, nihilation
less seriously mimics the straight world and straight relationships.

A group of women were driving up a mountainous road one evening. An
older couple was in the car ahead, moving slowly and not very expertly
maneuvering the car around rather sudden curves. Several women in the
car began to parody the conversation they imagined was taking place in
the car ahead, dubbing the couple Mabel and Fred, "two hicks from Iowa."
    "Oh Fred," chirped Mabel, "you're just so strong and masterful and I
really feel safe with you at the wheel taking care of your little wifey-
poo!" The parody went on for several minutes in this vein, mimicking
the supposedly adoring wife and blustering he-man husband. (Condensed
from field notes)

A common way of symbolically nihilating the straight world is to caricature heterosexuals, who are conventional in their sexuality, as ultra-con-
servative in all respects. Or the straight world may be effectively nihilated
and denied importance simply by the refusal to acknowledge straight
people, straight relationships, or straight concerns as legimiate topics for
conversation.

I was talking to L one night about her friendship with J [a woman]. She
described her happiness about the relationship and about their ability to
communicate with one another. I drew an analogy between her relationship with J and my relationship with a man. I became aware of L's deliberate inattention to what I was saying—a contrast to the easy conversation that we had been having. "I don't think there's any comparison,"
she said stonily and abruptly refocused the conversation on gay matters.
(Condensed from field notes)

Another instance of nihilation occurred one afternoon when a group of
women was gathered in the living room of a woman's summer home:

I mentioned that I had a son. One of the women who also had children
responded with interest, and we started talking about kids, school, and
so on. I heard one of the other women say in a quiet, disgusted tone,

"Oh, no! We have to listen to kid-talk now!" She and her friend got up and left the room. (Condensed from field notes)

Such accounts are not meant to suggest that "heterosexual topics" such as children or relationships with men are taboo in conversations with particular gay people or with personal gay friends. However, in groups gathered together for purposes of gay sociability, the emphasis is on gay issues and gay people and heterosexual issues are treated as intrusive.

In sum, groups within the lesbian subculture bring many different tactics to bear in their nihilation efforts vis-à-vis the straight world. On a theoretical level, sectors of the gay world—particularly the more politicized parts of that world—put forth the notion that everyone is fundamentally bisexual or homosexual, thus posing a challenge to the heterosexual scheme of things. In the context of day-to-day interaction in gay groups, nihilation takes place in fleeting instances of mockery, stereotype, and satire, thereby attempting to make stigmatizing society ineffectual and ridiculous. Nihilation tactics are extremely effective tools both for building solidarity within the subculture and for neutralizing stigma.

The homosexual assumption and gay referencing are subcultural ways of normalizing lesbians and lesbianism that implicitly provide support for alternative definitions of lesbian identity for the ingroup. The homosexual assumption works for the ingroup by providing a favorable milieu for gayness and for related issues, while nihilation is at least symbolically addressed to the outgroup—rebuking and challenging its stance toward the gay world. Similarly, two patterns of ideological justification emerge from the lesbian world: one addresses the self-image of the gay group; the other challenges the legitimacy of the larger heterosexual society.

Ideological Justifications

The two forms of ideological justification for lesbianism in the lesbian world correspond to the two different types of groups on which this study is based: that is, secretive and activist lesbian groups. These legitimating ideologies differ in their basic assumptions and in their stance toward the heterosexual community. The ideology of the secretive group emphasizes accommodation by gays to a minority status and stresses not disrupting relations with the heterosexual world. In contrast, the ideology of the activist group rejects the minority status of gays by openly challenging the legitimacy of the heterosexual order.

Among social groups in the subculture those most unwilling to challenge the minority status of gay people are some secretive groups of lesbians. Such groups, though they may well dispute the evaluation of gays by heterosexuals, favor interpretations of lesbianism that view it as a sexual preference rather than a life-style. Explanations for homosexuality within such groups tend to emphasize genetic, hormonal, or innate factors, as opposed to volitional explanations. Some lesbians attempt cosmological explanations that place lesbianism and homosexuality in the context of the larger heterosexual order of things. For example, they propose that lesbianism is a natural form of birth control to prevent overpopulation.

Such explanations provide interpretations of gayness that are not disruptive to relationships with heterosexuals or to commitments in non-gay spheres. Secretive groups that support these notions emphasize similarities between gays and heterosexuals in all spheres except that of sexual activity.

In most secretive groups, then, there is an emphasis on conforming to social norms in nonsexual aspects of life and a consequent minimization of the life-style implications of gayness and lesbianism. Indeed, concern with conforming to the heterosexual normative order may make relationships with obvious gay people problematic. In this regard, Humphreys points out that excessive concern with conformity can lead to an extremely conservative stance, which he calls "the breastplate of righteousness."[11] Whether these concerns with conformity and the minimization of gayness lead to conservative positions in other areas or not, secrecy entails accommodation to minority status.

Some secret groups, though not speaking directly to the issue of the larger society's treatment of homosexuals, assert the superiority of lesbian relationships over heterosexual relationships. While acknowledging the normativeness of heterosexuality, they nevertheless emphasize the distinctiveness and preferability of lesbianism. Lesbians, in this view, constitute a special minority.

The Aristocratization of Lesbianism

Some persons and groups in the secretive lesbian community, though claiming the superiority of gayness, do not challenge the rightness of the heterosexual social order. (Of course, radical groups who similarly assert that gays are superior do challenge the legitimacy of the heterosexual "oppressors.") This aristocratization ascribes special qualities and desirable attributes to gay people, going beyond the mere normalization of lesbianism.[12]

Aristocratization is accomplished in two ways: first, by asserting the superior nature of relationships between women as compared to relationships between men and women; and second, by attributing special qualities to women. Some lesbians focus both on characteristics traditionally attributed to women in our culture (like nurturance, sensitivity, empathy, warmth, and understanding) and on a second set of qualities related to the devalued status of women (like forbearance, strength, and endurance). Yet other lesbians claim qualities traditionally defined as male, such as competence, assertiveness, and aggressiveness.

Relationships between women are often presented in ideal terms as having a greater degree of egalitarianism, mutuality, and sensitivity than those between heterosexual male-female dyads. Community members characterize lesbian relationships as evincing an intuitive understanding between partners and having greater intimacy. Sexual relations are also characterized in the ideology of the subculture as having a greater degree of intimacy and sharing than is reputedly possible between the sexes, an intuitive understanding of the sensual possibilities of the other, and a high degree of emotional, as well as sexual, satisfaction. It is often stated, for example, that women understand how to please another woman sexually better than a man does.

There's little niceties among women. Being a woman you know the feelings of another woman. And just—even the gay men, as feminine as they are, I don't think they still have the sensitivity—a woman's sensitivity—I don't know how to put it. I guess it's the way we've been programmed for centuries. . . .I think just niceties and sensitivities and kindnesses that a woman can show another woman that a man, even if he's extremely nellie,[13] doesn't know . . . because you know what pleases you, and I think that the gentleness and the tenderness and the timing—well, say in sex and things like that, a woman knows. And that's why so many women have sexual problems with men. Sure—I had that problem, you know, when I was going with men. There was always a little something lacking there, and it was just that—just little things that women expect, you just innately know—what you can do for another woman and a man just can't do. (Tape-recorded interview)

Simmel remarks that separation from the larger society through secrecy has the tendency to promote aristocratization among those separated—a contention supported by my observations.[14] Within the lesbian subculture, definitions and understandings of lesbians and lesbianism move beyond normalization to ideal, aristocratized conceptualizations of lesbianism. Thus, in parts of the lesbian world, lesbians are characterized as a special group, endowed with special qualities and attributes.

Challenging the Heterosexual Order

The apogee of aristocratization is expressed in politicized, activist parts of the lesbian subculture. In such groups the whole relation between straight and gay worlds is called into question and the normativeness of the heterosexual social order is explicitly challenged. Groups supporting these views do not accept the preferability, naturalness, and inevitability of the predominating heterosexual order. They may attempt radical destigmatization and stigma confrontation through challenging the legitimacy of heterosexual sex roles and socialization. Radical destigmatization entails the tactic of rejecting the rejectors.[15]

This legitimating ideology has its roots in the gay liberation and feminist movements and prevails in groups where politics, feminism, and the concerns of gay liberation are paramount. Activist ideology sees the status of the gay world vis-à-vis the straight world as a function of political and social oppression. It holds that the current division of society into masculine and feminine roles is inherently disadvantageous to women (a view shared by many current sex role theorists.), expressing the political hegemony of males. Such groups propose that the qualities commonly conceived of as the province of a particular sex are in fact human qualities; they oppose assigning gender to human attributes. Social learning is considered the most important factor determining who and what a person is, while biological conditions or concerns are minimized.[16]

Masculine and feminine are prescribed ways of feeling—you're most comfortable feeling that way and anxious when you don't. So a lot of people are very anxious because those roles are not natural. Some of the things that are most fun are ruled out for the women, and they lose the sense of mastery over their own fate. The way women are defined in this society —they get all the loser traits—dependent, childlike, timid, soft. Lesbians have had a whole realm of experience that most women don't have. Lesbians had to stand on their own two feet—so they're not so easily fright-

ened. They've been scared by experts. That's why lesbians are so important in the feminist movement, because they're the only reservoir of wom-
en with so much risk-taking experience. Society tries to frighten women
with lesbians and tells them be safe, be feminine, and be OK. The movement tries to show straight women that that is a tool of the oppressor.
(Tape-recorded interview)

Some writers in the gay liberationist tradition state that it is important
for gay people to see their position in society in political terms; they attempt to stress the political implications of personal choices.

A major message for social scientists, originating in the Women's Liberation movement, and extended by the Gay Liberation movement, is that
the *personal is political.* Our individual frustrations, self-hatreds, and
neuroses are not just our own problems, to be temporarily alleviated by
therapy or to be accepted because "everyone else has problems." Rather,
the personal problems stem from the power relationships in the larger
society and for personal change to be more permanent, it must relate back
to larger society.[17]

Jill Johnston also proposes the necessity of interpreting the lesbian's position in society in the light of power politics:

Lesbians are defining themselves as political outcasts and as such constitute a political group legitimate by its own creation and challenging by
its very existence if not by any overt action the exclusive political domin-
ion of the heterosexual institution by which women are maintained as the
subservient caste. By this definition lesbians are in the vanguard of the
resistance. If driven back from a position as a group with political consciousness the lesbian would become again a private suffering fugitive
criminal, or sick person by psychiatric terminology, and permitted to
exist only under the old conspiracy of silence.[18]

The ideology that repudiates the status of homosexuals and lesbians in
the larger society takes a stance of confrontation with respect to the heterosexual society. This may be done in the arena of private conviction or
may take the form of political action, such as picketing at public places,
lesbian guerrilla theater, whereby gay people enter straight settings and
either act "flamboyantly gay" or perform elaborate parodies of straight
role-relationships, or other open challenges to the normative order.

Self-Oppression

Violations of the homosexual assumption in political groups are seen as upsetting not only because they signal problems in acceptance of gay identity but also because they are seen as instances of *self-oppression*. The concept of self-oppression suggests that an individual who rejects a gay identity thereby accepts the legitimacy of the larger social order, including its negative evaluations of lesbianism. Such an individual may be seen as refusing to accept the truth about herself and as implicitly condemning herself. Thus, ambivalence in identifying oneself as lesbian, especially in a politicized context, is seen as self-oppression.

Among women who repudiate the legitimacy of heterosexuality, bisexuality is seen as a betrayal of lesbians. In their perspective, to engage in relationships with men after having had lesbian experiences is tantamount to consorting with the enemy. Women who hold this view state that even if an individual heterosexual male is not oppressive to women, the overwhelming oppression of females in the larger society makes it impossible for a woman not to be oppressed in a heterosexual relationship. In the reasoning of radical lesbian feminists and feminist separatists, opting for heterosexuality or bisexuality is choosing to oppress oneself by being in oppressive relationships and symbolically to oppress one's sisters by giving aid and comfort to the enemy.

Separatism

In certain sectors of the lesbian subculture the political ideology indicated above eventuates in a separatist philosophy analgous to black separatist elements in parts of the black movement. Separatism may even imply a disjunction of common interest between lesbians and gay males. Although gay males may be seen as oppressed because of their homosexuality, gay females are seen as doubly oppressed, both as gays and as women. These separatist sentiments were well summarized in an open letter written in a feminist magazine.

I reject any concept that lumps us [gay men and women] together. Society may oppress us equally for our rejections of heterosexuality and label us both gay, but we as women are learning to reject concepts put upon us by straight society. Gay men oppress us as much as straight men. If all men were gay they would still oppress us in the society. We [all women] would still be the typists, the shit workers. Gay men as well as straight men must challenge male chauvinism, which Webster's defines as a "blind and unreasonable attachment to a false cause" [masculinity]. I do not identify with gay men because I refuse to allow society to say I am anything other than a woman. If you must label me, call me a lesbian. . . . I also refuse to identify with my oppressors [gay men] as part of my struggle for my freedom to be human, to form roleless relations with other humans. . . . But right now, although they too are oppressed, I identify no more with them than I do other oppressed men, etc. I want them to be free, but where their heads are at now, their freedom would be at my expense.[19]

One lesbian separatist remarked:

I'm a separatist in the sense that I think it's really important for people to keep the gay male world and the lesbian world separate in their minds. They are *not* the same. Whenever I speak to straight people I find I have to constantly point that out: *No* we don't have steamrooms and sex in bathrooms and leather bars and whips and chains. *No* we don't dig pornography—most lesbian pornography is put out for the titillation of straight men—It's the straight world's fantasy about lesbians. Lesbians have a separate ways of being and acting. Of course, I'm not separated from the straight world. I'm not able to do that at this time—I've got to live and that's reality. Right now I can't separate from the straight world. But I certainly do separate myself from gay men—this business of "we're all gay and we're all together" just isn't so. (Conversation from field notes)

Some women who hold a separatist philosophy emphasize the distinction between the lesbian and the male gay subcultures, others emphasize separation from the heterosexual society:

I worked for a big company for years. I was one of the boys. All into a big power trip, I was making tons of money. I hate to tell you—I was proud of my status. Power, money, being accepted—but it was fucked! Straight people's heads are fucked! About two years ago I decided I would never work for straight people again—ever. And I've been making it. I do things for women, gay women. I paint, do carpentry, and now I'm learning about cars so I can repair cars. I'm learning from men how to do this. I'm not trying to reinvent the wheel so I'll learn from the people who are in the position to teach me—I'm choosing that. But to work for them—I won't do it. I'm looking forward to the day when I can operate totally independently of the straight world—I almost manage to do that now. (Conversation from field notes)

Among some radical lesbians separatism entails proscribing relations between lesbians and all men, including gay men. Other separatist lesbians
proscribe sociable relations with heterosexual or bisexual women as well
as with men, a position elaborated in these remarks:

There is pressure from my friends, my radical friends, to only associate
with up-front [overt] lesbians. It's sort of a problem. If I experience any
conflict in my life, it's around that. I feel like I'm not, you know, that
because I don't think all—I mean there's a part of me that doesn't think
that all men are terrible. You know, that all men are shitty, awful people.
Because I've had these positive relationships with men. And yet I feel
like because I've been so socialized and conditioned that I still may be,
you know, fucked over about it. I still may not want to totally give up.
I still have fantasies about change, you know, revolutionary change, and
I feel like it just can't happen with women, it's got to happen with everyone, with—all the minorities in the world have to sort of like rise up.
And so with this contradiction with my politics in the past, I feel like
my politics have to change. And my influence is in terms of separatism,
like my lover is into it, and the women that she's friends with are. And,
you know, they say things—like my roommate and I and this man bought
our house and another house together. The man used to be her lover for
three years. And she's still friends with him—and these women don't
think my roommate is a lesbian because she still has this relationship with
a man. And there's something very weird about that to me. I mean, this
guy is a wonderful, wonderful person and my roommate had this long
friendship with him, and for her to totally not be friends with him because she's a lesbian is totally not real. I mean, it's—what she feels,
even though she feels she's a lesbian. So I feel that—like there's some dog-
matism within that real heavy radical lesbian movement that I don't feel
I fit into. Part of me would like to fit into it, and belong to them, and
feel that I totally agree with them. It would be a lot easier for me if I did,
and—well, I—if I have to talk to men, if they—the worst is if they saw me
with a man, they would probably say, "Uh-huh, Z has a man friend." I
actually don't have any men friends right now, off by the wayside. But
it's sort of like there is this thing, that to be trusted with being in their
circle of friends that you've given up men, have no ties with men, no conversations with men, and that you don't give any emotional energy to men,
and that you don't feed off any kind of relationship with men. . . . My
friends, for example, would never agree to be interviewed by you; they
wouldn't even come to this house. They consider X and Y [two women,
owners of the house where the interview took place, who define them-

selves as bisexual] to be too middle-class and they allow men in their
house. They put me down for participating in your research. But I was
interested because X and Y told me they had a really nice experience being interviewed. (Tape-recorded interview)

Among groups that hold separatist views, the perceived failure to come
to grips with lesbian identity and the continued maintenance of individual
definitions of the self as heterosexual or bisexual (and in some instances
even gay) are not tolerated. Such individualistic definitions of the self are
seen in terms of elitism and a maintenance of privilege by continuing to
associate with those capable of conferring status—men, including gay men.
All men are seen as oppressors. Such radical lesbians ultimately impugn the
legitimacy of heterosexual women, generating real pressure in some groups
not to associate with heterosexual women because they associate with
men.

Radical lesbian groups and separatist groups can provide strong ideological support for lesbian identities, but their support entails many constraints on individualistic interpretations of lesbian experience. Such
groups construe lesbianism in such a way that continued ties to the heterosexual community, if not looked upon as treason, are strongly suspect.
Identities such as heterosexual and bisexual for persons engaged in lesbian
relationships or involved in the lesbian community are considered politically reactionary and dishonest in radical, separatist groups.

The Principle of Self-Determination

Some activist gay groups, such as some feminist lesbian groups or gay
self-help groups, recognize that acknowledgment of gay identity is difficult because of the stigma attached by the larger society. Such groups
take this difficulty into account by explicitly allowing for a transitional
period during which a woman can come to terms with her gay identity
and by providing the potential gay woman with explanations and interpretations of her experience that support the acceptance of gay identity.

A feature of identity ideology in these groups—and a prevailing ethos
within the lesbian and gay male communities as well—is the principle
of self-determination. It means that persons have the right to define themselves in terms of any identity they wish. This principle is rooted in the
awareness that persons are often unjustly labeled by the outside world,
having identities assigned to them solely on the basis of sexual behavior

or cues derived from appearance, demeanor, or association. An individual in the gay community, therefore, should have the right to decide what her (or his) identity is. There is, however, an implicit expectation that the principle of self-determination will inexorably lead to the acceptance and acknowledgment of gay identity that is considered the essence of the individual. The thinking here is that persons will recognize the gay self "that has been there all along."

Self-Help Groups

Self-help groups within the gay community have developed under the combined aegis of gay liberation and feminism. Serving as bridges between the straight world and other gay groups—usually activist groups—these groups explicitly recognize the lack of socialization and positive support for gay or lesbian identity in the larger society. They therefore make their focus identity work, which is designed to help the potentially gay person to recognize and accept lesbian identity.

Identity work is implemented by providing role models of proud gays, explanatory rationales and positive interpretations of gayness, accounts of other gay peoples' experiences, as well as the opportunity for the novice to talk about her own experience of lesbianism.

I used to think gayness was bad before I came to the center [self-help group]. Now I realize it's something to be proud of—I mean I was proud but it used to bother me what society said about it. (Tape-recorded interview)

Specific activities and counseling sessions form part of the services offered by these self-help groups. They provide a place where persons who are concerned or simply curious about lesbianism can discuss these issues in a supportive environment.

It is presumed in self-help groups that the individual who seeks information about lesbianism really has feelings, attractions, emotional experiences, and possibly sexual experiences that have led her to consider gayness. Although it is not explicitly stated, these groups appear to assume, that if a woman has these feelings, it inevitably means she is really gay or lesbian. Gay people who "feel good about themselves" and their gayness can serve as positive role models for an individual who is investigating gayness, and this, in turn, will promote further exploration of the novice's presumed gayness. To this end, participants in these self-help groups are provided with opportunities to attend rap sessions or so-called gentle encounter groups where they can discuss their feelings, fears, and concerns about gayness and about related practical issues, such as how to handle work relations and relationships with families and straight friends.

In these sessions, persons from the self-help organizations and novices or newcomers share their experiences. The organization that I attended provided growth groups, modeled on the principles of an encounter group. The groups provided a guided series of experiences, some of which focused directly on the issue of sexuality. By and large these sessions were reminiscent of sensitivity groups and experiential groups that one might encounter elsewhere, providing a supportive atmosphere in which women could talk about themselves and their experiences.

On the assumption that acknowledging gayness is often traumatic in a society that either is actively anti-homosexual or ignores it, counseling is usually a feature of self-help groups. In addition, to the concerns of gay identity per se, self-help groups for women typically focus on identity as a woman and on feminist issues. Consciousness-raising sessions emphasizing the experiences common to women are featured, and, to provide an alternative to the gay bar as a meeting place, the organizations offer a variety of social activities—dances, dinners, parties, and other get-togethers.

Summary

Both secretive and activist groups within the gay subculture provide crucial support for emerging gay or lesbian identity. Both group types normalize gayness through the operations of the homosexual assumption and gay referencing. In addition, nihilation tactics—both serious and satirical—are aimed at diminishing the importance of heterosexual standards. Some activist groups, notably self-help groups, consciously set about the process of providing a positive milieu for the exploration of lesbian identity and engage in identity work.

Groups within both the secretive and activist lesbian communities vary in their tolerance for women who do not identify as gay but engage in lesbian relationships or are in the lesbian community over a long period of time. For some groups the risks to security seem too great to admit persons with "ambivalent" (that is, bisexual or heterosexual) identities; others, such as the self-help groups in the activist community, interpret ambivalence as a phase in coming to terms with gayness.

Some radical groups in the community move beyond the issue of mere acceptance of gay identity into questioning the authenticity and legitimacy of the heterosexual social order. Asserting the primacy of gay identity, they develop and emphasize rhetorics of oppression as an explanation for the difficulty in accepting the gay self. In groups such as these, women are encouraged to examine the heterosexual world in political terms and to see the role constructions of the heterosexual world in the context of power relations between men and women, relations considered disadvantageous to women in general and especially disadvantageous to lesbian women. Intolerant of identities other than lesbian identity, particular political groups see identity ambivalence as bad faith and bad politics. While such groups provide strong support for lesbian identity, their stance toward other identities tends to limit their appeal and effectiveness both in terms of the secretive gay community and even in parts of the politicized lesbian community. They nonetheless form the cutting edge of a community which is in the process of redefining itself and developing new standards for viewing lesbianism and lesbian identity and their relation to society.

The combination of the various types of gay groups outlined above form a distinctive subculture. Perhaps the most important function of the subculture vis-à-vis identity is its function as a source of alternative meanings of lesbianism.

THE SOCIAL CONSTRUCTION OF IDENTITY AND ITS MEANINGS WITHIN THE LESBIAN SUBCULTURE

The integration of groups within the lesbian subculture provides the basis for the emergence of alternate meanings of lesbian identity. The content of these alternate meanings is the first focus of this chapter. The second is a description of the way lesbian identity is socially constructed within the gay subculture, summarized in what I call the *trajectory of gay identity.*

The Meanings of Identity Words in the Lesbian World

In the lesbian world, the terms *lesbian, homosexual,* and *gay* have special meanings in the context of identity. The way these terms are used is important in distinguishing the lesbian subculture from the larger society and in making distinctions within the subculture itself. As commonly used, outside the lesbian world, these terms assume an equation between lesbian activity and lesbian identity. In the lesbian world, too, the terms might be used interchangeably in the course of conversation by many woman-related women. However, in the lesbian world these terms do have a variety of specific meanings and may connote political identity and personal stances.

Usage of the terms *gay, female homosexual, lesbian,* and *bisexual* as identity labels or descriptive terms is related to several interacting dimensions of an individual's involvement with the subculture. These include a woman's chronological age, her age of entry into the community, the historical time in which she enters lesbian life, the extent of her integration into the community, her degree of politicization, as well as the particular sector of the community with which she is affiliated.

Gay, homosexual, and *lesbian* are commonly perceived within both the lesbian community and the larger society as referring to essential identities[1] rather than as describing mere behavior. Extending in meaning beyond a mere equation between sexual object choice and sexual behavior, the words *lesbian, homosexual, gay,* and, occasionally, *butch* and *femme,* signify an orientation, a way of being, or the essence of the person so designated. In the perspective of the lesbian subculture these terms refer to *ontological status,* or a state of being. Thus one does not change into a lesbian or become one, according to this logic: one simply recognizes what has been there all along.

In some instances women in the lesbian community use identity words not only to designate themselves but also to indicate solidarity with other lesbians. For example, in political, radical, and self-help groups some women use these terms with reference to themselves in an effort to destigmatize and neutralize their meanings. Other women in groups with a feminist orientation may retain private definitions of themselves as not really lesbian and yet use lesbian as a public identity statement for political reasons. To some women referring to themselves as lesbian connotes the acceptance of an essential self. Yet other women in the lesbian community, particularly those connected with bisexual groups or groups that are permissive about the identity designations of their members, call themselves bisexual or sexual to indicate their difference from lesbians.

Warren observes that words serve to demarcate the gay world from the straight world: "In the absence of any distinction between straight and gay, say in a society where bisexuality is the rule, there would be no gay world."[2] Berger and Luckmann note the crucial role of language in elaborating a particular world of meaning by stating that incipient legimation of a world view may inhere in meanings and connotations of words. Special vocabularies not only serve a nomic or ordering function but may serve to legitimate the phenomena to which they refer.[3] The repetition and acceptance of gay terms within the subculture inherently serves to normalize and legitimate that world for its members.

Lesbian

The term *lesbian* has a historical tradition stemming from the days of the poet Sappho, who wrote odes celebrating love between women on the Isle of Lesbos.[4] Some women have a sense of connection with this historical tradition and have used the term *lesbian* to designate themselves for many years. However, most of the women over forty years old whom I met use the term *homosexual* or *gay* when referring to themselves.

I have always called myself a *lesbian*. To me it has always been a beautiful word and describes what I am—I occasionally use the term *Sapphist*, which I also like. I think it's important for lesbians to know that they have a history. The word *gay* seems silly to me, and *homosexual* doesn't fit quite—oh, I suppose in a strict sense. But *lesbian* suits me and is who I am. (Tape-recorded interview)

The Political Use of the Term Lesbian

At the present time, the term *lesbian* is having a renaissance; in certain political and feminist groups, it is the preferred term for all women-related women. *Lesbian,* in its traditional sense, has the connotation of essence and of primary and ontological orientation toward women. As used in political circles, *lesbian* describes a total life-style and solidarity with the women's community. Several of the women I interviewed and many whom I met were involved with feminism to some extent and had come to adopt the word *lesbian*—after many years of calling themselves gay or homosexual—as a political statement. These women consider *lesbian* to be an unequivocal statement about the self that affirms their alliance with women, and may consider *homosexual* and *gay* to be male terms. Political lesbians see the usage of the term *lesbian* as a move toward destigmatization and demystification of the word and the social category—in short, as a consciousness-raising device. (Refer back to the tape-recorded interview on pages 85-86.)

In some feminist, gay liberation, radical, and self-help circles, *lesbian* is used as a self-designation to signify support of and solidarity with lesbians not only by women who consider themselves to be gay but by women who privately refer to themselves as bisexual or heterosexual as well, as the following account illustrates:

I: Do you define yourself as a lesbian?
R: I think so. I define myself publicly as a lesbian. Privately I think I might be a bisexual.
I: What's the difference? Why the dichotomy between the public and private?

R: Because I feel it's a cop-out to call myself bisexual publicly. It's like a way of evading the stigma attached to being a lesbian. So I don't want to do a cowardly thing. In terms of accuracy about my feelings, I am involved with women right now and really expect to be involved with women in the future. But it's not inconceivable to me at all that I could also be involved with a man—you know, if things were right. (Tape-recorded interview)

The position of such women—who define themselves publicly as lesbian but who privately define themselves as bisexual or heterosexual and continue to have sexual-emotional affiliations with men—is somewhat equivocal in the view of other lesbians. On the one hand, they are viewed favorably, as supportive toward the community of lesbians. At the same time their continued personal and sexual relationships with men may be seen by some lesbians as puzzling, if not disloyal.

In the subculture, as in the larger society, lesbianism is regarded as an essential identity, though with a meaning quite different from that which the heterosexual world attributes to the essentiality. The idea of choice about lesbianism is incompatible with a notion of the essentiality or ontological status of lesbianism. The self-labeled political lesbian who is bisexual or heterosexual in practice is somewhat of a mystery to women who have always defined themselves as lesbians and see this as not something one chooses to be but something one simply is.

I must say that I do have some problem understanding women who *decide* to become a lesbian. Somehow I don't see how a woman can *decide to become* a lesbian. She can find out maybe late in life, early or late, she can find out that this was potential in her and she didn't know about it, but that's not *becoming* a lesbian, do you think? It's just finding out what has been repressed or suppressed. To make a political decision to become a lesbian, this seems to me a little farfetched, not to say arbitrary. (Tape-recorded interview)

Homosexual

The terms *female homosexual* and *homosexual* are prevalent usage in groups whose members are over forty years old and whose socialization into gay life took place early in their own lives. These terms are virtually unused among younger women. Those who entered gay life relatively recently—during the late 1960s and early 1970s—consider *homosexual* to be a technical or medical term or a word that is more appropriately applied to men. But among the women who use *homosexual* as a designation of identity, it is similar in connotation to the term *lesbian,* referring to a primary sexual orientation and to an ontological status. Women who call themselves *homosexual* tend to view themselves as having been "born that way" and are likely to invoke a hormonal or genetic explanation for their orientation. For example, in the following account, a forty-two-year-old woman-related woman posits an endocrinological explanation of her homosexuality:

I was actually having homosexual affairs before I was aware of the word *homosexual.* So when I became aware of the word as it pertained to me, I was a freshman in college. . . . I think it's a matter of different endocrinal pattern between homosexuals and straights. They don't know what comes first, the emotions that produce the pattern or the pattern producing the emotions. . . . I think with some homosexuals it's related to endocrine patterns. (Tape-recorded interview)

Whether the individual invokes an endocrinological or cosmological explanation to account for homosexuality, *homosexual* is similar to *lesbian* in its centrality and reference to individual essence.

Gay

The word *gay* is probably the most widely used of the three terms. *Gay* derives from the French, *gaie*—meaning a homosexual man. Transmuted into English, *gay* came to refer to a prostitute; its meaning then changed to connote once again a homosexual man. It has now come to refer to the elaboration of homosexuality into a subculture.[5] Its use is common in self-help and gay liberation groups and among younger women in the secretive lesbian community, while it is relatively less common in radical feminist lesbian groups.

Gay is frequently used in a generic and adjectival sense to describe the subculture, persons, life-styles, communities, relationships, places, and situations. *Gay* may also be used to connote an aspect of the self, as contrasted to an essential identity, among some women who are in gay relationships but do not have gay or lesbian identities.

Although *gay* is widely used in the community as a sort of slang or shorthand expression, it is perceived by some older women-related women as an inappropriate and not un-ironical term that does not truly reflect their life-styles or identities. *Gay* has a connotation that is not without pain for these women, because for them being a homosexual has meant isolation, secrecy, and a fear of discovery—which are in no sense gay. Nonetheless, *gay* has a wide currency among women-related women, particularly among younger women. *Gay,* like *homosexual,* is a term applicable to both men and women and many woman-related women consider gay to be milder and less stigmatizing a term than is *lesbian.*

In addition, some women use this term as an identity label to distinguish or differentiate themselves from what they consider to be real lesbians. A forty-four-year-old therapist exemplifying this view stated that she distinguishes herself from true lesbians and uses the term *gay* only as conversational shorthand so as not to disrupt the expectation of mutual gayness when she is with gay friends.

I call myself gay when I'm with my gay friends; otherwise, I don't. . . . Sometimes I think of myself as not exclusively gay, but as kind of playing a gay game. Like I'm not really gay . . . that . . . I'm really heterosexual, no really bisexual, I would say, and I don't really feel myself as exclusively gay as those lesbian women that I meet. Especially with the younger, more militant lesbians. I don't identify with them at all. . . . *Lesbian* itself has an old-fashioned, last-generation connotation to it, so I hardly every use that word about myself . . . I sort of do fit the word *gay,* but I sort of don't. Because I still have my whole adult history essentially being married and having children, which a lot of lesbians don't. And so that puts a whole other dimension to it, and the ones that are younger and exclusively gay, I can't identify with them any more than I identify with any other single, younger woman. (Tape-recorded interview)

Gay is used by other woman-related women, however, as a statement of identity in much the same sense as *lesbian* and *homosexual* are used. *Lesbian, gay,* and *homosexual* are not the only major identity tags in the lesbian world. "Butch" and "femme" are also ways of describing both the essential self, the activities, and the apparent identities of others.

Butch and Femme

Earlier it was mentioned that the term *role playing,* as used in the lesbian world, involves the adaptation of masculine and feminine roles, modeled after typifications of these roles in the heterosexual world. The woman who plays the masculine role is called the butch, while the femme plays the stereotypical traditional female role.

Butch and femme are interpreted by some women simply in terms of a role that one plays. Other women-related women interpret these roles as the external manifestation of the character of the self and thus see butch and femme in terms of identities.

Role playing is characteristic of a minority of women in the lesbian subculture today. Although it was more prevalent in the past, even then, as reported by respondents, it was practiced by only a small proportion of the women in the community. However, role playing is a prevailing stereotype of lesbian behavior in the heterosexual world and as such has importance as a kind of negative standard in the perception of the lesbians I met. It remains an issue that women in the lesbian subculture may take into account in the formulation of their own identities. Therefore, the following discussion of role playing deals with it as an image rather than as a practice.

Notions of what constitutes butch and femme vary among different groups in the subculture.[6] Many of the characteristics thought of as masculine are attributed to and expected from the butch. Such qualities as being logical (as opposed to emotional), factual, directive, capable of decision making, as well as being able to take care of tasks outside the home and to handle emergency situations are likewise expected of the butch. In some instances, the butch is expected to be the breadwinner although, according to the women interviewed, usually both butch and femme work.

In its most fully elaborated form the femme role embodies qualities of wifely virtue such as passivity, docility, and nurturance—the panoply of characteristics that comprise the expectations for stereotypical femininity in the heterosexual community. Not infrequently, the femme is described by respondents in disparaging terms as an exaggeration of a stereotypical female role.

Having been a role player for many years, I would have to say that role playing is where one assumes a more aggressive, more domineering, more masculine kind of role and the other assumes a more passive, more subservient kind of role. Not necessarily in terms of household duties or whatever but in terms of how you relate to one another. Somebody is the boss and somebody is not the boss. Femme is the woman who sees

herself in the societal pattern of wife. Femme is the more—I hate to use
the word *feminine*—I'll try and find a better word than that—the societal
sense of the ultra-feminine woman, the kind that has to put out that she's
not too bright, though she may be very bright. But in her head she's got
to let the butch be brighter and stronger than she is; less in the limelight,
she takes more of a back seat, more of a "back" role and is sexually passive. (Tape-recorded interview)

Various aspects of role playing are emphasized among different groups
of lesbians. Some lesbian groups stress the importance of appearance and
clothing styles. According to respondents, some butches adopt male clothing, wear close-cropped hair, and approximate a male physique by such
measures as binding their breasts and padding the genital area, though none
of the women I interviewed had done this. The more prevalent trend, however, is simply that the butch should affect a more tailored style than the
femme:

Well, I tend to be the more feminine. I like makeup and pretty feminine
clothes, not your frilly feminine, but more softer looking. And H tends
to be somewhat butchy, not really masculine, but more tailored than I
am, and she was always into sports and that type of thing when she was
younger. (Tape-recorded interview)

Among most middle-class role-playing lesbians, the modification of dress
codes for butch and femme are not necessarily expected to be apparent
to heterosexual audiences. In other role-playing lesbian groups, however,
women are expected to be identifiably gay in the straight world as well
as among other lesbians. A fifty-six-year-old lesbian recounted the range
of role-playing expectations that were made of her in various groups:

[Some crowds] that one got into expected more role playing and some
were very, very conservative, where everyone was very hard to identify.
And then there were groups where there was a great deal of group pressure to be easier to identify—and there was a kind of daring—did you dare
be that easy to identify all the time? I dared during the war, when I worked
in an aircraft plant. I enjoyed it, but it puts an awfully big strain on you,
you know. You have to decide how much you are willing to risk. (Tape-
recorded interview)

Modes and Meanings of Role Playing

Some groups, mostly in the secretive world, exert pressures with regard to role playing: some proscribe it and others expect it. Respondents in this study engaged in role playing with varying degrees of commitment both in the context of the community and as isolated individuals. They attributed a range of meanings to the roles they assumed—from roles being mere play to being an expression of the true self.

Role Playing as Play

A sense of playfulness, fun, and experimentation characterized the role adaptations of some women. They would quite consciously adapt the semblances of role playing with little or no sense of role commitment, exemplifying what Goffman has called *role distance*. That is, women participated in playing a role but with an ironical sense, as this account illustrates:

Role playing? Oh sure, I was into that. You know, I'm really a green country kid. I was. I didn't know anything about anything. All I knew was how I felt, and from adolescence on I felt inclined toward women. By the time I was twenty-four and ready to get involved with a woman, I went there [to a bar] not realizing that I had to be other than me. When I got there, to that bar, I saw that there was a very definite division. Some women looked very masculine and some looked very feminine, and I really felt that I looked kind of in-between, but people took me to be feminine, and I was *assigned* a role because of my appearance. It doesn't mean that I was overly feminine. It just means that I wasn't overly masculine. So I was classified. That was on the Missouri side in Kansas City. Uh—I got into realizing that I was restricted. I was limited in the kinds of people I could relate to, and I found the kinds of people that I was willing to relate to me as a femme were people that I was not really interested in. . . . It restricted me to a class of people that considered themselves butches, butches in the sense of how they look and how they dress. They were not really appealing to me. I had been on the receiving end of aggression from men for years, and I wasn't interested. . . . You know, it wasn't really that comfortable for me, and so it was a time when I really didn't know what to do. . . . So when I went to the Kansas side, I decided to experiment a little, and I got to the point where I cut off my hair, and so I would go the Kansas side, and I would dress very masculine in terms of men's pants, men's clothes, and men's sweatshirts and things like that, just jeans not really anything else, you know. Uh—I would go to the Kansas side, and I would slick my hair back, and I'd be a butch, and I could pursue more feminine women, as we see them, you know, and that was a little more satisfying, and I—so since that time—and people were calling me the "it" because, you know, they'd see me on one side and I'd be a butch, and in Missouri I'd look like a femme, but I didn't want to be restricted. I didn't want to put restrictions on who I could relate to (Tape-recorded interview)

The One-Way Butch

In some groups in the lesbian community, specific sexual expectations for the butch role are normative. For example, the expectations for the butch role sometimes include sexual self-denial. In the argot of the community—referring to the fact that they did not permit reciprocity in lovemaking—such women are called one-way butches or "untouchables." By the logic of role stereotypes the expectations of passivity for the femme and aggressiveness for the butch, taken to an extreme, preclude both sexual initiating behavior and reciprocity on the part of the femme, which would be construed as aggressive on her part. At the same time, the expectations that the butch be the aggressor preclude her from being sexually receptive. The butch was expected to be the lover but not the beloved: she would make love to femmes but not expect lovemaking in return.

Sexual self-denial, though practiced by some butch lesbians, is considered an anathema by other butches and is never practiced by them. The reasoning behind the self-denial is interesting. Most of the women who said that they played the untouchable in the past stated that they accepted that part of the role because they felt frightened to allow someone to make love to them. Others emphasized that it would have destroyed their ersatz maleness to allow reciprocity. In addition, the heterosexual logic of inversion—"If I like women, I must be masculine"—was operative in several instances.

The experience of one woman echoes the above themes in her account of playing a one-way butch role:

I: What about sexual role playing? Were you into that?
R: Yeah, I was. And I think it was, I think I cheated myself.
I: Are you familiar with the term *one-way butch?*
R: Yes, I'm familiar with the term, I was one. I didn't really like it, because, I again, I feel that I was cheated out of something that I should be

getting, more than what I was getting. Somehow I felt frightened because I felt that if I tore down that particular barrier and had a freer sexual exchange with people, they might be frightened, they might be frightened away.

I: What would frighten them?

R: Well, a lot of the people that I know, well, if I tried to have a freer—well, that would frighten them. Oh dear, what would frighten them was that I wasn't really a man and we were putting up a beautiful illusion, and that it wasn't real, and it wasn't true. And I was afraid that if we did anything other than the one-way butch trip that they would be frightened away and not—want—want me anymore.

The majority of the women with whom I spoke disparaged the one-way butch role. Even women, such as the one just quoted, who had engaged in this role in the past had come to feel that they had played it out of a sense of personal insecurity. The following respondent, however, presented a uniquely positive view of the one-way butch role, which she periodically plays:

I've been in relationships like that, where I suppose it sounds kind of weird and far out, but I don't believe that's so entirely the way it sounds —you can become so identified and so empathetic in making love that you can and do come. It's not a wild orgasm, but it certainly doesn't leave you wanting. There is something so exciting and gratifying and climactic about the orgasm of a person you love, it's like, as if you were to pick up on how people feel three or four minutes after an orgasm, that tremendous peace and serenity. So if you can leave out the moment of orgasm and move on a few minutes, that's a very possible thing. I've experienced it, so it isn't quite the same thing as the partner being left in wild need. It can be a very loving thing. I can understand how one could go through a series of relationships like that. I think if you are so empathetic to the other, that's when that happens, only if you love and adore the person who you were with—and then again there are some people who are so inhibited about their gayness that that may be the only thing they're about to do. Now people that run from one person to another, I think they're on a male trip. (Tape-recorded interview)

Most lesbians with whom I spoke emphasized the mutuality and reciprocity of lovemaking in lesbian relationships. Most women who had played a butch role among my respondents expressed a disassociation from the one-way butch role, as evidenced in the following:

I have some friends like that, and I think that's very strange, too. . . . And I used to say to them, "You don't know what you're missing, you know. I think you're missing something here." I don't see it. There again is role playing in some respects, and for some reason or another even the people that are—live a very butch and femme life. If the butch thought that I thought for a minute that maybe they enjoyed some femme making love to them, they would die of mortification (Tape-recorded interview)

As indicated earlier, for some women role-playing behavior was a short-lived adaptation to the patterns of relations they saw in gay bars. Interestingly, there is suggestive evidence that isolation from the community of lesbians may have tended toward role-playing behavior among self-labeled lesbians. One respondent remarked:

You have to remember that a lot of the women you are talking to now are urban women, sophisticated women. But twenty years ago, particularly rural women, farm women, country women who had no contact with any kind of gay community, these women tended to be very masculine, male-identified. They didn't have any other models to follow and so when they found themselves attracted to women, they really thought they must be like men. And this was true for some urban women like myself who were young and didn't know what was happening and had no gay community around. You knew you were gay or something, but you weren't even sure what that meant, apart from thinking that you were like a man. It's really meeting other lesbians and being in the community that teaches you that you don't have to be masculine to love another woman. (Conversation from field notes)

The majority of the women interviewed were disinclined to play roles at all. For example, women whose lesbianism had the meaning, to some degree, of disaffiliation with traditional women's and men's roles found the role options of the gay world equally unattractive. Some women, in light of the expectations of role-playing groups, purposely adopted a middle-of-the-road stance, refusing to conform to the expectations of either role. Among role players such women were called "Ki-Ki."[7] Being Ki-Ki—being unwilling to choose a role—was somewhat stigmatized in role-playing crowds. In a taped interview one woman remarked with regard to her Ki-Ki status, "No self respecting butch would have anything to do with you if you were Ki-Ki."

For other women this activity had implications for identity: role playing, particularly the butch role, seemed to satisfy their conceptions of themselves. Martin and Lyon refer to such women as having a "heterosexual consciousness."[8] That is, they perceive themselves as being really masculine in accounting for their attraction to women. Conversely, the femme conceives of herself as a really feminine woman who relates to manlike women. There is some evidence in the accounts of respondents that role-playing styles also characterized women who were isolated from an urban gay community. Rural women, they reported, were much more likely to model themselves after heterosexual standards. Role playing among lesbians would tend to be a more prevalent style in groups where male-female roles are perceived as dichotomous. For many women, role playing was simply a *modus operandi* in certain social (and sometimes sexual) situations. For others, butch and femme roles were enacted as identities in much the same way.

Role playing is clearly on the wane in today's lesbian community and was characteristic in the past of a minority of lesbians as a continuing pattern of behavior. For the respondents in this study, role playing was a temporary pattern of behavior, engaged in either playfully or seriously, in light of expectations they encountered in particular groups or relationships. Thus, it was a passing phase of becoming socialized into the life of the lesbian world.

In the past, more than is true today, the novice lesbian's avenue of access to the lesbian community was through lesbian bars, where role playing expectations frequently prevailed. The greater access to the community provided by political groups, the widespread questioning of the legitimacy of stereotyped sex roles in both straight and gay worlds, and the influence of feminism have served as forces toward diminishing and even proscribing role-playing expectations.

Bisexual

The identity status of bisexual is problematic in the lesbian community. Although women with whom I spoke call themselves bisexual when referring to their personal identities and in fact have or have had sexual and emotional relationships with men as well as women, bisexuality is a rather stigmatized identity label in the lesbian community. First of all, it is considered a "cop-out," an evasion of stigma, an attempt to keep one foot in the door of heterosexual respectability. Even more significantly, within the lesbian world as in the heterosexual world, lesbianism in whatever degree is considered more definitive of the self than is heterosexual activity or association. Bisexuality is thus considered an inauthentic identity statement in most parts of the secretive community. Identifying oneself as bisexual is seen as evidence of having problems in accepting "true" lesbian identity in the activist community.

Bisexual—it is a difficult term for me to believe. It's hard for me to understand how a person can truly relate personally, sexually, emotionally to members of the same sex and the opposite sex. I think you are one way or the other. It's like a child of mixed blood. Even those people who say they are bisexual *must* have something in them that relates to one sex more than the other. . . . I can't believe it's the same with both. . . . I can't understand it. I think people have the responsibility to make up their minds and not try and play both sides of the street at the same time. All I can say is, God help the lesbian that gets involved with one, and God help the straight man, too. (Tape-recorded interview)

As these comments illustrate, the bisexual is considered by many lesbians to be in an impossible position. An implicit assumption about bisexuality in the lesbian community is that the bisexual woman is untrustworthy and lacking in commitment in her relationships, particularly relationships with women. Further, the bisexual is frequently considered as really a lesbian who is caviling at the stigma involved in identifying herself as such.

You know, I think bisexual women should shit or get off the pot—they're ripping off lesbians. You know, they have a love affair with a woman and then go—revert to status—become heterosexual—when things get a little hot . . . and it's so easy for women to say they're bisexual. And it's very easy to say that. (Tape-recorded interview)

Perceptions of Bisexuals in the Lesbian Subculture

The experiences of some lesbians who have been emotionally involved with bisexual women have lent support to the negative valuation of bisexuals in the community. Accounts such as the one that follows become part of subcultural lore, particularly among lesbian activists, and ultimately serve to support polar definitions of heterosexuality and lesbianism and a continuing distrust of bisexuals.

I got involved with a few bisexual women which I felt really fucked over about, because I felt really put down because they would be with me one night, and they would be with men the next day, and I felt really put down by that. I felt like—I guess anybody can go to bed with them. And I didn't want to be used that way, and there were a lot of lesbians, especially when the woman's movement first started off, there were a lot of what I call political lesbians, not really lesbians but women who did it as a political statement. Like, "Now I've made it with a woman, I'm liberated." Really! And I felt used by those kind of women because they weren't really gay women, as far as emotional—as far as *really* being identified with lesbianism. They were like bisexual women, or they were liberated women. And I felt really oppressed by the, because I was really —I knew I definitely was gay. . . . But women that are into a big trip where they go back and forth, and they really hurt the lesbians, because emotionally the lesbian might get involved with them . . . . It makes me feel like I was just an experience; like, "I went to bed with a dyke last night." (Tape-recorded interview)

The assertion of bisexual identity while engaging in lesbian relationships is regarded by some lesbians with extreme disapprobation and, not infrequently, fear. A lesbian who becomes involved with a bisexually identified woman might experience the ending of such a relationship in terms of a fundamental betrayal, implying a rejection of the lesbian above and beyond personal incompatibility, such as is evinced in the preceding remarks. Relationships between bisexuals and lesbians frequently carry the connotation of the lesbian being objectified as an experience or as an experiment in the course of the bisexual's "liberation."

The Status of the Bisexual: A Paradox in the Subculture

Despite the disapprobation received in parts of the lesbian subculture, women-related women who do not identify themselves as lesbians most frequently assert that they are bisexuals. Two general conditions typically underlie the assertion of bisexual identity. First, the woman's past or present experience or future expectations of heterosexual relationships provide a legitimating rationale for bisexual identity. Second, and less frequently, some women maintain the idea of universal bisexuality, asserting that "everyone is a bisexual."

Within the lesbian subculture, the status of the woman who identifies herself as a bisexual is somewhat paradoxical. Bisexuality as an "ideal state," one of which all humans are capable "by nature," is an ideologically legitimate position among activist lesbians. Calling oneself a bisexual, however, is considered to be an evasion of stigma and a denial of one's real self by these same movement-allied, lesbian-identified women. Accepting bisexuality as an ideal while rejecting it in practice is a contradiction in gay ideology as expressed by gay movement people. This contradiction has its apologists, who maintain that emphasizing the differences between heterosexuals and homosexuals makes it possible to build a sense of unity or a collective consciousness among gays. The practical rejection of bisexuality is clearly acknowledged to be a political tactic, one seen as necessary because of the present oppression of gays. According to this logic, separatism is a necessary step in building a strong sense of gay pride.

Other women assert that basically everyone is bisexual but with the proviso that living a bisexual life-style is not practicable, given their perception of the disadvantageous position of women in relation to men.

The Social Construction of Identity in the Lesbian World

Sexual behavior is only one criterion for imputing a homosexual identity to the self or others in the lesbian community. In addition to sexual behavior, and ultimately more important than behavior, are feelings of sexual-emotional attraction to the same sex, *whether or not these feelings have been acted upon.*[9] Assumed motivations and feelings may be the basis for the attribution of lesbian or homosexual identity within the gay community, paralleling the notion of latency within the psychiatric community.

Within the lesbian subculture the emergence of lesbian-related identity, irrespective of the terms used and of its specific content, is interpreted within the framework of what I call the *gay trajectory* and the process of coming out. The gay trajectory and coming out constitute basic underlying images of the social construction of identity within the lesbian world. The term *trajectory* is used in a special sense to describe a set of trajectories of identities. Each one of four elements of the gay trajectory may be the starting point of a projected path that leads to the most critical element —the assumption of lesbian identity.

The trajectory of gay identity, the principle of identity construction in the lesbian world, functions similarly to the principle of consistency, the underlying assumption of the social construction of sex-related identities in the larger society. It is construed as a relationship among five elements of subjective experience and behavior, an atemporal series of elements. The first element is that the individual has a subjective sense of being different from heterosexual persons and identifies this difference as feelings of sexual-emotional attraction to her own sex. Second, an understanding of the homosexual or lesbian significance of these feelings is acquired. Third, the individual accepts these feelings and their implication for identity—that is, the individual comes out or accepts the identity of lesbian. Fourth, the individual seeks a community of like persons. Fifth, the individual becomes involved in a sexual-emotional lesbian relationship. Given one of these elements, irrespective of their order in time, it is commonly assumed in the lesbian world that the others will logically come to pass.

The first three—the subjective experience of sexual-emotional attraction to one's same sex, an understanding of the lesbian significance of these feelings, and the acceptance of lesbian identity—are considered primary elements in the subculture's perspective. Though the search for a community of like persons and an actual sexual relationship are expected to co-vary with the other elements, their absence can be circumstantially explained. It is presumed, however, that given the first three elements, the individual will experience a sense of strain toward the other two . Such individuals are presumed to be in search of community. With respect to a woman who has not had a sexual-emotional relationship but who conforms to other elements of the trajectory, again it is assumed that were she to have such relationships, by definiton they would be with women.

These identity experiences are usually located separately in time, and that their specific order of occurrence varies widely among individuals will become clear in chapter 6. In the experience of some lesbians, these elements are reported as occurring simultaneously. In these instances, it can be presumed that the lesbian significance of these behaviors and experiences is part of the individual's stock of knowledge.

The gay trajectory, as the assumption underlying the social construction of lesbian identity, functions as a biographic norm of the community.[10] Moreover, its normative power is most clearly manifested when rule breaking occurs—when an individual reports experiencing all the elements outlined above, save the acceptance of lesbian identity. For example, certain women with whom I spoke had subjective feelings of attraction for their same sex that they define as lesbian, were in the lesbian world, had lesbian relationships, and yet stated that they were not really lesbians but were bisexuals or heterosexuals. Such women do not accept the essentiality of their lesbian behavior. In the community's terms a bisexual would be explained as "having trouble dealing with her gayness." The self-definition would not be considered legitimate or authentic within the lesbian world, given that the individual has lesbian feelings and relationships. In brief, when women claim (or are thought to have) attractions to women, or have sexual relations with women, or are present in the lesbian community over time, or acknowledge a subjective sense of difference from heterosexual others, then the acceptance and acknowledgment of lesbian identity (at least in the company of other lesbians) are expected to follow.

Being in the Community

Unattached females who associate with gay groups by going to gay meeting places such as bars and clubs will probably have gayness ascribed to them. A vocabulary of motives is implicit in the way in which identities are socially construed within the lesbian community that leads to assumptions about persons who seem attracted to gay company.[11] The exceptions to these expectations are persons who are considered wise by the community, a status that is facilitated by membership in a heterosexual couple. Once established, the status of the wise straight person may not be suspect, but for some it may be difficult to achieve. For example, a single or unattached woman who seeks out and seems to prefer the company of gay women is likely to have gayness attributed to her or she may be said to be in the process of realizing her gayness, whether she acknowledges it or not. Protestations of a non-gay identity are likely to be interpreted in terms of having problems facing gayness, while counterclaims about identity are explained in terms of being in a transitional period in the gay trajectory.

Blumstein and Schwartz comment in their study of bisexuals and lesbians that

since most lesbians have had some heterosexual experience, and all have suffered some emotional strain from the process of "coming out" as homosexual, it is widely believed in the lesbian community that a "bisexual phase" really is only a manifestation of the ambivalent feelings associated with "coming out." Hence, a bisexual is often defined simply as a homo-sexual who has not yet been able to accept her true identity. In the ex-treme, some lesbians refuse to believe that true bisexuality (or even ambi-sexuality) exists. . . . Hence, women who claim a bisexual identity receive not only hostility from their lesbian peers, but are in a sense told that the identity they are claiming is not real, but rather a fantasy or a phase which will not endure experience.[12]

However, a woman may engage in sexual relations with another woman without having the motives that are deemed appropriate by the lesbian community and thus may not have lesbian identity assigned to her by lesbians. An example would be a woman who is perceived as experiment-ing with lesbian relationships, a practice considered reprehensible.[13] A certain seriousness in motivation and a transituational commitment to lesbian relationships are expected to obtain.

Explaining Deviations from the Gay Trajectory

Deviations from the expectations of the gay trajectory are explained in terms of having difficulty accepting gayness or in terms of program-ming by the larger society, such as explanations employing the concept of repression. For example, a woman may have a sexual-emotional rela-tionship with a woman and "not be aware" of previous feelings of attrac-tion for her own sex. During the process of learning to acknowledge her lesbian identity, she may learn to reinterpret her biography in such a way that previously "unrecognized" feelings are brought to light. Such reinter-pretations are supported by subcultural rhetorics of repression and op-pression. Subcultural ideology also provides explanations for events that seem incongruous or contradictory with lesbianism, such as lesbians having current heterosexual attractions as well as heterosexual pasts, which might tend to call into question the essentiality and pervasiveness of a gay iden-tity. These feelings are explained in terms of programming by the larger society that results in superficial conformity to heterosexual standards. In this regard, Blumstein and Schwartz note that "lesbians who have spent a long time in the homosexual community often socialize younger ones to treat any heterosexual feelings as delusions.[14]
The following forty-five-year-old respondent, for example, accounted for her twenty-five-year heterosexual marriage and other relationships with men to her lack of knowledge about approaching women sexually:

I've been attracted to girls sexually since I was fourteen. I was such a chicken shit that we always did minimal things. We'd neck and pet. It was never—I didn't know how to take it past that. I was hemmed in by convention so I could never find anybody who would go along with what I wanted. So I was forced to have sex with men, and to release with them what was stimulated by being with women, and the fact [is] that in this culture we aren't allowed or even know how to do these things with women. (Tape-recorded interview)

Identity Lag

Members of the gay community recognize that the acceptance of gay identity may be problematic for the individual. Such problems may be expressed in the term *identity lag,* that is, there may be a lapse of time between experiencing feelings of difference from heterosexual others, labeling the feelings, engaging in sexual behavior, and accepting and acknowledging lesbian identity. Dank notes in his observations of the male gay community that there is an average lapse of six years between an initial sense of attraction to persons of the same sex and the assumption of gay identity.[15] Identity lag has been institutionalized in the gay community. In the argot of the community, it is called coming out.

Coming Out

The initial process of indicating to the self that one is gay is called coming out. Another significant meaning of the term in the lesbian world relates to the interaction between gay actors and their audiences. In addition to indicating gayness to the self, coming out refers to disclosing a gay self before an expanding series of audiences. This second use is more characteristic of political groups, for whom disclosure is a political and ideological stance. But both secret lesbians and activists refer to coming out before various audiences; for example, "I came out with my parents" or "She came out with her straight friends at work."[16]

Coming out is conceived of as a process that takes place over time—a series of acknowledgments and self-labelings. The self is the first audience to the coming out process. Later the individual comes out to an ever expanding audience of people. One is virtually "all the way out" when most others with whom the individual is in contact are aware of her gay identity.

Full membership as a lesbian is often extended to participants whose identity status is problematic, under the rationale of coming out. It is expected in the gay community that some persons may have lesbian feelings and engage in lesbian acts and maintain a heterosexual or a bisexual identity for some time. Even though there is an expected congruence between acts and identity on the one hand and feelings and identity on the other hand, these breaches of expectations of the gay trajectory are explained in terms of the process of coming out, unless the individual is deemed an experimenter.

The community gives permission for a period of transition in which the individual's identity may not have caught up with her feelings and behavior. But one is not expected to tarry too long in the transitional phase. If a person continues to assert an identity that is perceived as incoungruent with feelings and behavior, sanctions ranging from mild disapproval to public denouncement (the latter in highly political circles) may ensue. Explanations for the person's identity lag will move from the rationale and permission of the coming out process to accusations of inauthenticity, stigma evasion, or fence-sitting. Thus although the elements of the gay trajectory may vary in their temporal order, the trajectory does include implicit time norms.

The following conversation with a lesbian refers to a woman that I had seen in gay settings many times over a period of two and one-half years.

I: Well, how is K? I usually expect to see her when I see you.
R: Oh, my god! She's such a closet case![17] It gets to be a real pain in the ass. She'll have a little to drink and then try and be affectionate. I'm no damned experiment! She's always getting crushes and then getting angry with the woman because she can't handle her own feelings. She's so scared about what someone will say. You know, she's been my friend for years, but it's gotten ridiculous lately. I just can't stand her lying and denying. I wish she'd just come out and get it over with. It's getting boring already. (Conversation condensed from field notes)

Thus, if over the course of time a woman "talks differently than she walks"—if she is perceived as being "long overdue" with respect to realizing her gay identity—she may become unwelcome in gay circles.

Individual Responses to the Gay Trajectory

Individual women within the lesbian community have a range of responses to the expectations of the gay trajectory as well as to the process of coming out. These responses can be typified in three general forms:

rejection of lesbian identity, public conformity with private reservations, and acceptance of the group's definition of identity, thus rendering social identity and personal identity congruous.

Some persons continue to construct individualistic conceptualizations of themselves and to reject the validity of the gay trajectory: they refuse to come out. In so doing, they implicitly reject the essentiality of gayness altogether.

I think that a person can love and relate sexually to a man or a woman—
if they'll let themselves. It's so arbitrary to have to put some label on it.
I suppose that there are some people who really are at the ends of the continuum and, like, who are really lesbian who never cared about men —ever—and I guess never ever would be attracted to men, and I suppose they are *really* lesbians, but even there it could be learning, don't you think? I mean they are *used* to relating to women and not men. (Tape-recorded interview)

Women who are in lesbian relationships but do not consider themselves to be lesbians may handle the expectations implied in the gay trajectory by publicly (that is, with other gay people) stating that they are gay or by not disrupting the homosexual assumption and yet maintaining their private interpretations of their personal identity.

Some women state that they believe gayness is an essential identity for real lesbians but that they are not real lesbians themselves. They often make this claim by virtue of either past heterosexual experience or pro-jected plans for heterosexual experience in the future. Alternatively, they may feel that lesbian identity does not correspond to their experiences of themselves. A fifty-year-old woman distinguishes her use of the term *lesbian* with reference to herself from her concept of real lesbians:

At my age I consider it expedient to be a lesbian. It's a smart choice for me. The chances of my meeting a man my own age aren't great, and I'm not interested in being involved in a "mother-son" relationship. My best chances, being realistic, for a good relationship are with a woman. So when I say I'm a lesbian, I'm saying that I choose to relate to women at this time in my life and that I'll probably continue to do so. But I'm not closed to relating to a man again. I'm certainly not. At the same time women who have always been lesbians, real lesbians, absolutely fascinate me. I believe they have a real different culture—like X and her friends—

so conventional in so many ways and yet really unconventional in their sexuality. You may not agree with me, but I think there is really something different about them. For me it's a choice, and I think a smart one— looking at the world around me. I don't call myself a bisexual because it's a cop-out, but I guess that's how I'd describe myself. (Conversation condensed from field notes)

It should be pointed out that identity statements vary over time, not simply in response to perceived pressures from others but also in response to varying interpretations of the self and the meaning of lesbianism to the individual. The fact that sexual object choices vary over time for many individuals stimulates efforts to interpret the meaning of sexuality and self. Obviously, women who have had subjectively meaningful experiences with both men and women might be expected to be in the most conflicted position, given the stigma accruing to lesbianism and the presumptions of essentiality of lesbianism in both the heterosexual and lesbian communities as well as the gay trajectory as an expectation in the gay community.

Acceptance of Lesbian Identity

Many women involved in the lesbian world over time come to accept the subcultural formulation of identity and to embrace the logic of the gay trajectory. Further, most of the women who do come to designate themselves as lesbians reinterpret their biographies in conformity with the gay trajectory. For many of these women contact with the lesbian subculture is experienced as finding one's own, finally having a framework for understanding themselves and placing themselves in the world.

Coming out was an absolute relief. I always knew I was different, but I didn't know what it was. It was like suddenly I was home. Searching for years, in this difference. Knowing I was different and not knowing how I could relate to this difference, and it was like all of a sudden someone lifted a whole load off me. I felt like I finally found a structure, an awareness of myself where I suddenly knew where I belonged in the world, as compared to constantly searching and knowing that no matter where I was, I didn't quite fit. Not knowing, not being sure where I was in relationship to the people I was around. (Tape-recorded interview)

Recognition and acknowledgment of gayness as the true self frequently involves attributing inauthenticity to acts and behaviors that do not conform to gay identity. Previous identity statements may come to be viewed as instances of mistaken identity, as indicated by the following remarks:

Coming out means that I used to *think* I was straight and now I *know* that I'm gay. (Tape-recorded interview)

As I became close to the [women's] movement, I thought every time I have these love feelings, it's always toward a man; you know, I took them as—I didn't question them, because I—they seemed so genuine. It was soft and loving and so seemed so much a part of me, but only because this part [the lesbian part] was all squashed down. (Tape-recorded interview)

Now I'm not the person I was before I got embroiled in this marriage trip [an eighteen-year marriage]. When I was married, I didn't even know who I was. When I left, I found that part of being my own person has to do with loving women. (Tape-recorded interview)

Summary

The gay trajectory and coming out provide a framework for interpreting the meaning of gayness and its relationship to identity. Coming out is experienced by many women as a process of conversion within the self and as a resolution of identity.

Ideological features of the lesbian subculture tend toward the adaptation of a lesbian identity as the essential and true self. Not having a lesbian identity when one does have other lesbian elements is perceived in the community in terms of difficulties in acknowledgment and acceptance of lesbian identity. Recognition of these difficulties has been institutionalized in the community in the process of coming out.

It is worthwhile to note the parallels between the conceptualizations and theories about lesbianism and homosexuality in the heterosexual and lesbian communities. The attribution of essentiality is an important element in formulations about lesbianism in both communities, for the belief in its essentiality reinforces the polarization of lesbian and heterosexual identities and conceptualizations about them. The principle of consistency is matched in its inexorability by the biographic norms suggested in the gay trajectory and in the coming out process. Of course, the positive value placed on lesbianism or gayness within the lesbian community radically distinguishes its theories from those of the heterosexual community. Nonetheless, both the stigmatizing perspective of the larger society and the idealizing perspective of the lesbian world are similar in conceptions about the pervasiveness of gayness and its relation to identity.

The trajectory of gay identity in the gay world is similar to the principle of consistency in the heterosexual world as both are used as a standard in terms of which variations in sexual identities are explained. The gay trajectory also provides a method for locating the true self, because here again gayness is considered definitive of the self in an essential way. The gay trajectory presumes the existence of the true self and presumes to know the character of the true self of individuals who supply the cues of feelings, sexual attractions, interests, or associations with gay people.

AFFILIATION BETWEEN THE INDIVIDUAL AND THE GAY GROUP

The previous chapter concerned the way in which identity is construed in the gay group. Here the focus moves to the individual to consider affiliation between the individual and the gay group. The gay group is considered both in terms of the social category lesbian and in the sense of actual members of a community.

In the first part of this chapter I will point out the features of the larger society and the gay world that make up the conditions of affiliation between the individual and lesbianism. Then two types of affiliation will be considered. The first, a more tangible kind of affiliation, is contact between the individual and the social category lesbian or with actual lesbians. The second concerns symbolic affiliation between the individual and gay group through fitting individual biographies with the biographic norms of the gay group. I shall explain below the special sense in which I am using *biography;* but by way of a preliminary definition I shall focus on individual biographies as reconstructions of past events and look at how they correspond to the construction of identity in the lesbian community, that is, to the gay trajectory.

Conditions of Affiliation

Individual affiliation with the social category lesbian and with the gay group is conditioned by the amount and kind of information available about lesbianism and lesbians in the larger society and by the invisibility of the gay world itself.

Warren points out in her analysis of labeling on the individual and categorical levels that "certain social categories of persons are part of the social stock of knowledge, both as categories and as stigmatized categories." But, she notes, both knowledge of the category and understanding of it as opprobrious are "differently distributed by socialization and structural factors."[1] Several features of the surrounding heterosexual society and the lesbian world itself affect the availability, distribution, and nature of knowledge about the lesbian world. In the larger heterosexual society, for example, one of the main ways of dealing with stigmatized statuses, such as lesbian and homosexual, is simply to ignore and dismiss them. A second way in which these statuses are handled has to do with the character of the available information concerning lesbianism and homosexuality in popular media, literary presentations, and scientific literature, which consists of stereotypes of sin and sickness. Within the lesbian world, features that affect the availability and character of knowledge about lesbianism are stigma and secrecy on the one hand and the age constraints of that world on the other. In the main, the lesbian world is an adult world.

Lack of Socialization about Lesbianism

Knowledge about lesbianism and homosexuality is frequently not a part of socialization in the institutions of the larger heterosexual society; in fact, lesbianism is rarely discussed in heterosexual settings. Social interaction in heterosexual circles is typically characterized by the heterosexual assumption. (See the glossary.) Typically, sexual identity is not even an issue: the heterosexuality of others is an unquestioned background assumption in heterosexual settings. While the heterosexual assumption does function to maintain secrecy and covertness about lesbian identity, it also limits access to information about lesbians and lesbianism.[2] Simon and Gagnon cite the interactive rule of ignoring the sexual aspects of most identities, which tends toward the maintenance of the heterosexual assumption.[3]

Stereotypic Information

Information about lesbianism and lesbians in the heterosexual world is limited in quantity and type. As was indicated in the review of the literature in chapter 2, the prevailing imagery about lesbians in the larger society is negative. From the perspective of traditional psychiatry, lesbianism is conceptualized in terms of a pathological condition. Many churches assert that lesbianism is sinful. In the legal sphere, laws against

lesbian sexual activity reinforce negative ideas about it in the heterosexual world.

The negative picture of lesbians and male homosexuals in the larger
society renders them caricatures and stereotypes. This means that both
heterosexual persons and novice gays are not trained to recognize actual
lesbians and homosexuals when they see them. Warren states that people
are "taught that homosexuality is bad and so are homosexuals, *but* [they
are also] taught to recognize homosexuals by lurid signs such as extreme
effeminacy (in the instance of lesbians, extreme masculinity) or a fiendish,
warped, or debauched appearance. Thus they are not equipped to recognize actual homosexuals."[4] The beliefs held about homosexuals in the
straight world serve to limit knowledge about the social category lesbian
and function to make actual lesbians unrecognizable. Knowledge about
lesbianism is also limited by the secrecy of most of the lesbian subculture.

The Invisible Lesbian World

Because of the secrecy that hides the gay world and gay people as such,
the individual's search for others like the self takes on a fateful cast. Secrecy profoundly affects the individual's ability to locate and affiliate
with other lesbians by concealing the gay world, and stigma promotes disidentification with the category. The lesbian world exists largely as an
adult world—a world of leisure to which many avenues of access are restricted. Further, most adult lesbians are interested in relating to their
contemporaries and would be unwilling associates and partners for younger
women and adolescents. Thus, adolescents and children have few opportunities to meet lesbian adults and have few personal models for lesbian
identity. Though respondents report some groups of gay adolescents of
an autonomous experimental type, these seem to be few in number, and
access to them is limited.

Another feature of the lesbian world that tends to limit information
about it, in contradiction to the male gay world, is the reluctance of many
lesbians to talk about sexual activity specifically. This reluctance reflects
in part the socialization practices in the larger society that prescribe limits
on the sexual explicitness deemed appropriate to women in conversation.
However, it is also related to a perception that many lesbians have of the
straight world. Lesbians perceive the heterosexual world as interested
almost exclusively in the question, "What can two women possibly *do*
together?" (And, indeed, the heterosexual image of lesbians does em-

phasize sexuality.) Women-related women who are involved with public
speaking on behalf of other lesbians report that this question is ubiqui-
tous with heterosexual audiences. Questions in this area, therefore, are
almost always treated with reserve, if not obvious discomfort.

In addition, features of community organization in particular parts
of the country may limit access to the gay world. Several women remarked, for example, that access to the gay world and to lesbians is problematic for many women, particularly the young, and in rural settings as contrasted with urban places.

The conditions outlined above limit the availability of information
about lesbianism, affect access to lesbians, and may have an impact on
the individual's ability to adopt lesbian identity within the context of
the heterosexual world. I describe this impact in terms of a hiatus in identity and the search for identity.

Hiatus in Identity

When persons come to feel that they are implicitly in violation of the
heterosexual assumption or experience themselves as not fitting the mold
of heterosexuality, they may begin to define themselves in opposition to,
or in contrast to, the heterosexual patterning around them. They may
feel or believe that they are *not* like these heterosexual others without a
clear notion of what it is they *are* like. A hiatus in identity is created:
they become unable to assert who or what it is they actually are. The
subjective perception of being different from heterosexual others may
occur with varying degrees of clarity about what constitutes the difference, ranging from a vaguely perceived sense of not fitting in to a certainty about sexual-emotional attractions to one's own sex. Depending
on the clarity and urgency of these feelings, there then ensues a search—
conducted with greater or lesser intensity—for explanations or rationales
that can close up the identity hiatus.

The Search for Identity

Women who report they had begun to identify themselves as lesbian
prior to any contact with other lesbians or to any contact with the lesbian
subculture typically state that they experienced themselves as different
from heterosexual others. This difference was experienced in several ways
and with varying degrees of specificity. Some young women experienced

themselves simply in oppositional terms, as not being interested in boys as they saw other young girls were. Others experienced a positive interest in girls accompanied by the perception that other young girls were interested in boys. In the absence of any information about the significance of these feelings, these girls experienced a hiatus in self-identification. Such a perceived difference between the self and others typically leads to a search for some framework in which to interpret their feelings.

Dank reported in his study of coming out in the male homosexual world that the acknowledgment of gay identity often signifies to the subject the end of a search for identity.[5] This search may take the form of looking in the library for information in novels or in psychiatric and psychological literature or of making other such "disembodied" contacts with the social category lesbian. Or it may entail simply a close observance of the world around them for possible cues and explanations.

Once information about lesbianism is secured, an individual typically makes one of three types of resolution of identity. First, a woman may identify with the social category and accept the given negative imagery as descriptive of the self. Second, she may disidentify with the category. Third (and most prevalent among the women with whom I spoke), the individual may identify with the category but change the meaning of the category. Each of these ways of handling a stigmatized identity will be considered in the following discussion of affiliation.

Styles of Affiliating with Lesbians and Lesbianism

There are three basic ways in which individuals may affiliate with or come into contact with lesbians or lesbianism. These are: first, disembodied affiliation with the social category of lesbian; second, affiliation with a particular other in a dyadic relationship; and third, affiliation with groups of others within the lesbian community.

Disembodied Affiliation

Lofland notes that affiliation with a social category in the absence of direct access to a group or community entails "disembodied access" to sources of information about the social category or group such as contact through literature or media presentations.[6] In a similar manner, some women first recognize a lesbian self through disembodied affiliation with the social category of lesbian. Persons may thus designate themselves as members of a social category without being so designated by others and also without being affiliated with concrete social groups.[7] Women who come to identify themselves as lesbian or homosexual before actually meeting any lesbians and prior to lesbian relationships do so in response to subjectively perceived feelings, emotions, or attributes that are interpreted as having lesbian significance.

Symbolic Self-Labeling

Symbolic self-labeling as a lesbian means identification with the social category in the absence of such designation by others. This often occurs in the absence of contact with or knowledge of lesbian persons or groups with which one can identify. It is also more likely among those who are geographically isolated from the gay subculture, such as rural women. Symbolic self-labeling typically takes place in childhood and adolescence but may occur in adulthood as well. Among the women I interviewed, about 20 percent began to identify themselves as lesbians at a very early age, during prepuberty or puberty. Many of these made this identification through disembodied affiliation.

Some women labeled themselves lesbians when they came into contact with positive information about lesbians, such as Sappho's poetry and a number of European novels that portrayed lesbianism favorably. A sense of connection with a noble tradition and a history of lesbianism was often expressed, as in the following recollection by a seventy-eight-year-old poet:

You see, as I told you, I didn't have any educational advantages, and everything I've learned has been through reading—through associating with my kind of people. I think I was about seventeen when I first heard of Sappho, so naturally I read anything I could find about her. Lesbian has an honorable tradition. It meant—someone who lived on Lesbos, the women who lived on Lesbos—a great many of whom were Sapphic. . . .*Lesbian* to me is a perfectly honorable and beautiful word and I like it. I've no objection to Lesbos being my spiritual home in a sense. (Tape-recorded interview)

The Well of Loneliness was frequently cited as a source of information by means of which some women began to identify themselves as lesbian. Identification with the social category lesbian through reading this book was sometimes experienced as traumatic:

I read *The Well of Loneliness,* and I knew I was a lesbian. I tried to kill myself. I thought "Shit! Who wants this life?" (Tape-recorded interview)

But for other women, reading the same book led to their identification as lesbian without the negative imagery:

I really identified with that book, but in the end when she gave up her lover to a man I thought to myself, "It sure wouldn't be that way for me!" I just rewrote the end of the book in my head and made it come out the way I wanted it to! [Laughter] (Tape-recorded interview)

Other women, like one I will quote below, discovered the concept of lesbianism very late in life. Quite by accident, this woman came across *The Well of Loneliness,* which suggested a way of relating to women that she had never considered. She had been married for many years and had never even heard about lesbianism. Her contact with this book started her on a subsequent search for other material, but she kept her lesbian interests secret from her husband and three children. After her husband died, she moved to another city, where she approached a gay organization, met a woman, and finally had her first lesbian experience, twenty years after her initial identification.

I picked up a book off of a bookshelf, and I read *The Well of Loneliness.* That was the very first time—this is an orange book sitting here, and I picked it up, and I read it, and I said, "Well, what in the world do women want—to do together?" 'cause I never had any concept. I knew of men, you know, so I didn't know what women did together. But the book was so fascinating, and as I went along, I read it, and I began to feel some kind of desire, you know—aroused, I would say. And I had three children, and I simply did not understand that, and I had a husband. As the years went along, we just drifted sort of apart, you know. We were getting older, I was getting older, and so was he. . . . Well, what I did was I started groping around in the book stores and looking for literature. As the years passed, it was coming up, 'cause I never came upon anything like that. . . . So then I—just really wanted to—it just got to be an obsession with me. I wanted to see what I could—find somebody that I could have that sort of relationship with. (Tape-recorded interview)

For some women, learning the concept of lesbianism was definitive:

I first became aware of being different, loving, being attracted to other women when I was eight or nine years old, and it just wasn't some impulsive idea that went through my mind. It made such an impression on me that it became part of my identity. Somehow I knew, when I heard the word *homosexual* that that was me. At that young age I didn't know any-thing about it. . . . For a while it didn't figure as important. I remember though, I was very intense and some of my little girl friends said, "You act like a boy." I was a tomboy, but they meant something else. (Tape-recorded interview)

Ascriptions of Masculinity

Identification as lesbian through disembodied affiliation may entail an ascription of masculinity to the self. This implies invoking the consistency principle and the idea of inversion. Reasoning from their sexual object choice, and in light of the imagery about lesbians as masculine women, these women began to identify themselves not only as lesbian but as mas-culine as well:

I guess I assumed that I would take the butch role and proceeded to act in that fashion. I assumed I was masculine . . . an overgrown tomboy. My attitude toward it at that point had to be very stereotyped. It had to do with duck haircuts and leather jackets and all that stuff. . . . I was more masculine than feminine. . . . I considered myself as masculine. (Tape-recorded interview)

Reinterpreting the Category

Coming into contact with the category lesbian through communica-tions media sometimes leads to self-labeling as lesbian long before knowing about the existence of a lesbian subculture. The following remarks illustrate affiliation with the social category lesbian in the absence of community and reinterpreting the meaning of the category.

I knew I was a lesbian at about twelve. I read voraciously . . . and I found some books in the library and discovered that the way I felt about a lot of things were symptoms of lesbianism, which I felt was OK. I read fables and scientific journals and clinical doctor's books. I read anything I could get my hands on. And I had my mother check things out for me that I was too young to get myself. . . . I felt strongly physically toward women, and I knew enough not to say anything to anyone about it at all. . . . It told me there was a thing for what I felt, but then some of it didn't make sense either because I wasn't sick; I didn't feel sick. It said I was sick . . . and deviate and stuff, and I thought, "Obviously written by an adult. Adults are fucked." I had trouble with adults. [Laughter] (Tape-recorded interview)

In contrast to this woman, others who would later identify themselves as lesbians initially handled the stigma associated with the category by dis-identifying with and rejecting the category as fitting for the self. As one woman expressed it, "They said homosexuality was sick; I knew I wasn't sick, so therefore I couldn't be a lesbian." Such women reported that they had some subjective evidence that the category might apply to them, but because of the images of sin and sickness they could not accept it as applicable to them. These women continued to experience themselves in a hiatus in identity, feeling that they did not fit in the heterosexual pat-terning of male-female relations but being unwilling to accept the alter-native self-definition lesbian because of its negative implications.

Thus, some women who came into contact with information about lesbianism that fit with their subjective experience of themselves symbol-ically labeled themselves as lesbians. Other women, although they felt the information they had about lesbianism applied to them in some meas-ure, found its negative character led to disidentification and to a hiatus in identity. Still others changed the meaning of the category and identi-fied themselves as lesbians in the absence of community and relationships with specific lesbian others. Most of the women who symbolically labeled themselves lesbian through disembodied affiliation were aware of the negative evaluation of lesbianism in the larger society and thus endeavored to keep their lesbian identity concealed from heterosexuals.

Dyadic Relationships

Another group of women reported that because of the negative char-acterization of lesbianism they encountered in the literature they disiden-tified with it even though they had feelings and attractions that they would later come to define as gay or lesbian. For many of these women, the crit-ical event in identifying themselves as lesbian was participation in a dyadic emotional and sexual relationship with another woman. For others, dyad-ic relationships were the sole means of affiliation with lesbians and lesbian-ism.

Dyadic relationships—in this context, an intimate emotional-sexual re-lationship between two women—can be considered under two principal types: isolated dyads that are not affiliated with the larger lesbian commu-nity and those which take place in the context of affiliation with the les-bian community or with specific groups in the lesbian community. Parti-cipants can interpret dyadic relationships as having or as not having implications for identity. In the latter case, such relationships are perceived as situated and temporary arrangements, or the gender of the partner is considered to be coincidental and unimportant. For others, sexual behavior does have identity connotations.

Isolated Dyads

Three general types of isolated dyadic relationships can be identified among the women with whom I spoke. These are 1) isolated young experimental relationships; 2) isolated commitment to a unique relationship; and 3) lesbian or homosexual contacts in the context of heterosexual relationships. All three types generally carry a presumption of ignorance about lesbians and lesbianism.

Type 1: *Young Experimental Relationships.* Tripp makes a point with reference to isolated young experimental relationships that was borne out in the reported experience of some of my respondents: sexual contacts between same-sex peers among the young, where lack of information about homosexuality would be most likely, are often experienced by participants as a type of conformity.[8] Given that heterosexual socialization typically does not address the issue of lesbianism but in contrast emphasizes the taboo against premarital heterosexual activity, young girls may enter into dyadic relationships with one another without knowledge of their homosexual significance. Whether or not these early same-sex experiences will come to be interpreted as really homosexual depends to some extent upon the satisfactions intrinsic to such relationships and their subsequent repetition in concert with learning the social meanings of lesbian behavior. Such isolated dyadic relations may lead to further experimentation with the same sex or they may not.

A woman who is currently engaged in an ongoing relationship with another woman and calls herself a bisexual describes how she interpreted her early experience with women and men:

I think . . . I was sixteen when I first got sexually involved for about four years on and off . . . . When she came to college, we were in different sororities. . . . I really tapered off because she got interested in a guy she married, and I got interested in the guy I married. . . . I never thought of homosexual as relating to women, only thought of it as related to men, and I really had no idea of what two men did together. And I'm not sure I really knew what a man and woman did together actually, except from what I read. . . . Homosexuality for men—I'm not even sure if that had a sexual meaning for me as much as it meant some kind of swishy caricature meaning . . . . I remember my relationship with K as very exciting and my being very vain about it because she was very pretty. . . . Our sexual relationship we kept to ourselves, and I was more excited about it than anything else. I just thought it was more of a delicious secret. And at the same time I had a mad crush on a guy. I didn't think of it as being anything weird. I just thought of it as being neat, really something terrific—I didn't feel sneaky. I just felt appropriate . . . I thought it was a unique thing we were doing. (Tape-recorded interview)

Thus, this woman did not view her early relationship as lesbian. She subsequently married, had children, and was reintroduced to a relationship with a woman in a *ménage à trois* with her husband about fifteen years after her initial experience. She saw herself as basically heterosexual during that period of her life. Now, in the context of an ongoing primary relationship with a woman, she views herself as bisexual.

Isolated experimental relationships among young girls may be interpreted in several ways. Typically, in the absence of further dyadic contacts with the lesbian subculture, these relationships may be dismissed as a stage, merely a part of the heterosexual developmental process. For other women, such dyadic relationships may lead to a continuing interest in such relationships. A third possiblity, more characteristic of the women I interviewed, was that these earlier relationships were reinterpreted in the light of later experience as precursors to lesbian identity or unrecognized (at that time) initiations into lesbianism, as is the case with this respondent:

I really wasn't aware consciously of my attractions for girls until I had my first experience with D. But I remember that I used to come in contact with all these lesbian articles—like I read a lesbian article in a magazine when I was twelve, and I used to always pay attention when somebody talked about it. My history teacher in high school was gay, and my aunt knew her and used to tell stories about her, and I'd always listen—really be interested. Like all those books that say teenagers have a homosexual experience. I used to sit around and wonder if I was going to have one. . . . When D and I started sleeping together, we discussed the next day if we were lesbians or not. We decided that we weren't. [Laughter] That we just loved each other. Now I know I'm a lesbian but before I just couldn't believe it. (Tape-recorded interview)

Type 2: *Commitment to a Unique Relationship.* Isolated commitments to a unique relationship differ in intensity and longevity from young experimental relationships. A long-term commitment to a dyadic relationship may or may not have implications for identity in the absence of connection with the lesbian community. If the relationship continues to be perceived by participants as unique and situational, and if the gender of the participants is perceived as incidental (that is; the person, rather than the gender, is stressed), the likelihood is that the participants will not identify themselves as lesbians. If, on the other hand, the emphasis and specialness of the relationship derives from its being between two women, the likelihood is increased that the participants will, with knowledge of the social category, label themselves lesbians.

Contact with that very small but visible part of the gay community characterized by role-playing styles may similarly promote disidentification or identification with the category lesbian for relatively isolated dyads. The couple may perceive the lesbian community in stereotypic terms that do not mirror their unique relationship. The woman quoted below, who had been in an ongoing relationship with another woman for ten years, refused the label lesbian for herself as inauthentic and unnecessary:

I reject the use of these labels to define a person; if she happens to have an interest in this person, it's not fair. If someone says a person is a lesbian, it's a critical word. I don't think that a private relationship between two people that are extremely interested in each other has any social significance. They are simply expressing what they feel. I dislike such terms as *lesbian*. They imply a certain acceptance of a certain group. It's like we have a convert. It's a group rhetoric. . . . I actually cannot function in a gay bar. I shake, I tremble, I am with people who are not real. I have a strong sense of unreality. I certainly do not have a gay identity. (Tape-recorded interview)

This individual is unique among the women that I interviewed in her rejection of lesbian or gay identity despite the length of her relationship with a woman and her exposure to the lesbian community. Interestingly, her former lover concurred with this woman's definition of herself as not really gay.

More typical of the women in ongoing, unique, lesbian relationships that originated outside the community is that over time they will begin to affiliate with the social category lesbian or will make contact with lesbian others. Sometimes precisely because of their isolation and lack of social validation for their relationship in the heterosexual community, couples eventually began to seek out others like themselves:

I still think that if X had been a man that I would still love her. . . .I never felt sexually different from other women. X and I are pretty much loners, and except for a few people we keep looking for, that we can have really good friendships with, that we're destined to stay that way. We were together for seven years before we met any gay people. . . . It came to the point where we wanted to acknowledge ourselves as a couple, and that was part of the reason we became involved in gay groups. (Tape-recorded interview)

Lesbian identity, then, may follow lesbian behavior by many years. Lesbian identity may be adopted not always because of a perceived connection between identity and behavior, but for more instrumental reasons, such as the need for an accepting milieu for interpersonal relationships.

Type 3: *Contacts in the Context of Heterosexual Relationships.* The third way in which dyadic affiliation with lesbianism isolated from the lesbian community may occur is within the context of heterosexual relationships:

My husband and I got involved with another couple, and actually my husband got involved with this woman . . . and the two couples spent a lot of time together and so the four of us, actually the four of us got sexually involved with each other . . . so we would have foursomes. That way I could be with her [the wife], sort of. And she didn't really relate to me exclusively. She related mostly to my husband. I used my husband as a vehicle to get to her and at the same time I think I used her to get to him. (Tape-recorded interview)

Homosexual or lesbian dyads in the context of a heterosexual relationship are subject to a variety of interpretations by the participants and have differential implications for lesbian identity. If, as above, the emphasis remains on the heterosexual relationship and the lesbian relationship or behavior is seen as secondary, the likelihood is that the women involved will continue to think of themselves as heterosexual, If, on the other hand, the relationships come to be relatively equally weighted in importance, the women participants may come to define themselves as bisexual. Of course, the third possibility is that a relationship between two women within the framework of a heterosexual relationship may bring about a reevaluation of the self and facilitate identification as lesbian.

In sum, then, dyadic relationships that take place in isolation from the lesbian community or in the absence of knowledge of the community do not usually in and of themselves eventuate in the adoption of a lesbian or gay identity. However, these relationships may over time become re-interpreted as lesbian in the light of further knowledge about the social category lesbian or through contacts with the community. Another pos-sibility is that early relationships between women may be experienced as satisfying, so other similar relationships are sought. These later relation-ships in turn may lead to redefinition of the self.

Lesbian Sexual Activities as Affiliation

Sexual activities between women are implicit in the discussion of dyad-ic relationships. However, there is no necessary correspondence between particular sexual activities and affiliation with the category lesbian. Sex-ual activities between women must be understood in the context of the meanings these experiences have for the women involved. To be sure, the fulfillment and satisfaction that women experience in relationship to · each other may be the fulcrum of affiliation and identity—but it would be erroneous to assume that sexual activity has specific or unidirectional implications for identity.

I indicated earlier that women-related women did not talk graphically about their actual sexual activities. Their emphasis, rather, was on the quality of relationships between women. They referred to the dimensions of mutuality and closeness, particularly emotional closeness, in describ-ing their relationships. This is not substantially distinct from the way that heterosexual women talk about their intimate relationships: they do not routinely talk in explicit sexual detail about their experiences but tend, too, to talk about the quality of relationships. Similarly, Klaich found that most of the women-related women she interviewed did not refer directly to their sexual activities.[9] Kinsey indicated that sexual con-tacts between women show a higher frequency of orgasm than do male-female sexual contacts, a fact that led him to state: "Heterosexual rela-tionships could become more satisfactory if they more often utilized the sort of knowledge which most homosexual females have of female sexual anatomy and female psychology."[10]

Klaich went on to define this knowledge:

It is the knowledge that women prefer considerable generalized body stimulation . . . that fingertips, mouth and tongue, external female geni-talia, an unfettered imagination are fine instruments with which to produce sexual arousal. It is the knowledge that breasts, ears, the inner surfaces of thighs, the throat, the palms of the hand, the armpits, the soles of the feet, the buttocks and so on are splendidly responsive areas of the body. It is the knowledge that the clitoris, the inner surfaces of the labia minora, the extension of these inner lips into the vestibule of the vagina, and the anus are the locations of the greatest concentration of nerve endings, nerve endings that respond readily to fingertips, mouth, teeth, tongue, breast or another set of external female genitalia. It is the knowledge that the vagina, whether full of fingers or full of a penis, feels good when it is full, but better still in combination with arousal of other areas where the nerve endings are more concentrated.[11]

Contrary to popular notions, Klaich reported that few of the women she interviewed made use of dildos or other artificial penis substitutes in their lovemaking. When such devices were used, it seemed that their use was occasional, more by way of experiment than as a regular accoutrement of sexual intimacy among women. Her contentions are supported by the findings of the present study.

The women who were respondents in this study reported various individual preferences with respect to engaging in particular sexual activities. They stated that specific activities changed in the context of particular relationships; mutual satisfaction being more important than any particular technique. Some women liked manual penetration and manipulation; others preferred oral-genital sex; more preferred to combine these techniques. Yet others preferred tribadism, or simultaneous genital stimulation.

But no matter what particular sexual technique was used, no matter which specific sexual practices these women-related women engaged in, the activity itself did not seem to be the sine qua non of affiliating with the category lesbian or of identifying as a lesbian. In other words, the women I spoke with engage in a wide variety of sexual behaviors with other women and identify themselves in a variety of ways—as lesbian, as bisexual, or as heterosexual. In the world of women-related women sexual activity does not lead unequivocally to the assumption of lesbian identity (a point to be treated at length in chapter 7). Much more important in determining the identity outcome of sexual relationships and experiences is the meaning and significance attributed by women to these relationships. The meanings of relationships in turn relate to whether or not sexual activity is construed as having implications for identity in the first place, whether the lesbian significance of such activity is known, and whether sexual activity is seen as a manifestation of an underlying orientation or as an emanation of the true self.

Among the women in my sample, engaging in sexual activity with another woman per se was infrequently the basis for identification as a lesbian. In fact, isolated dyadic relationships among women were often not conceived of as lesbian. Further, self-labeling (as well as labeling by others) often took place prior to or in the absence of sexual activity. So the connection between sexual activity and sexual identity is not a direct one, a fact that again points up the importance of the experience and understandings of the actor.

Community Affiliation and Identity

When a woman experiences herself as not heterosexual, a hiatus in identity may ensue; it is closed when the individual finds a framework in which she can interpret herself and her experiences. Some women, however, find themselves in the lesbian community, either as single individuals or in dyadic relationships, prior to having come to a lesbian resolution of their own identities. They are likely to experience pressures—both subtle and overt—from the subculture toward adopting a lesbian identity.

Modes of Affiliation with the Lesbian Community

Individual or dyadic affiliation with the lesbian community presupposes some knowledge of the community and is usually accomplished in one of four ways: 1) Friends within heterosexual networks may reveal themselves as really gay and thereby provide an avenue of access to the lesbian world; 2) women might come into affiliation with the lesbian community, or at least the feminist elements in the lesbian community, through a mutual interest in the issues of feminism; 3) gay contacts may be purposely sought by individuals or dyads in gay bars or gay meeting places; 4) affiliation with the lesbian community may happen under the aegis of gay activism or politics, for example, through self-help groups. Overt lesbian groups are more accessible to the novice than are secretive groups and may be sought out by the curious, by women who are tentatively exploring the idea of lesbianism, as well as by individuals who have already symbolically labeled themselves as a lesbian.

The first two modes named above imply an element of chance, whereas the latter two imply more of a purposive or active seeking and presuppose a conscious choice of community on the part of the dyad or the individual. Active seeking of the gay community may have a variety of motives, including curiosity, loneliness, a desire to be with one's own, a desire for friendship or for sexual contact.

Gay Friends in Heterosexual Groups

For some women who will later become part of the lesbian community themselves, affiliation with gay people takes place within the context of heterosexual affiliative groups. Gay persons may be openly gay in these groups but more typically pass for straight. The circumstances of disclosure of gay identity are subject to the considerations that were outlined in chapter 3. The revelation of gay identity to the potentially gay person may take place for purposes of sociability or may occur in the context of an intimate relationships, as was exemplified by the following respondent:

I: Did you go through a period when you thought you weren't gay, or you didn't know about being gay?
R: As I told you before, I dated, and I was engaged, and I went to work in between jobs [as a musician] working all day in an office, and I met a woman there that was about—oh, I imagine—twenty-five years my senior —twenty years, I guess—her husband was in the service, and we started buddying around together. You know, we'd go out and drink and just have a good time, and she was the one that really broke me in. And I still think that she was the greatest thing that ever happened, but you know it never occurred to me that there was anybody else in the world, and I still was dating, but, boy, she and I were going at it good, you know. I'd be at work, and in the evenings and when I didn't have a date, I was going —running around with her. And this is where it started, and I realized all of a sudden that I liked what I was doing, and then her husband came back from the service, and that was the end of that immediately. . . . Then for a little while I worked in a defense plant . . . and I met a girl there. And she and I started running around together, and I guess we fell in love; really that happened to me for the first time. And we went into the service together. And we stayed together for the whole time we were in the service . . . We made plans to come out here and go to college, and about a week before it was time to go I got a wire from her that said she got married. I couldn't believe it. (Tape-recorded interview)

After this second affair, the respondent started meeting more gay people through her work as an entertainer.

And then I started running around. At this point I ran around with gay people, and I—at this point knew that was the way it was going to be. So I just ran around with gay people from that point on. (Tape-recorded interview)

Contacts with gay people in the heterosexual world may be the occasion for entry into gay life for the potentially gay woman and may eventuate, as was illustrated above, in more extensive contacts with the gay community. In fact, such contacts are usually the only way in which an individual can enter secretive gay groups.

As indicated previously, many of the women who eventually define themselves as lesbian first felt different from heterosexuals because of their attraction to other women. Such women may describe a "shock of recognition" or an intuitive sense of kinship when they came into contact with other gay people. They report their initial contacts with gay people as instances of recognizing their own. For some of these women, contacts with their own may occur periodically in heterosexual settings. In the experience of one respondent, summer camp was the occasion of periodic gay affiliation over a period of eleven years.

When I was in high school, I had a kind of schizophrenic existence. I had school life all year long, where I was this fat, out-of-it, introverted person, who had two skirts that were both gray. And summers I'd go to camp. I went to camp for eleven years in a row. And in camp, I'd know the whole culture, I was a leader, the kids would adore me . . . . In that arena, where I really fit in and connected, it allowed me to develop my personality. In school I didn't develop on any level. . . . See, there were all these counselors that I had a very great interest in when I was a young camper. And I had a sense that they were gay, that they related to each other sexually. I never really saw it, but I always knew it was there. They intrigued me greatly, and I had the sense that I really wanted to get more physically involved with another counselor. (Tape-recorded interview)

For some women in their early explorations of lesbianism, the heterosexual group was the sole source of relationships with other women, as they avoided any contact with the lesbian community.

I never sought people out. I would meet individuals in all kinds of circumstances, at work or at school. Sometimes we would become really good friends and know each other for years and neither one would know the other was gay—till the woman's movement. Previously women I brought out [had an initial gay experience with]—both of us were realizing something emotional was going on between us. We would start doing more and more things together and eventually we would enter into a sexual relationship together. We'd visit each other's apartment. Never an open thing of invitation but through the course of friendship where both of us would sense a physical attraction for each other in addition to friendship that had brought us together. One of us would make a move. I'm a very cautious type of person—kind of a test—would this new turn in the relationship be acceptable? Then I might be aggressive physically. (Tape-recorded interview)

The heterosexual world does interact with the gay world, usually unwittingly. So, despite the constraints of secrecy and the risks entailed in disclosure, it functions for some women as the channel of affiliation with gay people and as a connection to the lesbian subculture. For others, it serves as the source of sexual-emotional relationships. These affiliations and relationships may continue over time within the context of the heterosexual community or, as was the case for all the women cited above, initial contacts with other gay people in straight settings may lead to affiliation with the lesbian community.

Affiliation with Lesbianism through Feminism

The feminist movement spans both the heterosexual and lesbian worlds and sometimes provides an avenue of affiliation with lesbianism and lesbians for the potentially gay woman. The feminist movement emphasizes the importance of women and by extension supports the validity of relationships between women. Contacts with the feminist lesbian community may be the occasion for solidifying commitment to a lesbian identity for women who were previously identified as bisexual or heterosexual as well as for those who had made an identification as lesbian. Again, such contacts might be the occasion for beginning to explore the notion of love relationships between women for women who had previously not entertained the idea:

I had become close to the women's movement and was involved in consciousness-raising groups and generally interested in the whole women's
rights issue. It started as kind of an intellectual statement I made to myself. I felt so comfortable with women and was really turned on by the
exciting changes I saw in women around me—they certainly seemed to
be changing and growing a hell of a lot more than the men of my acquaintance. I began thinking, well—what is so terrible? I mean why not extend
my feelings for women into the sexual area? Why not express my feelings
sexually with a woman? Than it so happened that a friend of mine and I
started talking about the idea of relating to women sexually, and it sort
of happened. Not like some cold experiment or anything, but with the
idea that we were trying a different way of being with each other. It so
happens that for me—I find relationships with women to be much more
equal and free from the kind of role playing that goes on between men
and women. For me it really started off as an idea that progressed to experience and now, I would say, is probably the way I'll live. (Tape-recorded interview)

For other women, the women's movement served to change the meaning
of the category lesbian from negative to positive and to promote identification with that category.

I was thirteen years old when I had my first experience [with a woman].
I had no category for it at that time. I was involved in religion, and what
I was doing had to be the A-Number-One sin! And in addition to that the
very person who brought me out[12] wouldn't even dare say the word *gay*
or *lesbian* or whatever. We were just different and meant to be together.
It was very very oppressive. It was so difficult for me. . . . to get over
feeling that I was what everybody says I was: scum of the earth, perverted,
sick—you know all the labels. I didn't feel that way about myself—that's
what really drove me over the edge—the terrific conflict of knowing that
I really was OK, and I was right, and I had a perfect right to be however
I was, and it was a tremendously important aspect of my life to me, and
yet I wanted other people to like me. I really wanted acceptance. We
would avoid any people we thought were gay; we would never know, of
course, because we'd never say anything, and they would never ask anything. The most important thing for me in accepting myself was getting
involved with the movement—seeing people who had their heads up—it
was so important to me—it gave me pride. In the closet, I was very very
fragmented. Now I feel like I have sisters instead of just having acquaintances. (Tape-recorded interview)

The women's movement may facilitate access to the lesbian world and may be the framework for initial experimentation with lesbian relationships. For other women, contact with the lesbian community through feminism may serve to support a tentative self-definition as lesbian and be the source of positive meanings for lesbian identity.

Seeking the Community

It should be emphasized that finding the secretive community can be problematic indeed, particularly for the isolated gay woman. Gaining entry into a secretive lesbian friendship network is dependent upon the vicissitudes of meeting people in straight settings and establishing trusting relationships with them.

Some women seek out the community after having become aware of the social category of lesbian and after having labeled themselves lesbian. Other women make a tentative identification with the social category or simply want to investigate gay life and themselves in relationship to it. I would concur with Simon and Gagnon that emotional-romantic ties usually precede the overt sexual aspects of relationships among women.[13] However, some women do set about seeking the community in order to make a sexual contact:

I was ready. I went to my first gay bar all by myself to meet other women. I was a minister's wife. I didn't even drink. I was scared shitless. I was so scared. My rationalization before going into the bar was that if there were any men in there, they wouldn't want to have anything to do with me, and if there were any women who wanted to do anything to me, I'm sure it can't be anything that I haven't done in my head. Because I had been suffering for two years because I was trying to conform to something I just couldn't get into. So my initial feeling was one of great excitement, because I knew I wasn't going to spend the rest of my life alone. . . . I didn't want to be alone—and I thought if I'm going to go to hell, I might as well have a good time doing it. I was actively seeking a relationship with a woman. . . . I'd gone into the bar thinking I would sleep with someone that night because I felt lesbians were really into sex. But it wasn't that easy. I had to go again to meet someone who wanted to be with me, and it didn't matter who she was or what she was, she was a woman, right? I wasn't into falling in love, I was really into meeting a woman. It turned out she was a butch—we spent some time together before we finally got to bed. And I was into my aggression. I really wanted a woman. It was two years of pent-up emotion. (Tape-recorded interview)

Gay bars are a relatively accessible avenue of affiliation with the lesbian community and frequently provide normalizing experiences for novice gays. Bar contacts, in turn, frequently provide contacts with friendship networks in the community, as illustrated in the following account by a woman who was involved in a dyadic relationship with another woman:

We knew that there were lesbians, but we thought it was truck drivers or the butch-femme thing or something. It didn't quite register. I didn't understand it. All I knew was my high school economics teacher was masculine-looking. . . . So this guy, a friend of mine, was going to gay bars a lot, and he said he would take us to the bar. So we all went. And we just *loved* it. We went to the bar; we were scared. We didn't know what was going to happen. We were scared to go to the bathroom! [Laughter] And then a woman came up and introduced herself to us—she was real nice—and then we went to the bar a few more times and met some of this woman's friends. From then on we just got into meeting gay people. (Tape-recorded interview)

The gay bar as an avenue of access to parts of the lesbian community has been supplemented in recent years by the gay self-help organizations and feminist groups.

Affiliation with the Lesbian Community through Gay Organizations

Gay organizations derive from a variety of concerns with gay life, such as educating the straight world, providing social services to gay clientele, and working to change the public image of gays. Whatever their ostensible purpose is, these organizations serve as an avenue to the gay subculture. Some persons already in the community use the gay organization as an alternative to the gay bar. For other women, the gay organization provides the initial introduction into the life of the lesbian community. As the following example will illustrate, the gay organization may serve a kind of broker function, or as a clearinghouse for information about various special gay groups in the community. The following account refers to the Daughters of Bilitis (D.O.B.); founded by Del Martin and Phyllis Lyon in 1956, it is the oldest lesbian organization in the country. Its purposes are many: furthering education, providing an alternative meeting place to the gay bar, and altering the public image of the lesbian. The following account is by the woman quoted earlier who had come upon the idea of lesbianism through reading *The Well of Loneliness.* She subsequently sought to find the lesbian community by contacting the D.O.B.:

R: Somewhere along the line I read about the D.O.B., and on a late-night interview I saw this woman from the organization. And she spoke about the D.O.B. Well, that never left my mind. . . . But I had seen it in a newspaper that it would be on TV, and I stayed up and watched it. So we had come here to visit, and one of the first things I did was I looked in the telephone book and found the D.O.B., and my husband was with me when they [lesbian-activists] were having a march down by the city hall there, and they were all gathered up there, and there were all the signs . . . and I said, "Oh, boy, what's going on here? Let's stop and go see!" [Laughter] Somebody in the car said, "Oh, that's those women," you know. And I said, "Well, I'm interested. I'd like to know what they—what it's all about." But anyway, they wouldn't stop. And it just stayed in my mind from then on—that one day I'd go back to San Francisco where I could really be free and find out. And so that's what I did. The first thing I did—it took me about six months to do it— I passed that D.O.B. office for about six months. I'd go every other week or so, and sometimes I'd just pass it five times in one night. [Laughter] And I'd go down the street a little farther, and then I'd come back and I'd stand at the door, and I'd say, "Well, just go in." And then I'd say, "No, I can't go in there." And then I'd get on the bus and I'd come home. And I'd do it again and again. And finally I said, "Well, I'm going in here tonight!" and I did. . . . Once I went in there all I could see was just young kids. They were nice and friendly and accepting, but they were young. I asked if there was any older group . . . and she said yes and gave me a telephone number. Anyway after I did that that night, well, it took me another month to call, and I did call. And in the conversation she told me there was a group of women who called themselves S.O.L.—Slightly Older Lesbians—and she gave me a telephone number . . . and then in the conversation I asked her—this is going to sound awful—anyway, I asked her where or was there somebody that she could recommend to me for counseling, you know, because I had begun to feel that maybe I'm nuts, you know.
I: What made you think you were nuts?
R: Well, here I am. I was way past fifty, and I'd never done anything like it before, and I knew none of my family to be oriented this way. [Laughter] (Tape-recorded interview)

Affiliation is a matter of contact. Contact with the social category, with gay people, and with the gay subculture may take place in many different ways, but ultimately raises the issue of affiliation through identity. Identity—the response to the question "Who am I?"—looks to the data of personal history and experience for the answer. This most personal level of experience, the experience of the self over time, far from being the inviolable determinant of the present, shifts and changes according to present demands. Reconstructed biography is used to support and sustain a current identity status by demonstrating to others and to the individual herself that who she presents herself as being is grounded in the past and makes sense in terms of the past. On the other hand, biography may be used to demonstrate that one is not indeed the person whom others assume her to be. Before going into these specific uses of biography as the personal historical level of affiliation, I shall define *biography* as the term is used here.

Biography

Though the term *biography* is commonsensically used to indicate the sum or the sequence of events over the lifetime of an individual, my use of this term is more specialized and has three main features: reconstruction, reinterpretation, and continuity.

All biographies, especially autobiographies, are reconstructions of the past on the basis of present demands, interests, problems, and questions. Biographical reconstruction involves the culling out of events and experiences and the shaping of these into an ordered sequence organized with respect to present purposes. Certain events in a biography are chosen as important, critical, and meaningful, whereas others recede into the background, are forgotten, or are not attended to for the purposes at hand.

Reconstruction is to be distinguished from reinterpretation. Reinterpretation of biography indicates that current meanings of previous life experiences are both different from the meaning of those life experiences at the time they happened and are superimposed on past events in such a way that these events are now seen as always having had pointed to the present state of affairs in the life of the individual.

There are four basic elements involved in the idea of biographical reinterpretation. First is taking the present self as the essential, true identity. Second is the definition of a former identity or identities as inauthentic, implying a lack of recognition in the past of the true character of the essential self. Third is a need for congruity of experience between past and present identities, eventuating in a sense of strain. This strain occasions the fourth element of biographical reinterpretation: a recasting of the past as leading to the present identity. Thus, reinterpretation of biography always implies consistency and congruence: the consistency of identity and the activity that forms the basis of the identity, and the congruence between past and present identities and actions. As Berger points out, the decision about what is to be included as well as the meanings imposed upon these events depend upon the present frame of reference. "The course of events that constitute one's life can be subjected to alternate interpretations. . . . We . . . go on interpreting and reinterpreting our own life. As Henri Bergson has shown, memory itself is a reiterated act of interpretation."[14] Thus, individuals reassess and reformulate their biographies in such a way that the present seems continuous with and emergent from the past. Importance is attributed to events in personal histories in such a way that they become congruent with present truths: "We have as many lives as we have points of view."[15]

This concept of biography raises the issue of continuity, a concern with the temporality of events. Berger and Luckmann have noted that "as the individual reflects about the successive moments of his experience, he tries to fit their meanings into a . . . biographical framework. This tendency increases as the individual shares with others his meanings and theories of biographical integration."[16]

Continuity, a temporal concept, is to be distinguished from consistency. The principle of consistency, the gay trajectory, and the notion of essentiality are all fundamentally atemporal concerns. Once given an element in either the gay trajectory or the principle of consistency, the other elements are simply assumed to co-occur or to vary together. Continuity has to do with the actual temporal ordering of life events. An individual's present identity may be congruent with her past identity and the temporal ordering of past life events may seem to progress inexorably from the past identity to the present identity. In other cases the actual sequence of biographical events in an individual's life may be discontinuous, and present and past identities may be radically different. Biographical reinterpretation may be used to handle such discrepancies.

In biographical reconstruction, life events are presented in a temporal progression so that they are seen as leading from the past to the present, the past implicitly causing the present state of affairs. Yet, in the *reinterpreted* reconstruction of biography entailed by recounting the progression of past events, the present implicitly determines the past.

Within the lesbian world there are three types of biographical reconstruction evinced in the accounts of the women interviewed. The first mode characterizes the *primary lesbian,* who presents in her biographical reconstruction a continuity of experience showing a consistency of identity throughout her life summarized by "I was always that way." The second mode of biographical reconstruction is that of the *elective lesbian*, who reinterprets discontinuous life experiences so that they demonstrate a true, underlying lesbian identity. The third mode characterizes woman-related women who have idiosyncratic identities and some who have lesbian identities. They are not concerned with biographical continuity and consequently have no strain toward biographical reinterpretation. Their reconstructed biographies lack the features of continuity found in the reinterpreted reconstructions characteristic of elective lesbians.

Primary Lesbians

The primary lesbian is so designated by virtue of early childhood or pubertal definition of herself as lesbian, gay, or homosexual and by her conformity to the biographic norms of the lesbian community. According to the primary lesbian, memories of sexual or emotional attractions to other women predate puberty. (However, this is not to suggest that the primary lesbian does not go through the process of coming out.) The primary lesbian typically experiences herself as completely oriented toward women and reports very few (or no) heterosexual experiences. Sexual activity with men, if any at all, was reportedly conceived of at the time of its occurrence as an experiment, a "making sure," or as a test of her true nature. Thus biographical reconstructions of primary lesbians exhibit the character of continuous consistency. Their descriptions of the emergence of lesbian identity are congruent with the gay trajectory. The following account, typical of the biographical statements of primary lesbians, illustrates the congruence between biographical reconstruction and the gay trajectory as well as continuity between past and present identities.

I first fell in love with a woman when I was about fifteen or sixteen. I fell in love with a woman who was about a year older. I don't know whether I used the term *lesbian* then; I knew that I loved women, and that was where I was and where I wanted to be. I didn't fall in love with men. I don't dislike or hate men as such, whether homosexual or otherwise. I've had many more men friends in my early life, and I have all my life, than lesbian friends. It just happened that way in work, I guess. It was not difficult—it was far from being difficult for me to accept myself as a lesbian. It was a joyous thing. I like the way women look. I like wom-

en as people, and I wanted to have women as lovers and I love women.
So—and I don't know why—of course I know—it's partly religion and
indoctrination and training and all the frightening that women get that
probably makes some women feel differently, but the people around me
didn't know enough to frighten me about it, even if they wanted to. It
didn't—probably never occurred to them. I don't know—I never had any
of that negative impression. (Tape-recorded interview)

Other primary lesbians, of course, were more troubled and directly affected by the stigma that accrues to lesbianism. This woman was unique in
having a bohemian, artistic group of friends and a family who admired
her for her artistic achievements as well as her personal qualities. They
were reportedly unconcerned about her sexuality, so she was not subjected
to the pressures about her lesbianism that many lesbians report.

Elective Lesbians

The elective lesbian is distinguished from the primary lesbian in several dimensions. She generally comes to identify herself as a lesbian at a
much later time in her life, during her twenties, thirties, forties, or even
fifties. She has had heterosexual experiences, often extensive, and usually
has had a heterosexual identity prior to her identification as a lesbian; she
may also have had a bisexual identity.

The signal features of the biographical reconstructions of the elective
lesbian are, first, a discontinuous, or mixed, history of sexual-emotional
relationships—heterosexual experiences followed by homosexual experience—and, second, an imposition of continuity of meaning via retrospec-
tive reinterpretation upon this discontinuous sexual history. The elective
lesbian reviews her heterosexual past and finds it fraudulent, obscuring
her true lesbian nature. Through the process of reinterpreting the meaning
of past events, the elective lesbian brings her biography into line with the
gay trajectory and presents evidence to support a continuous, albeit unrecognized, lesbian nature. For example, this thirty-five-year-old woman
talks about the meaning of her identification as a lesbian, which had occurred four years earlier:

Lesbian is my primary identity. Before I was somebody's old lady[17] I was
a chameleon. I only just found myself. My identity before was like a
cloak or a cape I put on. I don't think I had an identity before I came
out and recognized my lesbian identity. The first thirty-one years of my

life was a waste. It would have been nice if I discovered or recognized my lesbianism earlier. Before I came out, I had prior experiences with women. It was groovy, a *ménage à trois*. It was a swinging thing. I went to bed with women long before I even began to think in terms of lesbianism or gayness and enjoyed myself thoroughly in bed with women sexually. I remove the idea of sexuality from lesbianism now, because it had not had a major role in my identity as a lesbian. But when I met T, I knew and I called all my friends and told them, "I'm a lesbian." (Tape-recorded interview)

The following account is from a fifty-two-year-old woman who had been heterosexually married for twenty-two years, after which she had a relationship with another man. For the past three years, however, she has been involved in lesbian relationships, and she states that she is a lesbian. In talking about how she came to relate to women, she reflected on her past and found evidence of lesbianism from her early childhood.

I began at this point to become involved with women's consciousness-raising groups, and I began to hear . . . of the idea of women being turned on to each other. It was the first time I heard about it in terms of people that I knew . . . I met a woman who said in a workshop, "Well, there are older women who are finding other options for themselves." . . . I was receptive, but there was no previous, immediate history. Like there was a part of me that had been thinking about it, and thinking, "Gee, that sounds like intellectually that's a good idea." . . . To think of it in terms of an older woman saying it was very exciting to me . . . And then, of course, when that happened, I got in touch with my own background. And remembered that I had had these kinds of thoughts as a high school kid, that I had crushes on women, that not only that, that I had had two small sexual experiences with women, and both were cases where I had touched their breasts. And that there was a period in my all-girl's high school where I had worn men's shirts, and my mother was so scared by it that she took me to my social worker aunt to get me straightened a-round. . . . I was trying to dress as much like a man as I knew how, without really saying it consciously. . . . And I very much wanted to be like the—what I thought were very neat-looking, boyish-looking women. Now it didn't fit me too well because I'm big breasted and have big hips, but I tried. I wore a man's shirt and had my hair cut short. I had a boy's haircut. . . . At the time I felt I was a misfit, that whatever I wanted to do was not right. That I wasn't a proper girl. (Tape-recorded interview)

Biographical accounts of the elective lesbian reflect a basic discontinuity in their identities and the contents of their life events that is resolved by a reinterpretation of events incongruous with a lesbian identity and by the selective recalling of events compatible with lesbian identity. The past is refocused and the meanings of past events are changed by recounting them in the light of present identity concerns. Rationales—such as programming by the heterosexual society, unconscious motivations, and other similar concepts—are invoked to explain heterosexual affiliations and behaviors and to explain the late realization of true lesbian nature.

Idiosyncratic Identities

A number of women-related women in the lesbian community do not fit their biographies into line with the gay trajectory nor do they strive to approximate a continuous lesbian past. Some of these women identify themselves as lesbians though they identified themselves as heterosexual in the past. These women do not see lesbianism as an essential identity or experience their identification as lesbian in terms of a conversion or a change: "I used to be heterosexual, now I'm a lesbian." Other women, however, despite the fact that they are engaged in what they describe as meaningful lesbian relationships and are affiliated with the lesbian subculture, remain obdurate in identifying themselves as heterosexual, bisexual, or sexual in contradistinction to the identity rules in both heterosexual and lesbian worlds.

Though fewer in number than either primary or elective lesbians, these women do not identify as lesbian even in the face of many pressures to assume such an identity. Their biographical reconstructions exhibit, simultaneously, the discontinuity in their sexual-emotional lives and an apparent lack of strain toward continuity. In contrast to both the elective lesbian and the primary lesbian, as well as in refutation of both the principle of consistency and the gay trajectory, these women do not draw the identity conclusion that their behavior would seem to impose according to the logic of social construction of sexual identity in both heterosexual and lesbian worlds.

The woman quoted below is a forty-four-year-old clinician, currently involved in a long-term relationship with a woman. Although she uses the term *gay* to describe some of her relationships, she also had several emotional-sexual relationships with men.

It feels to me that bisexual is essentially what I am. I must be bisexual;
that's how I've lived my life. I don't just relate to women; I have not just
related to women. Although I'm with a woman now, for a long period
of my lifetime I was relating just to men. And sexually that's been most
of my life. . . . Right now I'm not having any relationship with a man,
but I certainly have the proclivity for it. I don't think of myself or my
friends as lesbians. They just seem to me like people who just love one
another. And that almost seems accidental. And for me also. That is my
most comfortable view of the whole thing. That it is really accidental
. . . and it's just where you happen to find yourself and who you happen
to be turned on to (Tape-recorded interview)

Women-related women with idiosyncratic identities, then, continue to
stress the circumstantial, accidental, and situated features of their lesbian
relationship. They do not accept the essentiality of lesbian behavior and
feelings for themselves though they may well perceive essentiality as a
feature of real lesbians. Seemingly, the notion of lesbianism as being definitive of personal identity or as having necessary identity implications
does not correspond with the experience these women have of themselves.

The primary lesbian, elective lesbian, and the idiosyncratically identified woman differ from one another along several dimensions: their etiological accounts of lesbianism, the meaning of lesbian activity and lesbian
feelings, and their age of entry into the lesbian community, as well as the
historical time of their entry.

Primary lesbians define lesbianism in terms similar to those implied in
heterosexual theories of lesbianism—as a master status trait with the character of essentiality. Given that primary lesbians define lesbianism in a
favorable, nonpejorative sense, nonetheless, their conceptualization of
lesbianism includes the idea of an immutable and pervasive condition of
the self.

Primary lesbians are more likely than elective lesbians to have made
their identification with the social category lesbian through disembodied
affiliation. Many stated that they felt unique in the world because of
their feelings of attraction to women. The acknowledgment of lesbian
identity, the naming of these feelings in the coming out process, was often
experienced as a relief:

Coming out was an absolute relief. I always knew I was different, but I
didn't know what it was. It was like suddenly I was home. Searching for

years, in this difference. Knowing I was different and not knowing how I could relate to this difference, and it was like all of a sudden someone lifted a whole load off me. I felt like I finally found a structure, an a- wareness of myself where I suddenly knew where I belonged in the world, as compared to constantly searching and knowing that no matter where I was, I didn't quite fit. Not knowing, not being sure where I was in rela- tionship to the people I was around. (Tape-recorded interview)

The primary lesbian is disposed to describe lesbianism as an orientation or condition that informs the whole character of her self. While elective lesbians may come to view lesbianism as a condition or an orientation, they are more likely to use the term *preference* with respect to their sex- ual-emotional behavior. Elective lesbians are likely to invoke the notion of the essentiality of their lesbianism (as do the primary), but unlike the primary they tend to embrace the idea of lesbianism as a voluntary choice.

Woman-related women who have idiosyncratic identities, on the other hand, may hold that lesbianism is the essential, pivotal feature of the identities of other women but only describes an aspect of themselves or refers to situated and circumstantial behavior that says nothing about their identity.

Etiological Accounts

Primary and elective lesbians differ in the etiological, or causal, ac- counts they propose with respect to lesbianism. The primary lesbian is most likely to offer a genetic or hormonal theory, and some conceive of lesbianism as part of a cosmological plan.

I: Do you feel that you had a choice about being a lesbian?
R: I think down deep I just was this way. I don't know. I've never under- stood why. And rationalizing things out, I think that in all probability there are gay people—it's because we either kill ourselves off with a war —I think in all probability, logically, it's a balance—gay people provide a balance. Maybe it's nature's way of saying that some of us weren't meant to have children. . . . Because if everybody raised a family, we'd be so overpopulated that—I think maybe it's nature's way of balancing things out. And I happen to be one of those balancing, you know. I don't think it's any particular choice of mine at all. Logically this is how I've come to the conclusion or how I rationalize it. Whether I'm right or not I don't know. I just sat down one day and figured maybe this was the way it's supposed to be. That if we don't have a war every twenty years and kill

each other off, we got to have some way or other to maintain a balance. Nature and animals and plants and everything else in its way maintains its own balance. Maybe this is the way humans are supposed to do it. I don't know. I just think I've been this way basically from the time I was born and didn't know it. . . . I didn't react the way my friends did. . . . Apparently through time there's been gay people, and if the good Lord didn't want it to be this way, I don't think we would ever have thought of it. Something had to make people this way. . . . I've thought that somewhere along the line that some of us had to be this way—nature's way—the Lord—somebody's way of balancing a little bit of the population instead of killing each other and having a war every twenty years to get rid of a gob of people. (Tape-recorded interview)

This account combines elements of an innate gayness theory with a cosmological account for gayness. Of course, such an explanation ignores the heterosexuality (and the children) of other lesbians. As evidence, above, however, primary lesbians typically formulate lesbianism in such a way as to exclude the possibility of heterosexuality.

The elective lesbian holds similar beliefs about the etiology of lesbianism, vis-à-vis its naturalness, its inborn quality, and its place in the world. However, the elective lesbian, unlike the primary lesbian, must explain a heterosexual past while holding the belief in the essentiality of lesbianism. This involves positing different levels of reality, the most apparent of which is not the most real; that is, the heterosexual past was not really what was going on. Reality is attributed to fantasy life or to the previously unrealized character of the self. The elective lesbian may state that she was not acting in accord with her real feelings when she led a heterosexual life-style.

I realize now I never liked men. I always related to women. I was simply doing what society told me to do when I got married. I was programmed for marriage. I have never been so satisfied with a man as I am with X, and I don't mean just sexually, either. We have so much; we have a perfect meeting of the minds. (Conversation from field notes)

The etiological accounts of lesbianism from the perspective of women-related women who have idiosyncratic identities have greater application to others than they do to the women themselves. That is, these women may hold the belief that lesbianism is an essential quality of the self for lesbian women and may posit a genetic, hormonal, or social learning theory with reference to others. However, the woman with an idiosyncratic identity generally does not invoke an etiological explanation for her own lesbian activities and relationships. Rather, she focuses on personal and idiosyncratic qualities of the relationship, irrespective of the gender of her partner.

I guess you might say I'm person-oriented, as opposed to being heterosexual or homosexual. I personally can't relate to the idea of being only with women or only with men. It depends on the person. One of the most important love relationships of my life was with a man, and I can only say that I would be with[L] whether she was a man or a woman. It is her as a person that I love. It doesn't matter to me what sex a person is, but what kind of person they are. (Tape-recorded interview)

Thus the idiosyncratically identified woman tends to give short shrift to considerations of etiology with respect to her own behavior and identity. Her own involvement in a lesbian relationship is accounted for more in terms of attraction to a particular personality, though she may well express deep commitment. In comparing relationships with men to those with women, she is likely to emphasize the special qualities of the latter, focusing, for example, on intimacy, communication, and empathy.

Sexually my relationships with men were equivalent to those with women, but not emotionally. In terms of showing all sides of myself. . . . Women get to see you in all your moods, and when there's that natural closeness that's always allowed women. . . . I think there is a possibility that men and women can be that close. I think it's the way we're raised. (Tape-recorded interview)

It should be noted that the idiosyncratically identified woman, like the primary and the elective lesbians, is influenced by the negative and pejorative connotations attached to lesbian behavior and may have gone through a period of questioning whether or not the label lesbian or homosexual applied to her. An important feature, then, in an individual with an idiosyncratic identity is not only her refusal to conform to the identity norms of both heterosexual and homosexual worlds but also her distinguishing herself from other women-related women by referring to her attachment to relationsips with men. In the perspective of the idiosyncratically identified woman, this continued affiliation with males— whether it is on the basis of present, past, or expected future contact—is incompatible with being a lesbian. She may be cognizant of and partially accepting of the etiological theories put forth by primary lesbians, while refuting their applicability to her.

Age at Entry, Chronological and Historical

The primary lesbian makes her identification as a lesbian at an early age, usually during childhood or puberty. The deterministic view of lesbianism held by the primary lesbian tends to be more prevalent among women who are forty years old and older and who were socialized into the community prior to the last five years or so. The elective lesbian tends to make entry into lesbian relationships and identification as lesbian at a much later age than does the primary lesbian. This style, in general, is characterized by voluntarism, particularly among elective lesbians who so designated themselves in the last five years.

There is some evidence for the position that the rhetoric of choice is far more prevalent in the community now than it was formerly and that the deterministic ideas appear to have far less currency among both younger women and lesbians who entered the life of the community relatively recently. This, however, is only a suggestion that bears further specific investigation.

Women with idiosyncratic identities vary greatly with reference to both their age of entry into lesbian relationships and the historical time at which they entered the lesbian community. Because the idiosyncratically identified woman specifically rejects the essentiality of lesbianism, she also implicitly rejects a deterministic explanation of her own behavior and, like the elective lesbian, would invoke the rhetoric of choice, irrespective of the historical time she began affiliation with the community.

Most of the women in my sample presented reconstructions of their lives that were in conformity with the biographic norms of the community, or the gay trajectory. A number of women, however, conformed neither to the identity rules nor to the biographic norms of the community. Though affiliated with the lesbian subculture, they seemingly felt no strain toward continuity in either their biographies or their identities.

The closer the focus moves toward the individual, the more varied become the possibilities and resolutions of identity and biography. In the final chapter I shall again focus on the individual and examine personal resolutions to identity in the light of the expectations of gay and straight worlds.

7

THEORIES AND EXPERIENCES OF IDENTITIES IN THE LESBIAN WORLD

The social constructions of lesbian identity from both the heterosexual and lesbian worlds are parallel, as we have seen. Both paradigms contain the notion of essentiality of lesbianism, albeit an essentiality that has quite different implications in the two perspectives.

The first focus of this chapter is to review the heterosexual and lesbian constructions of lesbian identity and to indicate their inadequacies in light of the ways in which identity is actually experienced by participants in the lesbian world. Second, I will present a typology of identities grounded in my research in the lesbian world and more useful for understanding identities among women who love women than either the heterosexual or the lesbian models. This typology provides a more fruitful perspective for understanding what goes on in the empirical world because it is close to the experiences and identities that women report. Although including identity/behavior categories that are described by the gay trajectory and the principle of consistency, it goes beyond these two models to encompass typical variations in sexual experience and sex-related identity among women-related women.

The Heterosexual Paradigm of Essentiality and the
Principle of Consistency

In the heterosexual paradigm, the essentiality of lesbianism focuses on sexuality. Sexuality is conceived of as pivotal to the individual, and all other aspects of the person are seen through the prism of this "deviant" sexuality. This is evident when theorists attribute many kinds of neuroses to virtually all homosexuals simply on the basis of their homosexuality or when theorists otherwise negatively characterize the individual on the

basis of lesbianism or homosexuality. Psychiatric theories of lesbianism
are the most fully elaborated examples of the heterosexual paradigm. In
traditional psychiatric writings, lesbianism is conceived of as a disease
that infects the whole personality with a variety of undesirable traits.
The underlying assumption of such theories is the principle of consistency, which, it will be recalled, assumes that sex assignment, gender identity, gender role or sex role, sexual object choice, and sexual identity vary
together. Following the logic of this principle, a disruption in expectations
with respect to one element presumably carries consequences for all the
other elements.

Theories seeking to explain such disruptions focus on problems or
errors in sexual socialization (or developmental disturbances) on the one
hand or anomalies in gender sex on the other. Because such theories uti-
lize the concepts of latency and the unconscious, they have the advantage of being irrefutable. If the biographical data of a particular case at
hand should be recalcitrant to such an explanation, the theoretician can
assert that the conditions of the paradigm were met at an unconscious
level. In addition, a "mistake" in sexual object choice—such as a man
choosing a woman—implies inversion in gender identity and in sex role
behavior as well. Women who choose women, according to this logic,
are necessarily masculine.

Formulations such as these presuppose the omniscience of the observer. The observer knows and understands the meanings of the individual's
experience better than the individual herself understands her subjective
life and may proffer explanations that strongly contradict the experience
of women-related women.

Many lesbians *claim* that they are happy and experience no conflict about
their homosexuality, simply because they have accepted the fact that they
are lesbians and will continue to live a lesbian type existence. *But this is
only a surface of pseudo happiness. Basically, they are lonely and unhappy
and are afraid to admit it, deluding themselves into believing that they are
free of all mental conflicts and are well adjusted to their homosexuality*
(emphasis added).[1]

The Lesbian Paradigm of Essentiality and the Gay Trajectory

Within the lesbian world, the source of essentiality moves beyond
sexuality, implying an expansion of the experience of self and a finding

of community. Lesbian sexuality is seen as an emanation from the essential self: lesbianism is a totality of which sexuality is a mere part. The expansion of essential lesbian identity into an alternative way of life and being is expressed in the following:

People used to say, "You're obsessed with your gayness," and now I realize that what I was doing is trying to achieve an equilibrium because something was wrong. You know, if there's one thing out of kilter, then you tend to focus on that place where you're hurt and try to repair it except that it goes beyond repair into creation, into creating something new and a rejection of what is past, and so what starts out as a kind of specialized thing, being gay, being a homosexual, is then moving to being a lesbian. It suddenly takes up your whole humanness because you know if you can get the lesbian community together with all kinds of good creative input, then you are creating a life-style—where you can express all your humanness. So that lesbian becomes more than relating to another woman, it becomes a way of life, that is, a . . . means to finding a new identity, not just for yourself, perhaps, but, you know, for all people, creating an alternative way of life. (Tape-recorded interview)

The preceding account captures some of the features of the lesbian community's view of essentiality, which reaches its peak in the combined political thrust of gay liberation and feminism. The sexual meaning of gayness is deemphasized, and a meaning inclusive of many aspects of life and of self is stressed. Gayness is no longer thought of as a subset of the straight or heterosexual universe or as something explained in terms of a deviation from heterosexual standards. In politicized parts of the gay community gayness is the standard of sexuality from which heterosexuality is seen as narrow, conventional, and unexplored.

The gay trajectory and the essentiality of lesbianism are well illustrated by a lesbian's reinterpretive reconstruction of her life. As the writer of the following quote was exposed to the theories of the lesbian community, she assumed the community perspective and the gay trajectory became the framework for interpreting herself and her history of experience. Her biography was brought into line with the logic of the gay trajectory. Her experiences were reinterpreted so that they seem to have been leading up to her now recognized gay self and gay identity.

Coming out as a lesbian has been the most difficult decision of my life—and perhaps also the wisest. Difficult because of the social stigma attached to it—so effective that it is *even possible for a lesbian to live her entire life without ever becoming conscious of her sexual-emotional bias for women.*

I am now thirty-six. *For most of my life I defined myself as hetero-sexual without seriously questioning the definition.* Coming out was a long process—a series of acts and changing stages of consciousness . . . for one must come out again and again in a world where heterosexuality is presumed; where it is equated with mental health, moral uprightness, and the ability to be a productive member of society.

I had lesbian feelings and experiences through childhood, adolescence, and young womanhood, but, incredibly, it was only after the final proc-ess of coming out in my thirties—politically, sexually, and emotionally—*when I knew with certainty and with my whole being that I was a lesbian, that I was able to recognize and name my early feelings.* It is as if a sane person were imprisoned in a mental institution for half her life and, after being released, found others who understood her feelings and said she had never been crazy. And I feel anger at the *lie of sameness* that kept me so long from *knowing who I was* and from the comfort of love and commu-nity with women (emphasis added).[2]

The principle of consistency and the gay trajectory contain assumptions that do not accurately reflect the multiple relations among feelings, activ-ity, and identity: assumptions of essentiality, congruence, and a notion of the true self. Essentiality and the gay trajectory from the gay perspec-tive and essentiality and the principle of consistency from the heterosex-ual point of view are biographical recipes used to fill in an individual's biography in the absence of information; or they may be used as cor-rectives for biographies that do not conform to their dicta. Both explan-atory models for constructing identity have internal mechanisms for dealing with disconfirming evidence that militate toward the survival of the theories. In the gay world, the rhetorics of coming out, oppression, and stigma are used to explain failures to follow the gay trajectory. In the heterosexual world, the inversion principle is invoked so that consistency of another kind is maintained.

Both the principle of consistency and the gay trajectory invoke the notion of a real self that carries the true sex-related identity. I suggest that the "true self" and the "real self" are convenient methaphors for the ex-perience of temporal continuity of the self. In reality, the self, sexuality, and identity change over the course of time, a fact that can be illustrated by pointing out empirical instances of these changes. As we will see, the "same" acts may imply different identities for different persons, as well as the converse: the "same" identities may eventuate in different behavior for different persons.

The images of identity in both the gay and straight worlds fail to take into account the complexities of relations between actions and identities. They are essentially ideological in character in that they are self-confirming and cannot be refuted by negative cases. Indeed, there is some empirical evidence to support both of the foregoing explanatory models. There are masculine women in the lesbian world, women who wish to be men, although in my experience these women are a distinct minority. Similarly, there are women for whom the gay trajectory exactly mirrors their experiences. However, these models do not adequately cover the variety of identities of women-related women.

Against the background of these images of identity construction in both heterosexual and lesbian worlds, I wish to move toward an empirical examination of identities in the lesbian world and to consider actual relations of feelings, activity, and identity. The typology of identities that follows is more comprehensive than the models presented above for the following reasons: first, it is able to encompass a greater variety of features found in the real world than can simplified, ideological imagery. Second, it moves away from the polar conceptualizations of lesbian and heterosexual to reflect more accurately the variations in relations among feelings, activities, and identities that obtain in the world. Third, it speaks to the fluidity of both sexuality and identity over time. Fourth, it does not contain any explanatory *deus ex machina* to bring negative cases in line with its underlying assumptions.

Identities within the Community

This investigation disclosed that feelings, activity, and identity may be congruent or may vary independently of one another. The following respondent, a woman in her fifties, had recently started relating sexually and emotionally to women after a long heterosexual marriage. She stated that she was not bisexual, gay, or lesbian, although she asserted that she would probably "not relate to a man again."

I: You said before that you don't call yourself lesbian or gay.
R: Well I don't. I never have. I mean, why would I be—I mean I don't know what the difference—what is it? why can't I just be—just me—me?

Just be me without being—naming—without being in a box? Just a human being. (Tape-recorded interview)

This same woman also said that most of her friends now are gay women. At the same time she had no need to identify herself with them. Another respondent, who in the last ten years has had sexual-emotional relationships with women but had previously been heterosexually married, stated:

I don't like the terms *gay* or *lesbian*. I'm a bisexual, and I think everyone is, basically. I don't see the point of being closed off to either sex. Of course, it's true that it would be difficult for me to meet a man who would meet my standards, but I certainly would be open to doing so. I like men, I really do, and I get along with them very well. (Conversation from field notes)

There are many possible permutations of sex-related identities, activities (or lack thereof), and feelings of sexual-emotional attraction. Blumstein and Schwartz make a similar point, asserting that their research on sexual identity provides "dramatic evidence that the way an individual organizes her or his sexual life often fails to possess the coherence and continuity that have always been taken for granted. . . . The diversity is impressive, especially since most of us—*including the people under study*—have been thoroughly trained to think in terms of polarities" (emphasis added).[3]

Distinguishing a lesbian from other women by virtue of the fact that the object of her affections is another woman is complicated by the fact that such a woman may not identify herself as a lesbian. She might identify herself as a heterosexual, engage in lesbian sexual activities, and experience feelings of sexual-emotional attraction to both men and women. It should be remembered that such an individual would probably be seen as a lesbian by the heterosexual community as well as by the lesbian community. Within the lesbian community she would be interpreted as having difficulties in accepting her true gay identity. But the woman herself may conceive of both feelings and activities as peripheral to her self-identification.

On the other hand, a woman who has not had a sexual-emotional relationship with another woman may identify herself as a lesbian. Thus, defining who really is a lesbian is problematic. This problem derives from divergence between activity and identity, each of which may be interpreted variously by the actors in the lesbian world.

The variation of relationships among feelings, activities, and identity may be described in four identity/activity combinations with attendant subtypes. These are: (1) lesbian identity with lesbian activity, which includes women who conform to the gay trajectory and the inversion assumption; (2) lesbian identity with heterosexual, bisexual, or celibate activity, including political lesbians and lesbians involved in heterosexual relationships; (3) bisexual identity with lesbian activity; and (4) heterosexual identity with lesbian activity. Within each type I shall discuss the sexual-emotional feelings that women-related women describe having and the relation of these feelings to sexual identity.

Lesbian Identity with Lesbian Activity

Many of the women with whom I met in both activist and secretive lesbian communities identified themselves as lesbian, gay, or homosexual. Their current sexual activity and emotional proclivities were with and toward other women. They made their identification as a lesbian at widely varying ages. Though there were exceptions—that is, women who made this identification during childhood or puberty—emotional commitments to women and lesbian activities usually predated, sometimes by years, a lesbian identification.[4] This identity/activity category includes the primary and elective lesbians described in chapter 6.

The women considered here are sexually and emotionally involved with women at the present time and state that they would probably continue to view themselves as lesbian irrespective of whether or not they were in such relationships. The likelihood of these women becoming involved with a man in the future is perceived as almost nil. They hypothesize that such an involvement would not change their sense of self or identity as gay. Thus, being a lesbian to most of these women is far more inclusive of an orientation and life-style going beyond mere sexual activity and a particular sexual-emotional relationship. I asked a twenty-six-year old respondent if she would consider herself gay if she became involved with a man in the future:

I would always consider myself gay, or a lesbian. I could not deny that in myself anymore. It wouldn't matter how I lived, whether I was celibate or with a man. Once you've experienced something, you can't take it back, and I think I would always relate to women. (Tape-recorded interview)

Similarly, another lesbian stated that were she to become involved with
a man in the future, her primary orientation would remain lesbian.

I would be afraid that though I might be very much in love with an individual man . . . I might see a woman and have that feeling, you know. It
would be something I'd always be worried about maintaining, and I would
just be completely trapping myself. I've thought about that a good deal,
and I've seen women who have tried to marry, and they felt the relaxation
of the pressure and the approval of society and everything, but they can't
make it all the way. (Tape-recorded interview)

Blumstein and Schwartz report that women in their sample who were
lesbian-identified and who had had previous heterosexual experiences
found their heterosexual experiences unsatisfactory.[5] Among the respondents of this study, this was true of women who construed their heterosexual contacts in terms of an experiment with heterosexuality or as a way
of assuring themselves of their true identity as lesbians:

The fact is I never found men interesting. I feel neutral about them in
general. Now women I always, since I was a little girl, found them to be
attractive to me. I finally did try making it with a man; I was drunk at
the time. Just to see what all the hooting and hollering was about. And
it was OK as far as sex goes. I had an orgasm and all that. But it's simply
not the same thing emotionally and all the other things that go along
with a sexual experience as it is for me with women. The first sexual experience I had with a woman was when I was fifteen years old in a corn-
field. It was so wonderful, so complete, there was never any question for
me that I was a lesbian, even though at that time I didn't know the word.
(Tape-recorded interview)

Other lesbians, however, especially those who made this identification
after a heterosexual or bisexual history (such as the elective lesbian),
describe a variety of feelings and attitudes with respect to their prior relationships with men. These range from statements that they enjoyed
their heterosexual relationships at the time to statements that they felt
they were living a lie as heterosexuals. Several of these women remarked
that though their heterosexual relationships themselves were pleasant
enough, they had become disenchanted with other expectations that they
perceived as characterizing heterosexual relations. Many of these lesbians,
in contrast with primary lesbians, emphasize choice in moving toward
relationships with women:

I think I always had a choice about being a lesbian. It didn't happen to me. *People* happened to me. I've had relationships with men and think the negativity of those relationships for me was not because I didn't enjoy sex with men but because I didn't like the other expectations that went along with it, the kind of role playing that happens in relationships with men. The kind of thing where his work should come before mine . . . I wasn't prepared to accept that. That was always perfectly clear to me. I knew exactly what a good wife was supposed to do and that it was not my bag. (Tape-recorded interview)

Women like this do not necessarily endorse the notion of the essentiality of lesbianism but state that lesbian relationships offer them a greater degree of egalitarianism than they have experienced as possible in heterosexual relationships. Although clearly some lesbians have found relationships with men to be rewarding in many ways, they experience lesbian relationships as yet more satisfying.

Some lesbians state that they experienced their heterosexual relationships as not as genuine or as real or as satisfactory as their relationships with women and have thus chosen lesbianism as an alternative to relations with men.

I consciously chose to be a lesbian. The fact [was] that I was so turned off by men, that I've been so uncomfortable with them all my life. In my sexual life with men, I could never really regard them as sexual relationships. All my sexual relationships with women were so satisfying . . . that I decided there was no way that I was going to make it with men. And so I started thinking about the whole concept of lesbianism, and since my relationships with men were absolutely not working, I started thinking about lesbianism for myself I thought maybe I could do that. . . . It was a conscious decision. . . . I wasn't around lesbians a lot, although I did have sexual feelings for women. (Tape-recorded interview)

For some lesbians in this category, the satisfactions they found in lesbian sexual activity were an important element in beginning to identify as a lesbian:

I was never able to have a relationship with men that I didn't feel paranoid about. I was always very paranoid in all the relationships that I ever had with men and could never have a sexual relationship without having the feeling of being used. . . . I was in [a big city] and went to [a gay organization] because I knew that I wanted come out, I knew I wanted to have

a sexual relationship with a woman, and there weren't any in my immediate community so I went there. Then I finally got into a sexual relationship that was purely sexual. . . . I was amazed at how easy and comfortable it was. It wasn't scary at all. I mean up to the point when it actually
happened, it was scary. I didn't know how it was going to be. But when
it actually happened, it was wonderful. It was great to feel I never had to
depend upon men again.

Essentiality

For many of the women whose identity, activity, and feelings are lesbian, lesbianism has the connotation of essence—an immutable, transituational quality of the self. They conceptualize gayness as pervading nonsexual aspects of the self as well. One woman, who had been active in the
gay movement almost since its inception, stated that to her gayness is an
essence that permeates her existence.

R: I don't have to be in a relationship with someone to consider myself
gay. Gay doesn't have to mean being involved with someone.
I: What does it mean?
R: It's just my whole life, my whole essence, my being, everything about
me I consider as gay, a gay person. I don't know if I could explain it; I'll
try. I seem to be surrounded at all times in always by who I am . . . by
what I am . . . that's sometimes in the question "who I am." I carry my
whole life around with me, and so . . . I think I never turn my mind off.
I never turn my life off. It goes with me wherever I go . . . and my life is
gay and where I go I take my gay life with me. I don't consciously sit
and think while I'm eating soup that I'm eating this "gayly," but, you
know, it surrounds me.

I asked her if she thought that there might be a time when she would not
consider herself gay.

No . . . it *is* me. And to change it you would have to completely kill me
off and start me all over again. . . . I think it's impossible. (Tape-recorded interview)

Among such activist women, lesbianism has the connotation of creation
of identity, continual creation of the self, whose parameters have not yet
been realized.

The notion of essentiality, however, is evident in nonpoliticized parts of the community as well, for example, both primary and elective lesbians. The aristocratizing of gayness, by attributing special qualities to persons on the basis of lesbianism or homosexuality, is another way of essentializing lesbianism.

I think gay people tend to be more intelligent and more sensitive than straight people. Gay people have experienced themselves more, they've had to be more honest than your average straight, and they're more in touch with their sexuality than straight people are. (Tape-recorded interview)

Thus, for women whose identity and activity are aligned, that identity is rarely limited in meaning to sexual activity. Gayness is conceived of as having an ontological status that encompasses both an orientation and a life-style. Though gay identity may have its beginning in sexual activity, it seldom ends there, and once adopted, it persists irrespective of activity for primary and elective lesbians.

The Gay Trajectory and the Inversion Assumption

Both the gay trajectory and the principle of consistency are empirically illustrated by participants in the lesbian world. Women who identify themselves as lesbians early in their lives—primary lesbians—are most likely to employ the gay trajectory in recounting their coming out process, although many women who make this identification later in life subsequently reinterpret the events of their "pre-lesbian" lives to conform with their current identity status—and with the gay trajectory— as well. Women who identify themselves as lesbians prior to having sexual-emotional relationships with other women also conform to the gay trajectory. Women whose behavior, identity, and feelings are congruent with the gay trajectory receive maximum support from the lesbian community.

Just as many women who evince lesbian identity and lesbian behavior do conform with the gay trajectory in their biographical accounts, there is a subset of women in the lesbian identity/lesbian activity category that illustrates the inversion assumption implicit in the principle of consistency.

The Masculine Lesbian

The inversion assumption, in keeping with the principle of consistency, puts forth the image of the masculine lesbian. Earlier, I indicated that lesbians involved with role-playing behavior adopt the butch (and femme) roles with widely varied degrees of commitment, from a limited and situated playing at roles to a conviction that the role is an expression of the true self.

Some lesbians account for their attraction to women by attributing masculinity to themselves. Three of the women interviewed stated that they felt they were masculine women, and the butch role corresponded to their conceptions of their true nature. Others previously thought of themselves as really masculine but had come to reformulate their self-images over time. Some women are in the process of questioning former self-definitions, as the following illustrates:

I: You mentioned before about identifying as more masculine, and I'm wondering what you mean by that.
R: Well, I think that probably goes back to my father and the very close relationship I had with him when I was young. To be out doing the farming instead of the dishwashing. Certainly feeling much more comfortable all my life in pants than in skirts. I felt like I was about half-undressed in skirts! I was very uncomfortable in dresses, let me tell you! . . . [But] the early childhood thing with my father probably had more to do with my looking at myself in that way and *wanting* to look at myself in that way. It has at times in my life been very hard for me to admit that I was a woman, and in some points maybe that's been good, because I certainly wasn't going to accept the limitations that society was trying to put on me because I was a woman. Just wasn't going to deal with that at all or admit . . . even admit it was there—just go ahead and do it anyway. So it's probably been good in that aspect, but is hasn't been good in some other ways . . . The woman I'm involved with now refers to me as "lady" or "wonderful woman," or something like that and I just never—nobody has ever referred to me in that way, and it took a little getting used to. . . . I'm beginning to work with those feelings, that in addition to being gay I am also a woman. . . . It's beginning to make me feel good. At first it felt very strange, very sort of alien. [Laughter] "Don't you call me a woman!" But I'm getting to say, "Uh-huh, that's fine. I am." I don't know how I looked at myself as being—not a man, certainly. But I—assume I had some sexist attitudes; and that being a woman meant something that I didn't want to be—you know, the apron, the kitchen, the kids, that sort of thing. (Tape-recorded interview)

For a few lesbians the adaptation of the butch role has the special significance of expressing the masculine character of the true self. The one-way butch represents the repudiation of all characteristics, behaviors, and attributes that are deemed feminine. The butch role as signifying a masculine identification characterized few of the women that I interviewed and reportedly few in the community. Further, the majority of women I met who were involved in role playing in the past have come to adopt an egalitarian mode in relationships.

Lesbian Identity with Bisexual, Heterosexual or Celibate Activity

Although those not familiar with the lesbian world and the impact of politics on identity might assume that lesbian sexual activities or inclinations are a requisite for lesbian identity, in fact this is not the case. A small yet increasing group of women within the lesbian community identify themselves as lesbians although their sexual-emotional relationships currently (and significantly) include men or are focused entirely on males as sexual-emotional partners. Others choose not to be in sexual-emotional relationships at all or are inexperienced yet identify as lesbians.

These women identify as lesbian in the absence of pressure from others; they sometimes make this identification in the face of claims from the lesbian community that they are not lesbians. The largest group of women who fall into this category of lesbian identity with bisexual, heterosexual, or celibate behavior are "political" lesbians.

Some political lesbians *are* involved in lesbian relationships. These women may have formerly identified themselves as gay or homosexual but have come to use the term *lesbian* as an unequivocal statement about the self and as an expression of solidarity with other lesbians. Thus political lesbian has two referents: women who are identified as lesbian or gay and have become politicized and women who, irrespective of their sexual-emotional activities and alliances, choose to label themselves lesbian. Thus self-labeling as a lesbian in these instances is an expression of a particular ideological position and may be accompanied by a variety of sexual-emotional commitments—lesbian, bisexual, heterosexual, or celibate.

The Political Lesbian

Sentiments from the women's movement as well as from the gay liberation movement have relevance for the numbers of women who are adopting the label lesbian as a political statement whether or not they are engaged in lesbian activity. The following quote is from a woman whose intimate relationships have been with women for the last ten years:

I use the term *lesbian* about myself. It's an arbitrary definition. . . . I don't think there really is such a thing as a lesbian. It's because of political reasons that we have to use the term. I think it's a political, arbitrary designation. I think in an ideal community we would not have to label each other. I would describe myself actually as person-oriented, although admittedly I know few male persons at the moment. (Tape-recorded interview)

Political lesbians like this one, then, do not necessarily accept the notion that lesbianism is essential or the notion that lesbianism necessarily has a behavioral referent. They do emphasize the political functions of the label lesbian: its consciousness-raising and radicalizing effects.

The politicization of sectors of the lesbian community has given rise to a consciously political use of the term *lesbian*. Women who call themselves lesbian in a political sense observe that the common usage of heretofore stigmatized or negative words tends to diminish the charge of these words and eventuates in such terms becoming legitimate references. Thus repetition functions as a destigmatization technique.

Perceptions of the Political Lesbian in the Subculture

As indicated above, a political lesbian may be a woman who would conventionally be defined as a lesbian in both lesbian and heterosexual worlds. Since she conforms to the identity rules of the lesbian world, her self-labeling as lesbian as contrasted to gay would have little impact. But political lesbians who engage in bisexual and heterosexual relationships are differentially viewed in the lesbian community. On the one hand, asserting a lesbian identity is viewed favorably—as an expression of solidarity with lesbians—by many women in the community. On the other hand, this regard is not unmixed with puzzlement and sometimes even hostility. The puzzlement stems from the belief in the essentiality of lesbianism and raises the issue of a woman's *deciding* to be a lesbian. The hostility is rooted in the perception that women who voluntarily wear the label lesbian while maintaining their commitments to heterosexual relationships and affiliations can also voluntarily drop the label to avoid the stigma with which committed lesbians must live.

Some political lesbians reportedly feel impelled by their ideological position to move beyond the adoption of the label to the adoption of lesbian relationships and a lesbian life-style. In brief, because of their political commitment, they feel that it is reactionary to continue to relate to men. One lesbian commented that she could not understand why women who were not emotionally motivated to have such relationships would try and "force" themselves to be lesbians for political reasons. She noted the conflict experienced by one woman who felt it was "politically correct" to love women but was, in fact, not sexually attracted to women.

I see people who are politically identified as lesbians. I can understand it, but for me it's too rigid and tight. I know one woman who is in that place, and she's still very attracted to men and not too much interested or attracted to women and that's not so important, but, dammit, it is part of it and something that you've got to face. She's conditioning herself to be turned on by women. Now that's mind-blowing! Why would someone force themselves to do that? She is simply not sexually turned on by women; she's not sexually comfortable with women. She's very uncomfortable making love to a woman, going down on a woman [making oral-genital love]. She thinks that's not nice. That's crazy! She identifies herself as a lesbian feminist. I wonder what she's doing. I see her pain—she says it's painful. Why would someone want to do that to herself? For me it certainly wasn't a political choice; it was my preference. (Tape-recorded interview).

These remarks should not be taken to indicate that women who become involved in relationships with women through politics generally dislike the experience. It illustrates, rather, the conundrum that can arise when politics, identity, and sexual-emotional preferences collide.

　　Other lesbians express their belief that the political lesbian who is really bisexual or heterosexual is basically uncommitted to lesbianism and is thereby untrustworthy—she can easily reclaim the privilege of her heterosexual status to avoid stigma. Thus, women who are committed to the community by virtue of political choice but not by mutual stigma may be perceived as fickle in their commitment. The political lesbian's voluntary verbal or symbolic stigma sharing, in the view of many lesbians, does not provide the same bonds of security and guarantees of mutual protection as does real stigma.

Lesbians in Heterosexual Relationships

　　The continued salience of lesbian identity in light of so-called incongruent activity illustrates the primacy of feelings in creating and sustaining sexual identity. Several of the women-related women I met identify themselves as lesbians although they are currently involved in intimate relationships with men. Before these heterosexual relationships, these women had related primarily to women. Although political motives explain continued lesbian identification for some of these women, the assumed essentiality of lesbianism explains the continued lesbian identification of other women in relationships with men. The following account exemplifies the division between identity and activity in the experience of one lesbian, who distinguishes the specific heterosexual relationships in which she is involved from her general sense of herself as a lesbian.[6]

I think of myself as a lesbian. I live with a man. I don't think of myself as a bisexual. I'm not interested in any other men. They are nonentities as far as I'm concerned. They don't exist for me. . . . Until the last three years I've related exclusively with women. I didn't even think there was any other way for me. It wasn't in my realm of thinking It seemed absurd. . . . It's coincidental that I'm with a man. . . . If something happens to the relationship I am in now—and I hope it doesn't—I really like him —more than I ever have anyone else—but if it doesn't work out, I am almost sure that I will return to women again. I will relate to women again because there's too much shit for me this way. It's been a big adjustment for me (Tape-recorded interview)

She describes her sense of a lesbian identity as corresponding more truly with her sense of self, despite what she perceives as an ongoing and important relationship with a man. The belief in the essentiality and immutability of lesbian identity supports her continued identification as lesbian though she is involved in a heterosexual relationship.

The importance placed on lesbian identity would tend to limit experimentation with heterosexual relationships once a woman had made the identification. Too, a lesbian who engages in relationships with men could expect censure from other lesbians, a censure that might be somewhat mitigated in particular support groups, such as indicated by a lesbian whose affiliative groups consist of gay and straight friends:

When I started relating to a man, I did get some pressure from my lesbian friends. Some friends were funny—like, "I don't care as long as I don't have to meet him," and "as long as we don't have to double date" kind of thing, I guess it's all right. I have a friend now who I think is threatened by it. She's just been out [defined as a lesbian] for a little while. I don't feel free to complain to her. She comes out with so much crap. She'll say, "Oh, you wouldn't have those kinds of problems with a woman." It's a

constant bullshit rhetoric. But I don't feel that much pressure. The people
I have always known are not locked in. They have to be flexible. It's hard
for me to deal with people who are dyed in the wool anything—and anyone
who says that being a lesbian is the only way—well, that's a crock of shit.
With people like that, well—I couldn't stay close for very long. It's too cut
and dried for me. When I told my friends about H [male lover], my friends
were shocked. They said, "of all people in the world you'd be the last one
to be involved with a man." This included my straight and gay friends.
. . . Afterwards, people said to me, "You know, I've been thinking about
that for myself and I'd like to ask you some questions." Of course, none
of them have actually done anything about it yet, but now they have someone to talk about it with. I certainly don't encourage it—no more than
I'd encourage anyone into homosexuality who felt they were heterosexual. I figure you ought to do what you want to do. (Tape-recorded interview)

Before leaving the issue of lesbian identity in the context of heterosexual
activity, it should be emphasized that not everyone who ceases lesbian
activity continues to regard herself as a lesbian. The prevailing stigma attached to lesbianism and the pervasive support for heterosexuality would
tend against the maintenance of a lesbian identity in the absence of overt
homosexual behavior. Whether or not identity changes when sexual object
choices change (at least in the context of a particular relationship) depends, of course, on the meanings ascribed to both behavior and identity
by the human actor. However, persons who either renounced lesbian i-
dentity or resumed a heterosexual identity were not included in the study.

Ex-Lesbians

The population of ex-lesbians is beyond the purview of this analysis,
and a systematic study of the identity resolutions of women formerly
identified as lesbian awaits another investigator. However, one woman
among those studied here had stopped affiliating with the lesbian community, is relating to a man, and no longer identifies herself as a lesbian,
though she had in the past. Her sense of her personal identity represents
one of the many possible interpretations of self and biography. It serves
not only to illustrate the variety of meanings that attend the experience
of lesbianism but also to counter the false assumption that lesbian identity is a one-way street, as suggested by heterosexual and gay paradigms.

In my own development, I have had women with whom I had a deep
love attachment. These attachments were necessary for me in order to

grow. After having a deep sexual commitment with a woman, I was able
to have connections with women without having to have a sexual experience. But I needed to go through that sexual phase with a woman in
order to go into another stage of my own development. . . . I was raised
in a New York ghetto where all the men I knew were violent, so it was very
appealing to think of being with a woman. So I started going down to
the Village. The first time I went into a gay club, I felt I belonged there,
and what I realized later, many years later, was that it had to do with
being peripheral rather than being homosexual. But it was the first time
. . . I could enter into a world and feel safe as a peripheral person. I still
don't belong in the straight world. . . . It took me a long time to come
back from the lesbian world. It was a very serious thing in my life. . . .
You have to remember that this was in the fifties in the Village . . . which
was the world of the suicidal lesbian . . . alcoholic, drug addiction . . . it
wasn't pretty. . . . It's much different nowadays . . . neither the straight
world nor the homosexual world was attractive to me. . . . It seems to me
that being myself at this time in my life does not have to do with merging with a woman; I've done that. . . . What's been hard for me is merging
with a man. I feel safe with women, I feel a very safe thing, and I don't
like that. For me it's dealing with the masculine that exposes me and is
my challenge. With the woman I was with and in all my relationships with
women, there was that kind of statement in the air with a woman friend
of mine, and I could feel the safety of it, I could feel the seduction of it,
and I knew also that wasn't the way for me to go, that I had to deal with
men. I had to go into that tension and deal with that aspect of myself.
(Tape-recorded interview)

I have quoted from this interview at length because despite its idiosyncratic
features, it suggests the multiple meanings that lesbian experiences (as
well as heterosexual experiences) may have for the individual actor. This
woman stated that her lesbianism had been very important in her life,
and yet it did not have the connotation of an essential identity. For her,
lesbianism was an aspect of herself and ultimately not a definitive identity. The approach to identity and sexuality detailed above serves to under-
line variations in the relationship of sexuality to identity and to point up
the changeability in the direction and meaning of sexuality and the strains
attendant to such transitions.

The Naive or Inexperienced Woman

Even prior to actual sexual experience, most young women define
themselves as heterosexual. Thus, it should not be surprising that some

young women choose to designate themselves as lesbian before having sexual relationships. Lesbianism is here again conceived of as an immutable characteristic of the self. Cues to the essential gay self, in such instances, clearly depart from the heterosexual equation between sexual activity and sexual identity but conform to the logic of the gay trajectory. Thus, a woman who identifies herself as lesbian in the absence of sexual experience would receive support from the lesbian community. Evidences of the gay self may be derived from feelings, physical characteristics, or other qualities that are believed to have lesbian significance.

Learning to interpret one's feelings and inclinations in terms of a lesbian identity may come about through contact with gay women, the community, or disembodied affiliation. At times, identification can be a consequence of having lesbianism attributed to the self by others. I asked one woman who had never had a lesbian relationship how she came to feel that she was really a lesbian.

R: Well, this girl at the hospital where I worked told me she could tell I was a lesbian.
I: How could she tell?
R: She just knew. I don't know how.

While this is not a typical mode by which a woman begins to identify herself as a lesbian, ascription by others can be a critical determinant in self-labeling. If the ascription is believed to correspond to feelings or inclinations of the woman so defined, it is possible that she may begin to think of herself as really lesbian prior to any sexual-emotional relationships with a woman.

Celibate Lesbians

In addition to the woman who is politically or ideologically committed to calling herself a lesbian, there are a few women who define themselves as celibate lesbians. These women are not currently engaged in relationships with women (or men) and yet choose to designate themselves as lesbians, like the women who designate themselves heterosexual although they choose not to have sexual relations. The designation celibate lesbian implies a conscious desire to abstain from sexual relationships although the individual making the choice considers herself to be a lesbian.

Celibacy as a voluntary choice may derive from a political ideology among some lesbian feminists who find, on the one hand, heterosexual relationships inimical and, on the other hand, see monogamous relationships with women unacceptable because they are perceived as based on a heterosexual model. At the same time, successful nonmonogamy is perceived as difficult, if not impossible, in a society where people both straight and gay are reputedly programmed for monogamous relationships. These political sentiments were expressed in a political lesbian monthly magazine:

> The reason people have been celibate in the past does not have much to do with why I am. I have found, as Rita Mae Brown [a radical lesbian feminist] said, "you can't live in a post-revolutionary fashion in pre-revolutionary times." In my head I have a dream of people being able to love each other openly and freely, whether it's sexual or not, with no problems arising from the progression of affection to the physical. This is the way I would like to live, but I found that it is not the time. There are too many complications. It is too heavy for me to try to live non-monogamously in our present culture.[7]

Celibate lesbians imply that certain political and social conditions must obtain in order for them to feel free to engage in nonmonogamous sexual relationships. Other celibate lesbians state that their choice of celibacy is dictated by more personal reasons, such as personal growth or self-exploration:

> For the past two years I have not been involved sexually with anyone. I've been getting to know me. For many years before this I was involved in long-term monogamous relationships—for seven years, and then before that for five years. I began to realize when the seven-year relationship ended that I needed some time to myself. I found that if I get involved in a relationship, I get really involved and put all my energies into the relationship and the other person. I needed to be in my own space and get into my own head. I spend lots of time alone and I need it. It feels good for me. Not being sexually involved released a lot of energy for other things I wanted to do. Now I'm beginning to open up to the world a little bit, starting to look around a little. But this period of being alone and not having to relate to anyone . . . it was a very freeing experience. (Conversation from field notes)

Thus some political lesbians, some inexperienced and celibate lesbians, as well as lesbians involved in heterosexual relationships express a dichotomy between sexual activity and the sexual identity.

Bisexual Identity with Lesbian Activity

Women involved in lesbian relationships but identifying as bisexuals make a distinction between doing and being that is not made in either heterosexual or homosexual constructions of lesbian identity.[8] Perhaps the central consideration in determining whether or not a women-related woman will identify herself as a lesbian is how the issue of essentiality of lesbianism fits with her subjective experience of herself as well as the relative importance she places on relations with men and women.

Some women interviewed, though they were involved in sexual-emotional relationships with women, did not identify themselves as lesbians. The most prevalent definition of self among these women was bisexual or simply sexual persons. Several of the women in this category were involved in their first relationship with a woman; others had had several relationships with women as well as having had relationships with men. Yet others had been involved in gay relationships for periods of time ranging from three to twenty years and had not been involved with men during that time.

The linkage between lesbian activity and feelings and a lesbian identity for this group of women was far from automatic. These women tended to see the demarcation between lesbianism and heterosexuality as much more fluid than did lesbian-identified women and also tended to see their own sexuality as changing and situated rather than as an expression of their true nature.

Illustrating the position that gay and straight are adjectival descriptions of temporary, situated states are the following comments:

To me, being gay is like having a tan. When you are in a gay relationship, you're gay. When you're not in a gay relationship, you're not gay. (Tape-recorded interview)

Another woman-related woman hypothesized:

If I were to have a relationship with a man, I would quit being gay. It just wouldn't be fair to the guy, to keep on being gay when you're supposed to be with him. (Tape-recorded interview)

Such statements point up the transitory, changing, and situated meaning that designations like gay have for some women as contrasted with the essential quality described by other women-related women. Too, women who perceived their involvement in lesbian relationships in voluntaristic terms tend to perceive the real lesbian as confined to her gayness. The women considered here sometimes refer to the notion of essentiality in order to distinguish themselves from real or true lesbians.

For example, a woman in her late fifties who had been living in an intimate sexual-emotional relationship with another woman for six years did not identify herself as a lesbian but rather as a sexual person, explaining the difference she perceives between herself and real lesbians in terms of a choice for herself and a lack of choice for real lesbians.

I can't help it. I guess I still have a feeling of me versus them. I guess I see it [lesbianism] in terms of choice for myself. I don't see them [real lesbians] as having a choice about where they are, but I feel I do have a choice. (Tape-recorded interview)

The following respondent, who defines herself as bisexual and is currently in a relationship with a man, differentiates herself from the woman who had been her lover on the basis of the latter's assumed lack of choice about being a lesbian.

We talk about choice. It seems clear to me that I have a choice; I've chosen to relate to women and I've chosen to relate to men. But L has no choice. Not really. She has never ever been *interested* in men. She's been having affairs with women since she was nine years old. I don't think that in any real sense you can say she has a choice. She could choose to be celibate, I suppose. But if a person is not interested at all and never has been in any other thing than the thing they are doing—and couldn't really conceive of another way for themselves—how can they have a choice in any meaningful sense of the word? (Tape-recorded interview)

Although from the standpoint of both the heterosexual and the homosexual communities women such as these might be impugned as having "false consciousness," these women continue to define themselves as bisexual (or, in some instances, as sexual), refusing to identify themselves in terms of lesbian sexual identity at all.

Well, I don't really—I don't really think of myself as a lesbian in that sense, the way some people would think. I don't think that I'm really different from any other person that happens to love somebody else. It just so happens that the person I love is a woman. (Tape-recorded interview)

Yet other women state that using the term *lesbian* connotes a polarity, an exclusivity they do not feel.

That's a sham, saying I am gay, I am lesbian, I'm this or that. I think "isms" are really dangerous. It puts you in a group of them and us. . . . I'm not against men; I'm not down on any particular group . . . but . . . let's stop trying to see who's the most oppressed, blacks or gay people. . . . I don't want to hook up with one little niche that doesn't recognize anybody else. That's why I'm against saying I'm gay. . . . It becomes them against us. As far as identifying with one little group of people, I refuse to do it. Others identify me as gay. . . . I don't identify myself that way. (Tape-recorded interview)

Some bisexually identified women in lesbian relationships distinguish themselves from women whom they consider real lesbians on the basis of either past or possible future relationships with men. One woman described her heterosexual marriage as one of convenience and focused on the concerns of child raising. Her present emotional life, however, she described as centering on a relationship with a woman, although she has had meaningful relationships with men in the past as well.

I'm always attracted to a personality. I guess I'm a true bisexual. . . . I'm turned on by a relationship between two people. A spark between two people, this is what turns me on and nothing else. . . . It depends on the man, of course, the love relationship—I feel closer to a woman—although I've felt close to men, too. . . . It's the other things about a woman, not the sexual things, that really matter. (Tape-recorded interview)

Similarly, the woman quoted below invokes a heterosexual history as evidence that she and her circle of friends are bisexuals—not lesbians.

Myself, the women I know, I would describe as bisexual. You know D was married for years, I've been married, M's been married. Many of us have children. I use the term *gay* sometimes as a kind of shorthand. But when it comes right down to it, I'd say I think everyone is basically bisexual. Of course lesbians and some diehard heterosexuals don't *believe* they are bisexual, but basically everyone is (Conversation from field notes)

I noted in chapter 5 the stigma attached to the bisexual in the lesbian community: bisexuals are usually considered really to be lesbians. According to the logic of the gay trajectory, any indications of lesbianism

would be expected to take precedence over heterosexuality. Yet many
of the women with whom I spoke make a private statement about themselves as bisexuals and point to their history of heterosexual relationships
or present heterosexual or bisexual experiences. When in the company
of other lesbians, however, these women do not generally make a point
of asserting bisexuality. Rather, they simply do not disrupt the homosexual assumption.

Heterosexual Identity with Lesbian Activity

Within the context of the lesbian subculture and lesbian relationships,
the identity of heterosexual is the most difficult to maintain over time.
The fact of a lesbian relationship serves to throw the heterosexual identity of the individual into doubt, if not in the eyes of the individual in
question, certainly in the perspectives of both heterosexual and lesbian
audiences.

Failing to adopt a lesbian identity when living a lesbian life-style or
being in a lesbian relationship will almost certainly be challenged by others, including people with whom the heterosexual woman is intimately
involved. To illustrate this, two of the women in my sample were heterosexually married but were involved in an intense affair with each
other. Both maintained that they were heterosexuals. However, both
attributed lesbianism to the *other.*

I don't consider myself gay. I simply can't relate to that for me. I need
a romantic involvement in my life, and it happens to be with [her woman
lover], but I was with a man before this. I love my husband in a way. I
need the kind of anchoring or stability he gives me, which I think only
a man can give me. But I also have a romantic side, too. I may be selfish,
but I want it all. There is a price to be paid . . . but I don't want to give
either up. (Conversation from field notes)

The woman's reasoning is perhaps not dissimilar to that of a married man
or woman who is having an extra-marital affair. But her identity in the
lesbian world is subject to quite [different interpretations by others—
including that of her lover, who stated:

I wish I could identify as a lesbian; isn't that strange? But somehow I
don't. But if there is one thing I know for sure is that she [her lover]
is a *real* lesbian. That's where she really gets her emotional gratification.

The real reason she stays with her husband is that she's afraid he'll take the kids away from her if she leaves and the kids mean a lot to her. (Conversation from field notes)

Thus, for neither member of the dyad does the mere fact of participation in a sexual-emotional relationship constitute sufficient evidence for self-identification as a lesbian. Yet paradoxically it provides for each the basis for attributing lesbianism to the other.

Women who claim a heterosexual identity while having relationships with other women generally are women whose relationship to the lesbian subculture is tangential. Blumstein and Schwartz describe some of these women as prostitutes who "party" or have sexual relationships with women at the behest of men and essentially for the titillation of men.[9] Although prostitutes were not represented among the women with whom I spoke, there were several women who had relationships with women in the context of heterosexual relationships or a *mènage à trois* or had lesbian contacts incidental to primary heterosexual relationships.

I think of Z [male partner] as my mate, and I think of having occasional delight with women, but I'd say I'm straight basically. (Conversation from field notes)

Heterosexually identified women such as this one emphasize the accidental quality of their relationships with women and tend to define their alliances with women in purely sexual terms or in terms of a special, situated relationship. Of course, the continued identification as heterosexual in the context of relationships with women would receive negative sanction from lesbians, particularly if a lesbian-identified woman was the partner to such a relationship. As one lesbian woman put it:

If two straight women want to experiment with each other, that's fine. But to take out after a lesbian is reprehensible. (Tape-recorded interviw)

Lesbian-identified women frequently speculate that women in a gay relationship who refuse a lesbian identity are having trouble facing their gayness or that they are in a process of coming out, the end of which will be the acceptance of their lesbianism. Nevertheless, other lesbian-identified women assert that lesbian activity per se does not mean lesbian identity. Some women get fascinated by a personality and get involved with a woman. They're not lesbians. It's when the relationship breaks up and who it is that she then gets involved with that you know whether she's a lesbian or not. (Tape-recorded interview)

Thus, in the perspective of some lesbians exceptions to the rule of the gay trajectory of identity do exist. Nevertheless, dichotomizing between identity and activity is commonly viewed as a cop-out both inside and outside the gay community. Those who do not say that they are lesbian when they "act it" or claim that it is mere circumstance that they are with a woman instead of a man are accused of denying their true selves.

Women involved in a gay relationship who do not identify themselves as lesbian find themselves in a situation of strain because of their nonconformity with both heterosexual and gay paradigms. They tend to be secretive with other heterosexuals about their gay experiences largely because they believe that others are likely to make the equation between identity and activity, even if they themselves do not. They tend to hold the view that others would see them only in terms of that identifying label. However, heterosexually identified women (as well as bisexuals) do continue to construct a definition of themselves that is at variance with defining rules in both the heterosexual and gay communities in which they interact and in the face of pressures, both subtle and overt, from others. Central to maintaining idiosyncratic identities, of course, is the way in which they perceive lesbianism, which is usually limited to current sexual activity or as a definitive quality only of others.

The majority of these heterosexually identified women had their initial and/or significant lesbian experiences later in life than did the majority of lesbian-identified women, although many of this latter group began to identify themselves as lesbians during their thirties and forties. As noted in the previous chapter, heterosexually identified women in lesbian relationships evince little strain toward making their biographies continuous and consistent. One woman summed up this notion by saying,

I think of myself as a sexual person as opposed to a homo-, bi-, or heterosexual person. I happen to be involved with a woman at this time in my life, but I can't undo the fact that I was married for twenty years to a man. (Tape-recorded interview)

Such women make a separation between their sense of identity and the relationships in which they are involved. For such idiosyncratically identified women, the sources of personal identity lie outside sexual-emotional relationships. The identity rules of both heterosexual and lesbian worlds presume continuity in individual sexuality and mandate consistency between sexual behavior and sexual identity. The women described above, in breaking these rules, point up the varied character of identity making on the level of the individual.

The fluidity and changeability of both identity and activity on the level of the individual may elude classification within the frameworks of the paradigms available from the heterosexual perspective and from the viewpoint of the lesbian world.

The four combinations of identity and activity—lesbian identity with lesbian activity, lesbian identity with heterosexual, bisexual, or celibate activity, bisexual identity with lesbian activity, and heterosexual identity with lesbian activity—and their subtypes indicate the principal variations between identity and activity that prevail in the lesbian world. These combinations are ideal types of identity resolutions of experience, biography, and identity made by individuals, and each type has empirical referents. It is important to point out, however, that the boundaries of each category are permeable and that women-related women can and do move from one category to another as definitions of themselves and their experiences change over time.

Some of the features of the larger society (such as feminism) and of the gay world (such as gay liberation, feminism, and radicalism) have complex effects on movement both within and among these categories. On the one hand, these features cut across categories and serve to open up and make the social category of lesbians and the lesbian subculture more accessible. On the other hand, the mandate of various political philosophies may serve to make certain identity categories less accessible. The belief in essentiality, too, may serve to increase commitment to lesbian identity or it may lead toward disidentification with lesbian identity. The variety of resolutions among biography, activity, and identity point up the importance of the individual as a source of meanings of identity.

The Self: A Social Source of Identity

In the foregoing pages I analyzed identities in the lesbian world on three levels: the larger society, the affiliative group, and the individual. I pointed out the underlying assumptions of essentiality and the principle of consistency as informing the images of lesbian identity held in the heterosexual world. I identified the root image of lesbian identity within the lesbian community as essentiality in concert with the trajectory of gay identity and attempted to point out the ideological character of both of these models for constructing lesbian identity.

The imagery of straight and gay worlds serves to perpetuate polar definitions of lesbianism and heterosexuality. These polar definitions are maintained by analyses of lesbians that take either of these assumptions as their root image and thereby treat the issue of what and who a lesbian is as unproblematic.

In contrast, I have endeavored to remain close to the meanings that identities have for the actors in the lesbian world. Doing so revealed the highly variable nature of individual resolutions to the questions of sexual and personal identity. The individual as the focus of analysis proves very resistant to dichotomous classification. Staying close to an actor's meanings of experience, biography, and identity serves to emphasize the centrality of the actor as a source of these meanings and to highlight her ability to develop quasi-independent definitions of the self.

The analysis of identities in the lesbian world must necessarily take into account the social contexts of those identities but must focus as well on the perspectives of the individuals in that world who select, reject, refine, and change the meanings of identity, of themselves, and of their world.

GLOSSARY

Bisexual—An individual who has sexual-emotional relationships or is self-defined as bisexual on the basis of her openness to sexual relationships with both men and women. She does not conform to the models of identity of either heterosexual or lesbian worlds. A bisexual is typically conceived of in the gay community as "refusing to accept her gayness" or as "sitting on the fence" between heterosexuality and homosexuality; she may be seen as a person who is equally attracted to both sexes to the point where choice between the two is impossible.

Bring Out—To introduce an individual to lesbianism or homosexuality, either by acquainting them with gay people or through a sexual affair.

Butch—A lesbian adopting a "masculine" style.

Celibate Lesiban—A woman who identifies as lesbian but who chooses to abstain from sexual relations.

Closet—Being secretive about gay identity. There are degrees of being in the closet: for example, being "all the way in the closet" refers to the individual being the only audience to the gay self.

Closet Case—An individual who is assumed to be gay but who will not acknowledge it.

Coming Out—Acknowledgment of gay identity to the self and to others. In the political sense, it has the connotation of revealing gay identity to others. Coming out may also refer to an initial same-sex sexual experience.

Counterfeit Secrecy—A semblance of secrecy in which the gay self is not acknowledged but there is tacit knowledge of gay identity by other audiences.

Dropping Pins—Reference to gay persons, gay places, gay events in order to ascertain if another person is gay. If an individual "picks up the pin"—responds by acknowledging acquaintance with said event, person, or place—a tentative gay hypothesis is formulated for further testing. Usually

dropping pins occurs in heterosexual settings that would preclude direct-
ness about sexual identity.

Dyke—Lesbian. The term is considered derogatory, especially if used by
outsiders. It has the connotation in some groups of "strong lesbian"; in
others, of "masculine" or male-identified lesbian. In some political circles,
the term is used as stigma confrontation, to raise consciousness and to
destigmatize the term.

Elective Lesbian—A woman who is self-defined as a lesbian, usually later
in life. Her sexual-emotional history includes heterosexual relationships,
frequently extensive. Although her sexual-emotional history exhibits
change, she presents an underlying consistency in commitment to lesbianism and sees her heterosexuality as not as real nor as significant in defining
the self as is lesbianism.

Essence—A quality of a person given great social importance in defining
the individual. An essence is commonly presumed to have ontological
status, a status of being; essences are construed as immutable, central, and
pivotal to who an individual is; essences give rise to essential identities.
Essences may be deviant or charismatic. Acts may give rise to the ascription
of essences, but essences are seen as transcending and preceding acts.

Essential Identities—Definitive identities; who an individual "really is."
Examples of essential identities include lesbian, homosexual, genius, liar,
murderer. Essential identities are conceived of as emanating from immutable qualities of the individual—essences. Ancillary qualities are typically
presumed to adhere to essential identities. The individual's acts are interpreted through the lens of the ascribed essential identity.

Etiquette of Disclosure—Methods and techniques of disclosing the gay
self.

Femme—Lesbian who plays a stereotypical female role in relation to a
butch; a stereotypically feminine woman.

Gay—Lesbian, homosexual, used in both the adjectival and nominative
senses; considered a "male" term by politicized lesbians, yet it remains the
most frequently used general term for homosexuality in the lesbian community.

Gay Referencing—The practice of indicating whether events, places,
and persons are gay in gay conversations.

Gay Trajectory—A set of paths that are presumed to lead inexorably
to gay identity; the model for social construction of gay identity in the
lesbian world. Feelings, sexual activities, or association with the lesbian
community may be the starting point of the trajectory.

Go down on—Engaging in oral-genital sexual relations.

Head, Giving Head—Being the active partner in oral-genital sexual
relations.

Heterosexual Assumption — An unquestioned assumption in hetero-sexual interaction that participants are heterosexual.

Hiatus in Identity — A period during which an individual has not clearly formulated or is unsure about a sexual identity.

Homosexual — Lesbian or gay male; usually considered a technical term and, particularly in political lesbian circles, a "male" term.

Homosexual Assumption — An unquestioned assumption among gay people in gay places that participants are gay.

Identity Work — Techniques, strategies and methods that have as their purpose effecting a change in the meaning of a particular identity or a change in the identity itself.

Idiosyncratic Identities — Identities of women who define themselves as heterosexual, bisexual, or sexual and who engage in lesbian relationships.

Inversion — Reversal of "expected" — that is, stereotypical — gender role behavior; an individual exhibiting behaviors or qualities deemed appropriate to the opposite sex — passivity in males, aggressiveness in females, usually with reference to sexual behaviors. The term is frequently confused with homosexuality. In Tripp's terms it refers to passing, momentary enactment of the passive or active role in sexual relations for men and women, respec-tively; a characteristic of both heterosexual and homosexual activity.

Inversion Assumption — the idea that inversion is a concomitant of lesbi-anism (and male homosexuality).

Ki-Ki — A term used in role-playing groups connotating a woman who will not play either the butch or femme role; a woman who takes a middle-of-the-road stance with respect to role playing and does not adopt an iden-tifiable butch or femme style.

Lesbian — A term understood to mean a woman who relates sexually and emotionally to other women. Because of the political connotations that have come to accrue to this category, I use it as a nominative category referring to women who define themselves as lesbian irrespective of sexual-emotional alliances.

Lover — Partner in an intimate sexual-emotional relationship between two women; related terms are *friend, roommate, partner.*

Political Lesbian — A lesbian who has become politicized, usually through feminism, and/or gay liberation. Or a woman who irrespective of her sexual-emotional ties (heterosexual, bisexual, celibate) defines herself as lesbian for political reasons.

Primary Lesbian — A woman who defines herself as lesbian and who describes herself as always having been a lesbian. Her sexual-emotional history has consistently been focused on relationships with women.

Principle of Consistency — A common-sense assumption about the direction of and relations among sex-related identities that underlies both folk and common-sense theories of heterosexuality and lesbianism. It is presumed that sex assignment, socialization, gender identity, gender role, sexual object choice, and sexual identity vary together—that the sexual identity outcome is "naturally" heterosexual. The principle of consistency functions as a standard from which deviations are measured and constitutes an underlying assumption in theories explaining heterosexual and homosexual development. Homosexuality is explained in terms of "mistakes" either on the biological level or in the area of socialization.

One-way Butch—A lesbian who takes a "masculine," aggressive role in lovemaking and will not permit reciprocity.

Out of the Closet—Being open about one's gay identity before audiences to the self. One is "all the way out of the closet" when virtually everyone with whom the individual is in contact knows about the gay self.

Own—Members of an in-group.

Queer—A derogatory term for lesbian or male homosexual.

Straight—Heterosexual, sometimes with the connotation of conventional.

Tribadism—Variation of lesbian lovemaking, involving mutual genital contact.

Turn Out—To be the agent of an individual's "turning gay." The term usually connotes having an initial lesbian relationship.

Wise—An outgroup member who has gained the trust of an ingroup and who knows its secrets; a person who is not a member of a particular ingroup but is accepted as a member and has a member's right to access to information.

Women-related Women—Women who relate sexually and/or emotionally to women, who feel identified with women. Such women may define themselves in several different ways: as lesbian, bisexual, heterosexual, lesbian celibate, sexual. The term was developed to embrace the variety of relations among activity and identity in the lesbian world.

NOTES

Introduction

1. Herbert Blumer, *Symbolic Interactionism: Perspective and Method* (Englewood Cliffs, N.J.: Prentice-Hall, 1969), p. 62.

2. Erving Goffman, *Stigma: Notes on the Management of Spoiled Identity* (Englewood Cliffs, N.J.: Prentice-Hall, 1963), p. 2.

3. George McCall and J. L. Simmons, *Identities and Interactions* (New York: Free Press, 1966), pp. 138-40.

4. McCall and Simmons, *Identities and Interactions,* pp. 90-91.

5. Jack Katz, "Essences as Moral Identities: Verifiability and Responsibility in Imputations of Deviance and Charisma," *American Journal of Sociology* 80 (1975): 1369-90.

6. Jonathan Katz, *Gay American History: Lesbians and Men in the U.S.A.* (New York: Thomas Y. Crowell Company, 1976), p. 446.

7. Anselm Strauss, *Mirrors and Masks* (New York: Free Press, 1959).

Chapter 1

1. Carol A. B. Warren, "The Use of Stigmatizing Social Labels in Conventionalizing Deviant Behavior," *Sociology and Social Research* 58 (1974): 303-11.

2. Barney Glaser and Anselm Strauss, *The Discovery of Grounded Theory* (Chicago: Aldine Publishing Co., 1967).

3. Howard S. Becker, *Outsiders: Studies in the Sociology of Deviance* (New York: Free Press, 1963); John Lofland, *Analyzing Social Settings* (Belmont, Calif.: Wadsworth Publishing Co., 1971).

4. Carol A. B. Warren, *Identity and Community in the Gay World* (New York: Wiley Interscience, 1974).

5. Carol A. B. Warren, "Observing the Gay Community," in *Research on Deviance,* ed. Jack D. Douglas (New York: Random House, 1972), pp. 139-63.

6. Evelyn Hooker, "The Adjustment of the Male Overt Homosexual," in *The Problem of Homosexuality in Modern Society,* ed. Henrik M. Ruitenbeek (New York: E. P. Dutton & Co., 1963), pp. 141-61.

7. Jack Douglas, *The American Social Order* (New York: The Free Press, 1971).

Chapter 2

1. Dolores Klaich, *Woman + Woman: Attitudes toward Lesbianism* (New York: William Morrow & Co., 1974), p. 11.

2. John Money and Anke A. Ehrhardt, *Man and Woman, Boy and Girl: The Differentiation and Dimorphism of Gender Identity from Conception to Maturity* (Baltimore: Johns Hopkins University Press, 1972), p. 4.

3. Ibid., pp. 1-2.

4. Ibid., p. 2.

5. Ibid., p. 4.

6. Goffman, *Stigma.*

7. Lucile Duberman, *Gender and Sex in Society* (New York, Prager Publishers, 1975), p. 26.

8. Ibid., p. 28.

9. John H. Gagnon and William Simon, eds., *Sexual Deviance* (New York: Harper & Row, 1967), p. 247.

10. C. A. Tripp, *The Homosexual Matrix* (New York: McGraw-Hill, 1975), p. 22.

11. Ibid., p. 35.

12. Ibid., p. 72.

13. D. J. West, *Homosexuality* (Chicago: Aldine Publishing Co., 1968), p. 73.

14. Martin Hoffman, *The Gay World: Male Homosexuality and the Social Creation of Evil* (New York: Basic Books, 1968), p. 104.

15. Jane Rule, *Lesbian Images* (Garden City, N.Y.: Doubleday & Co., 1975), p. 13.

16. Leviticus 20:13.

17. Rule, *Lesbian Images,* p. 18.

18. The Reverend Dr. D. S. Bailey suggests that the controversial "to know" refers to attitudes toward strangers and that the Sodomites wanted "to become acquainted with" the heavenly messengers rather than "to know" them in the Biblical sense; cited in Wainwright Churchill, *Homosexual Behavior Among Males: A Cross-Cultural and Cross-Species Investigation* (Englewood Cliffs, N.J.: Prentice-Hall, 1971), p. 200.

19. In fact, bisexuality was acceptable. There is evidence to support that Sappho herself, though undoubtedly a lover of women, was bisexual in contrast to lesbian, as this latter term is usually understood.

20. Romans 1:26.

21. Rule, *Lesbian Images*, p. 19.

22. Ibid., p. 21.

23. Ibid., p. 22.

24. Rev. Robert L. Treese, "Homosexuality: A Contemporary View of the Biblical Perspective"; cited in Rule, *Lesbian Images*, p. 27.

25. Del Martin and Phyllis Lyon, *Lesbian/Woman* (New York: Bantam Books, 1972).

26. Churchill, *Homosexual Behavior Among Males*.

27. Hoffman, *The Gay World*, p. 98.

28. Churchill, *Homosexual Behavior Among Males*, pp. 202-03.

29. Ibid., p. 204.

30. Ibid., p. 205.

31. E. Westermark, *The Origin and Development of Moral Ideas* (London: Macmillan, 1906).

32. Churchill, *Homosexual Behavior Among Males*, p. 206.

33. West, *Homosexuality*, p. 74.

34. Churchill, *Homosexual Behavior Among Males*, p. 210; West, *Homosexuality*, pp. 74-75.

35. West, *Homosexuality*, pp. 74-75.

36. Churchill, *Homosexual Behavior Among Males*, p. 206.

37. Ibid., p. 210.

38. West, *Homosexuality*, p. 82.

39. Churchill, *Homosexual Behavior Among Males*, p. 216.

40. Ibid., p. 215.

41. Ibid., p. 216.

42. Ibid., p. 221.

43. *Family Law Reporter, Current Developments* 2 (November 1975-October 1976): 2715-16.

44. Churchill, *Homosexual Behavior Among Males*, p. 216.

45. *Family Law Reporter, Current Developments* 2 (November 1975-October 1976): 2408.

46. Churchill, *Homosexual Behavior Among Males*, p. 240.

47. William Simon and John Gagnon, "Homosexuality: The Formulation of a Sociological Perspective," *Journal of Health and Social Behavior* 8 (September 1967).

48. Rule, *Lesbian Images*, p. 33.

49. Klaich, *Woman + Woman*, p. 60.

50. Ibid., pp. 59-60.

51. Ibid., p. 67.

52. Rule, *Lesbian Images*, p. 33.

53. Havelock Ellis, *Studies in the Psychology of Sex* (New York: Random House, 1936), 2: 218.

54. Ibid., p. 217.

55. Sigmund Freud, "The Psychology of Women," in *New Introductory Lectures on Psychoanalysis* (New York: Norton, 1933), p. 153-85; Sigmund Freud, *Three Essays on the Theory of Sexuality,* trans. James Strachey, (New York: Basic Books, 1962).

56. Ibid.

57. Sigmund Freud, *Collected Papers* (New York: Basic Books, 1959), 3: 206.

58. This is not intended to lay either credit or blame for the proliferation of this image on Freud. He intended his theories with respect to sexuality to be heuristic guides for research, not a rigid doctrine.

59. Frank S. Caprio, *Female Homosexuality: A Psychodynamic Study of Lesbianism* (New York: Citadel Press, 1954).

60. Judd Marmor, personal communication, 1976.

61. Caprio, *Female Homosexuality,* p. 304, viii, 40.

62. Edmund Bergler, *Homosexuality: Disease or Way of Life?* (New York: Collier Boales, 1956), pp. 245-48.

63. Ernest Jones, "The Early Development of Female Sexuality," *International Journal of Psychoanalysis* 8 (1927): 459-72.

64. R. de Saussure, "Homosexual Fixations in Neurotic Woman," *Revue Francaise Psychoanalytique* 3 (1929): 50-91.

65. Helene Deutsch, "On Female Homosexuality," in *The Psychoanalytic Reader* (New York: International Universities Press, 1932), 1: 237-60.

66. David M. Rosen, *Lesbianism: A Study of Female Homosexuals* (Springfield, Ill.: Charles C. Thomas, 1974), pp. 6-7.

67. Sandor Rado, "Fear of Castration in Women," *Psychoanalytic Quarterly* 2 (1933): 425-75.

68. C. L. Bacon, "A Developmental Theory of Female Homosexuality," in *Perversions: Psychodynamics and Therapy,* ed., S. Larand (New York: Random House, 1956), pp. 131-59; Freud, "Psychology of Women," p. 178; Deutsch, "On Female Homosexuality."

69. Rosen, *Lesbianism,* p. 8.

70. W. H. Perloff, "Hormones and Homosexuality," in *Sexual Inversion: The Multiple Roots of Homosexuality,* ed. Judd Marmor (New York: Basic Books, 1965), pp. 124-76.

71. Marmor, ed., *Sexual Inversion.*

72. M. E. Romm, "Sexuality and Homosexuality in Women," in *Sexual Inversion,* ed. Marmor, pp. 291, 298.

73. H. E. Kaye et al., "Homosexuality in Women," *Archives of General Psychiatry* 17 (1967): 633.

74. Rosen, *Lesbianism,* p. 9.

75. Charlotte Wolff, *Love Between Women* (New York: Harper & Row, 1971), p. 12.

76. Ibid., p. 172.

77. Naomi Weisstein, "Psychology Constructs the Female," in *Woman in Sexist Society,* ed. Vivian Gornick and Barbara K. Moran (New York: Signet, 1972), pp. 210-11.

78. Thomas S. Szasz, *The Myth of Mental Illness* (New York: Harper & Row, 1961), p. 2.

79. Ernest Van den Haag, "Roles in Homosexuality," in *Homosexuality in Modern Society,* ed. Ruitenbeek, p. 297.

80. Judd Marmor, "Homosexuality and Sexual Orientation Disturbances," in *Comprehensive Textbook of Psychiatry,* ed. Alfred M. Freedman, Harold I. Kaplan, and Benjamin J. Sadock, 2d ed. (Baltimore: Williams & Wilkins Company, 1975), 2: 1516-18.

81. Marmor, "Homosexuality and Sexual Orientation Disturbances," p. 1517.

82. Judd Marmor, personal communication, 1976.

83. Ellis, *Studies;* and Havelock Ellis, *My Life* (Boston: Houghton Mifflin, 1939).

84. Alfred Kinsey et al., *Sexual Behavior in the Human Male* (Philadelphia: W. B. Saunders Company, 1948); Alfred Kinsey et al., *Sexual Behavior in the Human Female* (Philadelphia: W. B. Saunders Company, 1953).

85. Kinsey et al., *Sexual Behavior in the Human Female,* p. 447.

86. V. Armon, "Some Personality Variables in Overt Female Homosexuality," *Journal of Projective Techniques and Personality Assessment* 24 (1960): 292-309; Rosen, *Lesbianism,* p. 11.

87. J. H. Hopkins, "The Lesbian Personality," *British Journal of Psychiatry* 115 (1969): 1436.

88. Mark J. Freedman, "Homosexuality among Women and Psychological Adjustment," *Ladder* 23 (May 1968): 2-3; M. R. Saghir and E. Robins, "Male and Female Homosexuality: Natural History," *Comparative Psychiatry* 12 (1971): 503-10; N. D. Thompson, B. R. McCandless, and B. R. Strickland, "Personal Adjustment of Male and Female Homosexuals and Heterosexuals," *Journal of Abnormal Psychology* 78 (1971): 237-40.

89. J. Loney, "Background Factors, Sexual Experiences, and Attitudes toward Treatment in Two 'Normal' Homosexual Samples," *Journal of Consulting and Clinical Psychology* 38 (1972): 57-65.

90. M. Seigelman, "Adjustment of Homosexual and Heterosexual Women," *British Journal of Psychiatry* 120 (1972): 479.

91. David A. Ward and Gene G. Kassebaum, *Women's Prison: Sex and Social Structure* (Chicago: Aldine Publishing Co., 1965); Rose Giallombardo, *Society of Women: A Study of a Women's Prison* (New York: John Wiley & Sons, 1966); Rose Giallombardo, *The Social World of Imprisoned Girls: A Comparative Study of Institutions for Juvenile Delinquents* (New York: John Wiley & Sons, 1974).

92. Giallombardo, *Social World of Imprisoned Girls.*

93. William Simon and John H. Gagnon, "On Psychosexual Development," in *Handbook of Socialization Theory and Research,* ed. David A. Goslin (Chicago: Rand McNally & Company, 1969), p. 736.

94. Ibid., p. 734.

95. Ibid., p. 746.

96. William Simon and John H. Gagnon, "The Lesbians: A Preliminary Overview," in *Sexual Deviance,* ed. Gagnon and Simon.

97. Carol A. B. Warren, "Women Among Men: Females in the Male Homosexual Community," *Archives of Sexual Behavior* 5 (1976): 156-75.

98. Mary McIntosh, "The Homosexual Role," *Social Problems* 16 (1968): 182; Simon and Gagnon, "The Lesbians;" Robert T. Bell, *Social Deviance: A Substantive Analysis* (Homewood, Ill.: Dorsey Press, 1971).

99. Warren, *Identity and Community,* pp. 146-47.

100. Martin and Lyon, *Lesbian/Woman.*

101. Rule, *Lesbian Images,* p. 188.

102. Ibid., p. 50.

103. Indeed, among the women with whom I spoke, *The Well of Loneliness* was frequently mentioned as one of the first sources of information a young woman had about lesbianism with which to reflect upon herself and the meaning of her own lesbianism.

104. Rule, *Lesbian Images,* p. 55, 56.

105. Ibid., pp. 54-56.

106. Ibid., p. 58.

107. Ibid., p. 60.

108. Martin and Lyon, *Lesbian/Woman,* p. 22.

109. Ibid. See Rule, *Lesbian Images,* and Klaich, *Woman + Woman,* for complete treatments.

110. Claire Morgan, *The Price of Salt* (New York: Bantam Giant, 1958); Isobel Miller, *A Place for Us* (New York: Bleecker Street Press, 1969); Han Suyin, *Winterlove* (London: Jonathan Cape, 1970).

111. Martin and Lyon, *Lesbian/Woman.*

112. Juanita Williams, *Psychology of Women: Behavior in a Biosocial Context* (New York: W. W. Norton & Company, 1970), pp. 90-120.

113. Harold I. Leif, "Introduction to Sexuality," in *Comprehensive Textbook of Psychiatry,* ed. Freedman, Kaplan, Sadock, 2: 1349.

114. Klaich, *Woman + Woman,* p. 95, citing *Time,* January 21, 1966, and "The David Suskind Show," October 10, 1971.

115. David Reuben, *Everything You Always Wanted to Know About Sex** (New York: David McKay Co., 1969), p. 217.

Chapter 3

This chapter is published, in slightly different form, as "Secrecy in the Lesbian World," in *Sexuality: Encounters, Identities, and Relationships,* a special issue of *Urban Life,* October 1976.

1. Georg Simmel, *The Sociology of Georg Simmel,* trans. and ed. Kurt H. Wolff (New York: Free Press, 1950), pp. 345-46.

2. Ibid., pp. 361-62.

3. Ibid., p. 339.

4. Cf. Joan Emerson, "Nothing Unusual is Happening," in *Human Nature and Collective Behavior,* ed. T. Shibutani (Englewood Cliffs, N.J.: Prentice-Hall, 1970), p. 211.

5. Goffman, *Stigma.*

6. Stanford M. Lyman and Marvin B. Scott, *A Sociology of the Absurd* (New York: Appleton-Century Crofts, 1970), p. 78.

7. Simon and Gagnon, "The Lesbians," p. 262.

8. Warren, *Identity and Community,* p. 175.

9. Ibid., pp. 32-34.

10. Simmel, *Sociology,* p. 360.

11. Ibid., p. 365; Warren, *Identity and Community,* p. 141.

12. "Marriage" refers to an ongoing lesbian relationship in this instance.

13. Barney Glaser and Anselm Strauss, "Awareness Contexts and Social Interaction, *American Sociological Review* 29 (1964): 669-78; Barney Glaser and Anselm Strauss, *Awareness of Dying* (Chicago: Aldine Publishing Co., 1965), pp. 64-78.

14. Emerson, "Nothing Unusual."

15. "Friend" means lover in this context.

16. Simmel, *Sociology,* p. 335.

17. This respondent had married a gay man—a marriage of convenience, or a cover, for both.

18. This issue of counterfeit secrecy—in fact, the issues involved in relationships in general between children and lesbian mothers—awaits another investigator. Data from the present study indicate that children

of women-related women accept their mothers' relationships with equanimity, though most frequently the sexuality of these relationships is not specifically discussed (as would be the case for most heterosexual relationships.)

19. Simmel, *Sociology*, p. 330.

20. Ibid., p. 337.

21. Ibid., p. 356.

22. Ibid., p. 337.

23. Erving Goffman, *The Presentation of Self in Everyday Life* (Garden City, N.Y.: Doubleday & Co., 1959).

24. "Turned out" means to have an initial gay affair, usually with the connotation that the individual who is turned out becomes gay.

25. Simmel, p. 360.

26. Ibid.; Warren, *Identity and Community*.

27. Simmel, p. 360.

28. Warren, *Identity and Community*.

29. Simmel, p. 369.

30. Ibid., p. 333-34.

31. Ibid., p. 334.

32. Goffman, *Stigma*, p. 20-31.

33. Simmel, p. 333.

34. Ibid., p. 346.

35. Laud Humphreys, *Out of the Closets: The Sociology of Homosexual Liberation* (Englewood Cliffs, N.J.: Prentice-Hall, 1972).

36. Warren, *Identity and Community*, p. 18.

Chapter 4

1. Daniel Glaser, *Social Deviance* (Chicago: Markham, 1971), p. 35.

2. Goffman, *Stigma*, p. 19.

3. I met several wise women in different settings in the lesbian community. The wise status of those women who were involved in relationships with men was unproblematic. Others who were not involved in heterosexual relationships at the time and were known not to have been involved in a relationship with a man for some time experienced "slippage" in their wise status; i.e., they were assumed to be really gay.

4. I am indebted to Joe Styles, for the notion of identity work. Identity work refers to the processes and procedures engaged in by groups designed to effect change in the meanings of particular identities. Identity work usually connotes the acceptance of a particular identity and alteration of the meaning of the identity through providing role models who have accepted the identity. Such role models share their experiences in coming

to accept the identity and thus act as guides to the novice. Self-help activist gay groups engage in identity work. Other examples of identity work would be Alcoholics Anonymous, Synanon, and various therapies whose aim is helping clientele to come to terms with various social identities. Also see Goffman's *Stigma* for a discussion of the professionalization of stigmatized persons.

5. There are, of course, notable exceptions to this etiquette of mutual protection, as exemplified by the plight of Kate Millett, who, it appears, was coerced by radical lesbians into making a public statement of lesbian identity that provided the basis for subsequent scurrilous attacks in the press on her work and her credibility.

6. Goffman, *Stigma;* Warren, *Identity and Community.*

7. William Simon and John Gagnon, "Femininity in the Lesbian Community," *Social Problems* 14 (1966): 218.

8. Peter L. Berger and Thomas Luckmann, *The Social Construction of Reality* (Garden City, N.Y.: Doubleday & Co., 1967).

9. Warren, *Identity and Community,* pp. 126-30.

10. Martha Shelley, "Gay if Good," in *Out of the Closets: Voices of Gay Liberation,* ed. Karla Jay and Allen Young (New York: Douglas Book, 1972), p. 34.

11. Laud Humphreys, *Tearoom Trade: Impersonal Sex in Public Places* (Chicago: Aldine Publishing Co., 1970), pp. 131-48.

12. Cf. Simmel, *Sociology;* Warren, *Identity and Community.*

13. "Nellie" means effeminate.

14. Simmel, *Sociology,* pp. 364-66.

15. Cf. Gresham M. Sykes and David Matza, "On Neutralizing Delinquent Self-Images," in *Deviance: The Interactionist Perspective,* ed. Earl Rubington and Morton S. Weinberg (London: Macmillan & Co., 1968) p. 369.

16. The ideas of the feminist lesbians with respect to relativization of sex roles and the deleterious effects of strict sex role definitions reflect and are reflected in the writing of current students of sex roles. An examination of the traditional sociological literature on sex roles reveals certain consistencies in depictions of the attributes that have long been perceived as appropriate for males and females: dominance and aggression for males, and passivity and submissiveness for females. The female role is seen in terms of the affiliative roles of wife and mother and emphasizes female sexuality in its procreative aspects. Women as childbearers are expected to have qualities, such as nurturance, that facilitate the mother role. Other attributes considered appropriate and natural for women are dependency, receptivity, and emotionality. Men are expected to be aggressive, dominant,

and achievement-oriented, embodying instrumental qualities appropriate
to the relation between the family and the outside world.

In women these qualities were frequently judged inappropriate or
deviant. Parsons and Bales (1955) summarize this sexual division of
labor between men and women under the rubrics "instrumental" and
"expressive," respectively. They maintain that this division of labor is
functional, a necessary condition for the maintenance of the family and,
ultimately, of society. Other sociologists, though agreeing that these
characterizations of male and female roles describe an actual role division
between men and women, question both the inevitability and the functionality of this division. This critical tradition in the analysis of sex roles is
concerned with the dysfunctions and latent consequences of the widely
shared meanings of women's sex roles; however, it should be noted that
these critical treatments underscore the prevalence of the depiction of
women as passive, dependent, nurturant, and helpless.

As do feminist lesbians, these critical studies point to the dysfunctional
effects of the stereotypic meanings of women's roles on the self-esteem
of women. Gove and Tudor (1973), for example, trace the relationship
between rates of mental illness for women and relate these rates to women's
sex roles, concluding that women are more likely to have emotional
problems than men. Chesler (1971) sees this fact developing from a lack
of recognition of the oppressive character of depictions of, and expectations for, women. Along similar lines, some writers note the lack of major
role alternatives for women and the frustration that women experience if
they try to assume instrumental roles (Bernard, 1971; Lopata, 1971).
Goode (1960), Parsons (1942), Angrist (1969), and Rose (1951) assert
that the expectations confronting women (with the exception of the previously noted affective expectations) are unclear and diffuse—a condition·
that creates problems for women. Rose (1951), Angrist (1969), Epstein
(1970), and Bardwick (1971) assert that women's role consists in adjusting
to contingencies and adapting themselves to men's roles. Yet other theorists
assert that the cultural meanings and expectations for women are contradictory and place women in a double bind in their experiences of themselves (Mead, 1949; Komarovsky, 1946; Friedan, 1963; Steinmann and
Fox, 1966; and Bardwick, 1971).

McKee and Sheriffs (1957, 1959); Sheriffs and McKee (1957); Gurin,
Veroff, and Feld (1960); Rosenkranz, Vogel, Bee, Broverman, and
Broverman (1968)—all emphasize the fact that women have negative images
of themselves, while Farberow and Schneidman (1965), Stengel (1969),
and Maris (1969) note that women have higher rates of suicide attempts
than men. Gove and Tudor (1973) suggest that the pattern of variation in

rates of mental illness reflects unequal social positions and differential societal valuation of males and females.

In short, there appears to be widespread concurrence about the meanings of women's sex roles but considerable disagreement as to the functionality of these roles.

17. Burke and Edelman, cited in Sharon Raphael, "Coming Out: The Emergence of the Movement Lesbian" (Ph.D. dissertation, Case Western Reserve University, Cleveland, Ohio, 1974), p. 78.

18. Jill Johnston, *Lesbian Nation: The Feminist Solution* (New York: Simon & Schuster, 1973), pp. 277-78.

19. Cited in Raphael, "Coming Out," p. 42.

Chapter 5

1. Cf. Jack Katz, "Deviance, Charisma, and Role-Defined Behavior," *Social Problems* 20 (1972): 186-202; Jack Katz, "Essences as Moral Identities."

2. Warren, *Identity and Community*, p. 101.

3. Berger and Luckmann, *Social Construction of Reality*, pp. 92-94.

4. Klaich, *Woman + Woman*, pp. 129-60.

5. Bruce Rodgers, *The Queen's Vernacular* (San Francisco: Straight Arrow Books, 1972), p. 93.

6. There is some suggestive evidence from respondents' reports that the adaptation of role-playing styles may vary inversely with social class. One would thus expect a greater degree of role-playing behavior and commitment to that behavior in groups whose members derive from heterosexual groups or milieus that dichotomize strongly between male and female roles. Hedblom's work suggests regional variations in the adaptation of role-playing styles—the Midwest being the most conservative (that is, participating in role playing) and the two coasts displaying considerably less role playing. See Jack H. Hedblom and John J. Hartman, "Comparative Dimensions of Lesbianism Over Time, Place and Data Collection Techniques", (Paper read at the Annual Meeting of the Midwest Sociological Society, 1976).

7. "Ki-Ki" means a lesbian who will not adopt or declare a masculine or feminine role. See Sidney Abbott and Barbara Love, *Sappho Was a Right-On Woman: A Liberated View of Lesbianism* (New York: Stein & Day Publishers, 1972), pp. 93-94.

8. Martin and Lyon, *Lesbian/Woman*.

9. Cf. Warren, *Identity and Community*.

10. Warren, "Observing the Gay Community," p. 144.

11. Cf. C. W. Mills, "Situated Actions and Vocabularies of Motive," *American Sociological Review* 5 (December 1940): 904-13.

12. Philip W. Blumstein and Pepper Schwartz, "Lesbianism and Bisexuality" (Manuscript, University of Washington, 1974), p. 17.

13. Experimentation may be perceived essentially in two ways depending on the motives attributed to the experimenter—the first in conformance with the gay trajectory and the coming out process. A woman may be seen as experimenting as an expression of her underlying true lesbian identity, of which she is unaware. On the other hand, a woman may be seen as a heterosexual whose experiments example callousness—who in effect is "using" lesbians for her own pleasure with no sense of commitment to relationship.

14. Blumstein and Schwartz, "Lesbianism and Bisexuality," p. 18.

15. Barry Dank, "Coming Out in the Gay World," *Psychiatry* 34 (May 1971): 180-97.

16. For an elaboration of the many meanings of "coming out," see Dank, "Coming Out in the Gay World."

17. "Closet case" means someone who is assumed to be gay but will not acknowledge it.

Chapter 6

1. Warren, "Women Among Men," p. 161.

2. See chapter 3 for a discussion of the heterosexual assumption.

3. Simon and Gagnon, "The Lesbians," p. 247.

4. Warren, *Identity and Community*, p. 155.

5. Dank, "Coming Out in the Gay World," p. 180.

6. John Lofland, *Doomsday Cult: A Study of Conversion, Proselytization and Maintenance of Faith* (Englewood Cliffs, N.J.: Prentice-Hall, 1966), pp. 65-69.

7. Warren, "Women Among Men."

8. Tripp, *The Homosexual Matrix*, p. 87.

9. Klaich, *Woman + Woman*, p. 49.

10. Kinsey et al., *Sexual Behavior in the Human Female*, p. 468.

11. Klaich, *Woman + Woman*, p. 46.

12. To "bring someone out" is to be the agent of their "realizing" they are gay; it usually refers to an initial same-sex sexual-emotional relationship. The term also means an individuality of lesbianism (or male homosexuality).

13. Simon and Gagnon, "The Lesbians."

14. Peter L. Berger, *Invitation to Sociology: A Humanistic Perspective* (Garden City, N.Y.: Doubleday & Co., 1963), pp. 54-57.

15. Ibid., pp. 56-57.

16. Berger and Luckmann, *Social Construction of Reality*, p. 64.

17. "Old lady" means wife or girlfriend.

Chapter 7

1. Caprio, *Female Homosexuality*, p. 43.

2. Joan Larkin, "Coming Out: 'My Story is Not about all Lesbians,'" *Ms.* 9 (1976), p. 72.

3. Blumstein and Schwartz, "Lesbianism and Bisexuality."

4. Cf. Simon and Gagnon, "The Lesbians"; Dank, "Coming Out in the Gay World."

5. Blumstein and Schwartz, "Lesbianism and Bisexuality," p. 9.

6. This illustrates ironical use of the logic employed by heterosexuals and bisexuals involved in lesbian relationships. These lesbians state that their current relationships with men are situated and coincidental.

7. The Politics of Celibacy," *Lesbian Tide;* cited in Raphael, "Coming Out," p. 61.

8. Warren, *Identity and Community*.

9. Blumstein and Schwartz, "Lesbianism and Bisexuality".

BIBLIOGRAPHY

Angrist, Shirley. "The Study of Sex Roles." *Journal of Social Issues* 25 (January 1969): 215-32.

Armon, V. "Some Personality Variables in Overt Female Homosexuality." *Journal of Projective Techniques and Personality Assessment* 24 (1960): 292-309.

Bacon, C. L. "A Developmental Theory of Female Homosexuality." In *Perversions: Psychodynamics and Therapy,* edited by S. Larand. New York: Random House, 1956, pp. 131-59.

Bardwick, Judith. *The Psychology of Women: A Study of Biocultural Conflicts.* New York: Harper & Row, 1971.

Becker, Howard S. *Outsiders: Studies in the Sociology of Deviance.* New York: Free Press, 1963.

Bell, Robert T. *Social Deviance: A Substantive Analysis.* Homewood, Ill.: Dorsey Press, 1971.

Berger, Peter L. *Invitation to Sociology: A Humanistic Perspective.* Garden City, N.Y.: Doubleday & Co., 1963.

Berger, Peter L., and Luckmann, Thomas. *The Social Construction of Reality.* Garden City, N.Y.: Doubleday & Co., 1967.

ᵉrgler, Edmund. *Homosexuality: Disease or Way of Life?* New York: Collier Boales, 1956.

Bernard, J. *Women and the Public Interest.* Chicago: Aldine-Atherton, 1971.

Blumer, Herbert. *Symbolic Interactionism: Perspective and Method.* Englewood Cliffs, N.J.: Prentice-Hall, 1969.

Blumstein, Philip W., and Schwartz, Pepper. "Lesbianism and Bisexuality." Manuscript. University of Washington, 1974.

Brecher, Edward. "History of Human Sexual Research and Study." In *Comprehensive Textbook of Psychiatry,* edited by Alfred M. Freedman, Harold I. Kaplan, Benjamin J. Sadock. Baltimore: Williams & Wilkins Company, 1975, 2: 1352-57.

Broverman, D. M., et al. "Roles of Activation and Inhibition in Sex Differences in Cognitive Abilities." *Psychological Review* 75 (1968): 23-50.

Caprio, Frank S. *Female Homosexuality: A Psychodynamic Study of Lesbianism.* New York: Citadel Press, 1954.

Chesler, Phyllis. "Patient and Patriarch: Women in the Psychotherapeutic Relationship." In *Woman in a Sexist Society,* edited by Vivian Gornick and Barbara K. Moran. New York: Basic Books, 1971, pp. 362-92.

Dank, Barry. "Coming Out in the Gay World." *Psychiatry* 34 (May 1971): 180-97.

de Saussure, R. "Homosexual Fixations in Neurotic Woman." *Revue Francaise Psychoanalytique* 3 (1929): 50-91.

Deutsch, Helene. "On Female Homosexuality." In *The Psychoanalytic Reader.* New York: International Universities Press, 1932, 1: 237-60.

Douglas, Jack D. *The American Social Order.* New York: The Free Press, *1971.*

Duberman, Lucile. *Gender and Sex in Society.* New York: Praeger Publishers, 1975.

Ellis, Havelock. *My Life.* Boston: Houghton Mifflin, 1939.

———. *Studies in the Psychology of Sex.* New York: Random House, 1936, Vol. 1.

Emerson, Joan. "Nothing Unusual is Happening." In *Human Nature and Collective Behavior,* edited by T. Shibutani. Englewood Cliffs, N.J.: Prentice-Hall, 1970, pp. 208-22.

Epstein, Cynthia. *Woman's Place.* Berkeley: University of California Press, 1970.

Farberow, Norman, and Schneidman, Edwin. *The Cry for Help.* New York: McGraw-Hill, 1965.

Freedman, Mark J. "Homosexuality among Women and Psychological Adjustment." *Ladder* 23 (May 1968): 2-3.

Freud, Sigmund. *Collected Papers.* New York: Basic Books, 1959, Vol.2.

———. "The Psychology of Women." In *New Introductory Lectures on Psychoanalysis.* New York: Norton, 1933, pp. 153-85.

———. *Three Essays on the Theory of Sexuality.* Translated by James Strachey. New York: Basic Books, 1962.

Friedan, Betty. *The Feminine Mystique.* New York: Norton, 1963.

Gagnon, John H., and Simon, William. *Sexual Deviance.* New York: Harper & Row, 1967.

Giallombardo, Rose. *The Social World of Imprisoned Girls: A Comparative Study of Institutions for Juvenile Delinquents.* New York: John Wiley & Sons, 1974.

———. *Society of Women: A Study of a Women's Prison.* New York: John Wiley & Sons, 1966.

Glaser, Barney, and Strauss, Anselm. "Awareness Contexts and Social Interaction." *American Sociological Review* 29 (1964): 669-78.
———. *Awareness of Dying.* Chicago: Aldine Publishing Co., 1965.
Glaser, Daniel. *Social Deviance.* Chicago: Markham, 1971.
Goffman, Erving. *The Presentation of Self in Everyday Life.* Garden City, N.Y.: Doubleday & Co., 1959.
———. *Stigma: Notes on the Management of Spoiled Identity.* Englewood Cliffs, N.J.: Prentice-Hall, 1963.
Goode, William. "Norm, Commitment and Conformity in Role Status Obligations." *American Journal of Sociology* 66 (November 1960): 246-58.
Gordon, Chad. "Self Conceptions: Configurations of Content." In *The Self in Social Interaction: Classic and Contemporary Perspectives,* edited by Chad Gordon and Kenneth J. Gergen. New York: John Wiley & Sons, 1968, 1: 115-37.
Gove, Walter R., and Tudor, Jeanette F. "Adult Sex Roles and Mental Illness." In *Changing Women in a Changing Society,* edited by Joan Huber. Chicago: University of Chicago Press, 1973, pp. 50-74.
Gurin, Gerald; Veroff, Joseph; and Feld, Sheila. *Americans View their Mental Health.* New York: Basic Books, 1960.
Hall, Radclyffe. *The Well of Loneliness.* New York: Covici, Friede, 1928.
Hooker, Evelyn. "The Adjustment of the Male Overt Homosexual." In *The Problem of Homosexuality in Modern Society,* edited by Henrik M. Ruitenbeek. New York: E. P. Dutton & Co., 1963, pp. 141-61.
Hopkins, J. H. "The Lesbian Personality." *British Journal of Psychiatry* 115, (1969): 1433-36.
Humphreys, Laud. *Out of the Closets: The Sociology of Homosexual Liberation.* Englewood Cliffs, N.J.: Prentice-Hall, 1972.
———. *Tearoom Trade: Impersonal Sex in Public Places.* Chicago: Aldine Publishing Co., 1970.
Johnston, Jill. *Lesbian Nation: The Feminist Solution.* New York: Simon & Schuster, 1973.
Jones, Ernest. "The Early Development of Female Sexuality." *International Journal of Psychoanalysis* 8 (1927): 459-72.
Katz, Jack. "Deviance, Charisma, and Role-Defined Behavior." *Social Problems* 20 (1972): 186-202.
———. "Essences as Moral Identities: Verifiability and Responsibility in Imputations of Deviance and Charisma." *American Journal of Sociology* 80 (1975): 1369-90.
Kaye, H. E., et al. "Homosexuality in Women." *Archives of General Psychiatry* 17 (1967): 626-34.
Kinsey, Alfred; Pomeroy, W. B.; Martin, C. E.; and Gebhard, P. H. *Sexual Behavior in the Human Female.* Philadelphia: W. B. Saunders Company, 1953.

———, et al. *Sexual Behavior in the Human Male.* Philadelphia: W. B. Saunders Company, 1948.

Klaich, Dolores. *Woman + Woman: Attitudes toward Lesbianism.* New York: William Morrow & Co., 1974.

Komarovsky, Mirra. "Cultural Contradictions and Sex Roles." *American Journal of Sociology* 52 (November, 1946): 184-89.

Kuhn, Manford H., and McPartland, Thomas S. "An Empirical Investigation of Self-Attitudes." In *Symbolic Interaction: A Reader in Social Psychology,* edited by Jerome G. Morris and Bernard N. Meltzer. ed Boston: Allyn & Bacon, 1972, 112-24.

Larkin, Joan. "Coming Out: 'My Story is Not about all Lesbians.' " *Ms.* 9 (1976), p. 72.

Leif, Harold I. "Introduction to Sexuality." In *Comprehensive Textbook of Psychiatry,* edited by Alfred M. Freedman, Harold I. Kaplan, and Benjamin J. Sadock. Baltimore: Williams & Wilkins Company, 1975, 2: 1349-52.

Lemert, Edwin. *Human Deviance, Social Problems, and Social Control.* Englewood Cliffs, N.J.: Prentice-Hall, 1976.

Lofland, John. *Analyzing Social Settings.* Belmont, Calif.: Wadsworth Publishing Co., 1971.

———. *Deviance and Identity.* Englewood Cliffs, N.J.: Prentice-Hall, 1969.

———. *Doomsday Cult: A Study of Conversion, Proselytization and Maintenance of Faith.* Englewood Cliffs, N.J.: Prentice-Hall, 1966.

Loney, J. "Background Factors, Sexual Experiences, and Attitudes toward Treatment in Two 'Normal' Homosexual Samples." *Journal of Consulting and Clinical Psychology* 38 (1972): 57-65.

Lopata, Helen Z. *Occupation: Housewife.* London: Oxford University Press, 1971.

Lyman, Stanford M., and Scott, Marvin B. *A Sociology of the Absurd.* New York: Appleton-Century Crofts, 1970.

McCall, George, and Simmons, J. L. *Identities and Interactions.* New York: Free Press, 1966.

McIntosh, Mary. "The Homosexual Role." *Social Problems* 16 (1968): 182-92.

McKee, John, and Sheriffs, Alex. "The Differential Evaluation of Males and Females." *Journal of Personality* 25 (March 1957): 356-71.

———. "Men's and Women's Beliefs, Ideals, and Self Concepts." *American Journal of Sociology* 64 (January 1959): 356-63.

Maris, Ronald. *Social Forces in Urban Suicide.* (Homewood, Ill.: Dorsey, 1969).

Marmor, Judd. "Homosexuality and Sexual Orientation Disturbances." In *Comprehensive Textbook of Psychiatry,* edited by Alfred M. Freedman,

Harold I. Kaplan, and Benjamin J. Sadock. 2d ed. Baltimore: Williams & Wilkins Company, 1975, 2: 1510-20.

————, ed. *Sexual Inversion: The Multiple Roots of Homosexuality.* New York: Basic Books, 1965.

Martin, Del, and Lyon, Phyllis. *Lesbian/Woman.* New York: Bantam Books, 1972.

Mead, George Herbert. *Mind, Self, and Society.* Edited by Charles Morris. Chicago: University of Chicago Press, 1934.

Mead, Margaret. *Male and Female.* New York: Mentor, 1949.

Miller, Isobel. *A Place for Us.* (New York: Bleecker Street Press, 1969.

Mills, C. W. "Situated Actions and Vocabularies of Motive," *American Sociological Review* 5 (December 1940): 904-13.

Money, John; and Ehrhardt, Anke A. *Man and Woman, Boy and Girl: The Differentiation and Dimorphism of Gender Identity from Conception to Maturity.* Baltimore: John's Hopkins University Press, 1972.

Money, John; Hampson, J. L.; and Hampson, J. G. "An Examination of Some Basic Sexual Concepts: The Evidence of Human Hermaphroditism." *Bulletin of the Johns Hopkins Hospital* (1955): 97.

Morgan, Claire. *The Price of Salt.* New York: Bantam Giant, 1958.

Parsons, Talcott. "Age and Sex in the Social Structure of the United States." *American Sociological Review* 7 (October 1942): 604-16.

————. "The Position of Identity in the General Theory of Action." In *The Self in Social Interaction: Classic and Contemporary Perspectives,* edited by Chad Gordon and Kenneth J. Gergen. New York: John Wiley & Sons, 1968, 1: 11-25.

Parsons, Talcott, and Bales, R. F. *Family, Socialization, and Interaction Process.* (Glencoe, Ill.: Free Press, 1955.

Perloff, W. H. "Hormones and Homosexuality." In *Sexual Inversion: The Multiple Roots of Homosexuality,* edited by Judd Marmor. New York: Basic Books, 1965, pp. 124-76.

Rado, Sandor. "Fear of Castration in Women." *Psychoanalytic Quarterly* 2 (1933): 425-75.

Raphael, Sharon. "Coming Out: The Emergence of the Movement Lesbian." Ph.D. dissertation, Case Western Reserve University, Cleveland, Ohio, 1974.

Reuben, David. *Everything You Always Wanted to Know About Sex*.* New York: David McKay Co., 1969.

Romm, May E. "Sexuality and Homosexuality in Women." In *Sexual Inversion: The Multiple Roots of Homosexuality,* edited by Judd Marmor. New York: Basic Books, 1965, pp. 282-301.

Rose, Arnold. "The Adequacy of Women's Expectations for Adult Roles." *Social Forces* 30 (October 1951): 69-77.

Rosen, David M. *Lesbianism: A Study of Female Homosexuals*. Springfield, Ill.: Charles C. Thomas, 1974.

Rosenberg, G. G., and Sutton-Smith, Brian. *Sex and Identity*. New York: Holt, Rinehart and Winston, 1972.

Rosenkrantz, Paul; Vogel, Susan; Bee, Helen; Broverman, Inge; and Broverman, Donald. "Sex-Role Stereotypes and Self-Conceptions in College Students." *Journal of Consulting Psychology* 32 (1968): 287-95.

Rule, Jane. *Lesbian Images*. Garden City: Doubleday & Co., 1975.

Saghir, M. R., and Robins, E. "Male and Female Homosexuality: Natural History." *Comparative Psychiatry* 12 (1971): 503-10.

Schur, Edwin. *Labeling Deviant Behavior*. New York: Harper & Row, 1971.

Schutz, Alfred. *Collected Papers: Studies in Social Theory*. Edited by Arnid Broderson. The Hague: Martinus Nijhoff, 1971, Vol. 2.

Seigelman, M. "Adjustment of Homosexual and Heterosexual Women." *British Journal of Psychiatry* 120 (1972): 477-81.

Shelley, Martha. "Gay Is Good." In *Out of the Closets: Voices of Gay Liberation*, edited by Karla Jay and Allen Young. New York: Douglas Book, 1972, p. 34.

Sheriffs, Alex, and McKee, John. "Qualitative Aspects of Beliefs about Men and Women." *Journal of Personality* 25 (June 1957): 450-64.

Simmel, Georg. *The Sociology of Georg Simmel*. Translated and edited by Kurt H. Wolff. New York: Free Press, 1950.

Simon, William, and Gagnon, John H. "Femininity in the Lesbian Community." *Social Problems* 14 (1966): 212-21.

———. "The Lesbians: A Preliminary Overview." In *Sexual Deviance*, edited by John H. Gagnon and William Simon. New York: Harper & Row, 1967.

———. "On Psychosexual Development." In *Handbook of Socialization Theory and Research*, edited by David A. Goslin. Chicago: Rand McNally & Company, 1969.

Steinmann, Anne, and Fox, David. "Male-Female Perceptions of the Female Role in the United States." *Journal of Psychology* 64 (November 1966): 265-79.

Stengel, Erwin. *Suicide and Attempted Suicide*. Baltimore: Penguin Press, 1969.

Strauss, Anselm. *Mirrors and Masks*. New York: Free Press, 1959.

Suyin, Han. *Winterlove*. London: Jonathan Cape, 1970.

Sykes, Gresham M., and Matza, David. "On Neutralizing Delinquent Self-Images." In *Deviance: The Interactionist Perspective*, edited by Earl Rubington and Morton S. Weinberg. London: Macmillan & Co., 1968, pp. 367-70.

Szasz, Thomas S. *The Myth of Mental Illness.* New York: Harper & Row, 1961.

Thompson, N. D.; McCandless, B. R.; and Strickland, B. R. "Personal Adjustment of Male and Female Homosexuals and Heterosexuals." *Journal of Abnormal Psychology* 78 (1971): 237-40.

Thorsell, Bernard A., and Klemke, Lloyd W. "The Labeling Process: Reinforcement and Deterrent." *Law and Society Review* 6 (February 1972): 393-403.

Tiryakian, Edward. "The Existential Self and the Person." In *The Self in Social Interaction: Classic and Contemporary Perspectives,* edited by Chad Gordon and Kenneth J. Gergen. New York: John Wiley & Sons, 1968, 1: 75-87.

Tripp, C. A. *The Homosexual Matrix.* New York: McGraw-Hill, 1975.

Van den Haag, Ernest. "Roles in Homosexuality." In *The Problem of Homosexuality in Modern Society,* edited by Henrik M. Ruitenbek. New York: E. P. Dutton & Co., 1963, pp. 97-124.

Ward, David A., and Kassebaum, Gene G. *Women's Prison: Sex and Social Structure.* Chicago: Aldine Publishing Co., 1965.

Warren, Carol A. B. *Identity and Community in the Gay World.* New York: Wiley Interscience, 1974.

———. "Labeling Theory: The Individual, the Category, and the Group." Manuscript. University of Southern California, 1976.

———. "Observing the Gay Community." In *Research on Deviance,* edited by Jack D. Douglas. New York: Random House, 1972, pp. 139-63.

———. "The Use of Stigmatizing Social Labels in Conventionalizing Deviant Behavior." *Sociology and Social Research* 58 (1974): 303-11.

———. "Women Among Men: Females in the Male Homosexual Community." *Archives of Sexual Behavior* 5 (1976): 156-75.

Warren, Carol, and Johnson, John. "A Criticism of Labeling Theory from the Phenomenological Perspective." In *Theoretical Perspectives in Deviance,* edited by Robert A. Scott and Jack D. Douglas. New York: Basic Books, 1972, pp. 69-93.

Weisstein, Naomi. "Psychology Constructs the Female." In *Woman in a Sexist Society,* edited by Vivian Gornick and Barbara K. Moran. New York: Signet, 1972, pp. 210-11.

Wolff, Charlotte. *Love Between Women.* New York: Harper & Row, 1971).

INDEX